WESTERN CONCEPTS OF CHINA
AND THE CHINESE, 1840-1876

Western Concepts of China and the Chinese, 1840-1876

By

MARY GERTRUDE MASON

HYPERION PRESS, INC.
WESTPORT, CONNECTICUT

Library of Congress Cataloging in Publication Data

Mason, Mary Gertrude, 1900-
    Western concepts of China and the Chinese, 1840-1876.

    Reprint of the author's thesis, Columbia.
    Vita.
    Includes bibliographical references.
    1. China. I. Title.
DS755.M3 1973   301.15'43'91503   73-890
ISBN 0-88355-083-0

Published in 1939, New York.
Copyright 1939 by Mary Gertrude Mason.

First Hyperion reprint edition 1973

Reproduced from a copy in the collection of the University
of Illinois Library

Library of Congress Catalogue Number 73-890

ISBN 0-88355-083-0

Printed in the United States of America

To

ANNA MASON
AND
HAYES MASON

FOREWORD

THE purpose of this monograph is to state the Western concepts of China as a country and of the Chinese people during the years from 1840 to 1876. The year 1840 marks the outbreak of the first Anglo-Chinese War which is a turning-point in the history of China as well as for Chinese and Western relations. This war is the beginning of the end of China's isolation and aloofness. As a result of the partial opening of the country in 1842, Europeans gained a greater opportunity to get first-hand information. The date 1840 is also the point of departure for the breakdown of old concepts and the gradual formation of new ideas about China which gathered momentum slowly through the remainder of the nineteenth century. By the decade of the seventies, the general descriptive works on China indicate that foreigners have more accurate information and no longer express some of the more absurd notions about the Empire and its people. Although Western knowledge was increasing noticeably by 1876, this date is a more or less arbitrary limit for this study. There is no definite shift in European or American interest in China. The missionaries have steadily and persistently continued their work in somewhat the same manner until the present. The traders and capitalists throughout the nineteenth century expanded and enlarged their interests. With the revival of imperialism particularly in England and France, Western statesmen, merchants, and traders realized the importance of China for markets and as a place for the investment of capital.

This is not an interpretative study of China and the Chinese. I am interested primarily in showing the part China played in Western thought and also in setting forth the ideas which Europeans entertained of the Orientals and their country. Whether or not Western opinion of China is correct or incorrect is of no moment in so far as this particular study is concerned, but in many instances later research upon a particular point is cited.

This monograph is, therefore, largely a summary of the curious and absurd generalizations of a large number of badly informed writers and also of the observations of many shrewd and intelligent missionary and lay scholars, consular officials, and travellers. It is impossible to use quotation marks to designate their opinions which are generally summarized instead of quoted, but the names of the authors of such statements are cited in notes and frequently in the text itself.

The method of treatment is both topical and chronological. In so far as it is possible, each subject is discussed chronologically to disclose the gradual changes which different concepts underwent in this period. It is very difficult to trace any progressive advance in the spread of correct ideas on China because it was described by authors with such different training, backgrounds, outlooks, and interests. A curious mixture of fantastic statements based on seventeenth and eighteenth century popular works and upon superficial researches and casual observations exists along with information based upon scholarly researches and upon accurate and systematic observations.

A survey of the literature indicates that Westerners were interested in China from various points of view, but especially from that of intellectual curiosity. Descriptions of social customs with emphasis upon the unique and unusual occupy much space in books and articles. Many Occidentals were concerned with the commercial and industrial life of China, and the missionaries gave special attention to philosophy and religion.

As the output of literature on the subject of China during this period is enormous, a certain amount of selection in the use of materials has been absolutely necessary. A large number of general works and travellers' accounts was read. The entire field of periodical literature could not be examined, but the more important periodicals were investigated. Newspapers were not consulted. Although they yield information on shipping to and from the Orient, on diplomatic relations with China, and on other subjects, few opinions on China and the Chinese are expressed. State Papers for the entire period were not examined, but *Hansard's Parliamentary Debates* are an important source for the opinions of statesmen on the opium question, and the *Journals of the California Legislature* afford an insight into the American attitude toward Chinese immigrants.

I hope to publish the bibliography of more than four thousand entries which was compiled in connection with this study. It will include general descriptive works, travellers' accounts, translations of Chinese literature, Chinese grammars and dictionaries intended for the use of Western students, articles in general periodicals and the publications of learned societies, and miscellaneous material written during the period from 1840 to 1876.

The research for this book has been done in large part in the Library of Columbia University, in the New York Public Library, in the Wason Collection, Cornell University, and in the Essex Institute, Salem, Massachusetts. Sources in other libraries, such as the Baker Library, Harvard University, the Boston Public Library, the Library of Congress, and the Mission Research Library and the Library, Union Theological Seminary have been consulted. Acknowledgments are made to the staffs of these libraries.

This study was begun in a seminar under the late Professor William R. Shepherd to whom I am very much indebted for assistance in the classification of the material and in making the general plan for the book. After Professor Shepherd's death, June 7, 1934, Professor James T. Shotwell became sponsor of the study. I am also indebted to Professor Shotwell for his encouragement and valuable criticisms. To Professor J. J. L. Duyvendak of the University of Leyden and Visiting Professor of Chinese, Columbia University, I am very grateful for many criticisms and suggestions which have inestimably improved this work. Professor C. H. Peake of the Department of Chinese has given many excellent suggestions both on content and style which I appreciate.

I also wish to thank Dr. Arthur Christy of the Department of English who read a portion of the material in its early stages, Professor L. C. Goodrich of the Department of Chinese, Miss I. G. Mudge, Reference Librarian, Columbia University, and Dr. A. W. Hummel of the Library of Congress for helpful suggestions.

MARY GERTRUDE MASON

New York City
June 20, 1938

CONTENTS

ABBREVIATIONS

Abh. d. bay. Ak. d. W. . . . . Abhandlungen der philosophisch-philologischen Classe der königlich bayerischen
Akademie der Wissenschaften, München.

All the Year . . . . All the Year Round, London.

Asiat. J. . . . . The Asiatic Journal, London.

Ath. . . . . The Athenaeum, London.

Atlan. . . . . The Atlantic Monthly, Boston.

Blackw. . . . . Blackwood's Edinburgh Magazine, Edinburgh.

BSG . . . . Bulletin de la Société de Géographie,
Paris.

CJ . . . . The China Journal, Shanghai.

C. & J. Repos. . . . . The Chinese and Japanese Repository,
London.

CR . . . . The China Review, Hongkong.

C. Recorder . . . . The Chinese Recorder and Missionary
Journal, Foochow.

C. Repos. The Chinese Repository, Canton.

Cal. Leg., Jols. of Sen. and Ass. . . . California Legislature, Journals of the
Senate and Assembly.

Cath. W. The Catholic World, New York.

Chamb. J. Chamber's Edinburgh Journal, Edinburgh.

China Critic . . . . The China Critic, Shanghai.

Colburn . . . . Colburn's New Monthly Magazine, London.

Cornh. . . . . The Cornhill Magazine, London.

Corres. . . . . Le Correspondant, Paris

Cosmo. . . . . The Cosmopolitan, New York.

CSPSR . . . . The Chinese Social and Political Science
Review, Peiping.

D. Monatsschrift . . . . Deutsche Monatsschrift für Litteratur,
Leipzig.

Daheim . . . . Daheim, Leipzig.

De Bow . . . . The Commercial Review of the South
and West (J. D. B. De Bow, ed.), New
Orleans.

Denk. d. Ak. d. W. Wien . . . . Denkschriften der kaiserlichen Akademie
der Wissenschaften. Philosophisch-histo-
rische Classe, Wien.

Didaskalia .... Didaskalia, Frankfurt am Main.

Dub. R. .... The Dublin Review, London.

Dub. Univ. M. .... The Dublin University Magazine, Dublin.

Ecl. M. .... The Eclectic Magazine, New York.

Ed. R. .... The Edinburgh Review, Edinburgh.

Europa .... Europa . . . von Gustav Kühne, Leipzig.

For. Quar. R. .... The Foreign Quarterly Review, London.

Fraser .... Fraser's Magazine, London

Galaxy .... The Galaxy, New York.

Hansard .... Hansard's Parliamentary Debates.

Harper .... Harper's New Monthly Magazine, New York.

House. W. .... Household Words, London.

Hunt .... Hunt's Merchants' Magazine, New York.

Illus. London News .... The Illustrated London News, London.

Illustrirtes Familienbuch ..... Illustrirtes Familienbuch, Triest.

JA .... Journal Asiatique, Paris.

J. d. Lit. .... Jahrbücher der Literatur, Wien.

JNCBRAS .... Journal of the North China Branch of the Royal Asiatic Society, Shanghai.

JRAS .... The Journal of the Royal Asiatic Society, London.

J. Savants .... Journal des Savants, Paris.

Knicker. .... The Knickerbocker, New York.

Land u. Meer .... Ueber Land und Meer, Stuttgart.

Liv. Age .... Littell's Living Age, Boston.

Mission Field .... Mission Field, London.

Mo. Chron. .... The Monthly Chronicle, Boston.

Monde Illus. .... Le Monde Illustré, Paris.

Morgenbl. .... Morgenblatt für gebildete Leser, Stuttgart.

N. & Q. .... Notes and Queries, London.

N. & Q. on C. & J. .... Notes and Queries on China and Japan, Hongkong.

Nat. M. .... The National Magazine, New York.

Nat. Quar. R. .... The National Quarterly Review, New York.

Nation .... The Nation, New York.

Neue Europa .... Das Neue Europa . . . von August Lewald, Stuttgart (after 1840, Karlsruhe).

New Eng. .... The New Englander, New Haven.

No. Amer. R. ....The North American Review, Boston.

No. Brit. R. ....The North British Review, Edinburgh.

NSEQ ....Nankai Social and Economic Quarterly, Tientsin.

Once a Week ....Once a Week, London.

Overland ....The Overland Monthly, San Francisco.

Penny M. ....The Penny Magazine, London.

Philo. u. hist. Abh. d. Ak. d. W. ...Philologische und historische Abhandlungen der königlichen Akademie der Wissenschaften zu Berlin.

Phoenix ....Phoenix (James Summers, ed.), London.

PSQ ....Political Science Quarterly, New York.

Quar. R. ....The Quarterly Review, London.

RDM ....Revue des Deux Mondes, Paris.

Sat. R. ....The Saturday Review, London.

Scrib. ....Scribner's Monthly, New York.

Sitz. d. Ak. d. W. Wien ....Sitzungsberichte der philosophisch-historischen Classe der kaiserlichen Akademie der Wissenschaften, Wien.

Sitz. d. bay. Ak. d. W. ....Sitzungsberichte der philosophisch-philologischen und historischen Classe der königlich bayerischen Akademie der Wissenschaften zu München.

TP ....T'oung Pao, Leiden.

Unsere Zeit ....Unsere Zeit, Leipzig.

Unterhaltungen ....Unterhaltungen am häuslichen Herd, Leipzig.

Verh. Ges. Erdk. ....Verhandlungen der Gesellschaft für Erdkunde zu Berlin.

Westermann Mh. ....Westermann's Jahrbuch der illustrirten deutschen Monatshefte, Braunschweig.

Westm. R. ....The Westminster Review, London.

Z. allg. Erdk. ....Zeitschrift für allgemeine Erdkunde, Berlin.

ZDMG ....Zeitschrift der deutschen morgenländischen Gesellschaft, Leipzig.

Z. Ges. Erdk. ....Zeitschrift der Gesellschaft für Erdkunde zu Berlin.

WESTERN CONCEPTS OF CHINA
AND THE CHINESE, 1840-1876

CHAPTER I

INTRODUCTION

A S NINETEENTH-CENTURY knowledge of China was
greatly indebted to the researches of the three preceding
centuries, a short sketch of the relations of China and Europe
during that time is essential to understand Western attitude
toward China from 1840 to 1876. Through the activities of
navigators, travellers, and missionaries of the sixteenth, seventeenth, and eighteenth centuries, much new knowledge of China
came into Europe. During these centuries, the Jesuits were an
important bond between the East and the West, and by the
latter part of the seventeenth century they held first place as
authorities on China.[1] In the following century the writings
and translations of the Jesuits popularized the Orient to such
an extent in the West that in 1769 it was somewhat extravagantly stated that "China is better known than some provinces
of Europe itself."[2]

[1] For the history of Jesuit researches, see Theophilus Sigfridus Bayer,
Museum Sinicum (1730), Praefatio, pp. 1-145; Stephanus Fourmont, *Meditationes Sinicae* (1737), Praefatio, p. xxvi; Virgile Pinot, *La Chine et la
formation de l'esprit philosophique en France 1640-1740* (Paris, 1932), Livre
premier; Adolf Reichwein, *China and Europe* (New York, 1925), pp. 15-22,
75-153; Louis Pfister, *Notices biographiques et bibliographiques sur les Jé-
suites de l'ancienne mission de Chine* (Shanghai, 1932, 1934), vols. I, II;
Henri Cordier, "Notes pour servir à l'histoire des études chinoises en Europe,
jusqu'à l'époque de Fourmont l'aîné," *Nouveaux mélanges orientaux* (1886),
2 sér., 19, pp. 399-429; "Fragments d'une histoire des études chinoises au
XVIIIe siècle," *Centenaire de l'école des langues orientales vivantes* (1895),
pp. 223-93; "Half a Decade of Chinese Studies (1886-1891)," *TP* (1892),
3, pp. 532-63; "Les Études chinoises (1891-1894)," *ibid.* (1894), 5, pp.
420-57; (1895), 6, pp. 99-147; "Les Études chinoises sous la révolution et
l'empire," *ibid.* (1918), 19, pp. 59-103; J. J. L. Duyvendak, "Les Études
hollando-chinoises au 17ième au 18ième siècle." *Quatre esquisses détachées
relatives aux études orientalistes à Leiden* (1930), pp. 21-44; "Early Chinese
Studies in Holland," *TP* (1936), 32, pp. 293-344; "Le Développement des
études sinologiques," *Orient et occident* (1934-35), nos. I, II, IV, V, VI, VII.
[2] Reichwein, *op. cit.*, p. 78; *Oeuvres complètes de Voltaire* (Paris, 1829),
XXIX, 344.

The Jesuits learned from experience that it was not necessary to make professions of humility and asceticism in China as self-abasement and austerity were not, in the eyes of the Chinese, indications of superior virtue. Adapting themselves to the life as it was then lived, they even dressed like the Chinese. The other religious orders wore their customary religious habits in the Far East and adhered rigidly to their principles of asceticism.

Outwardly conforming to the customs of China, the Jesuits also made an effort to understand Chinese philosophy. They thought it was possible to compromise with Confucianism because it was a moral doctrine rather than a religious code and contained nothing contrary to Christian ethics. The ancient Chinese religion was, therefore, accepted by the Jesuits as fundamentally in harmony with Christian doctrine. The identity of faith was even believed to extend to a worship of the same God as that of the Christians.

More difficult was the harmonization of Christianity with the worship of ancestors. A great danger confronted the missionaries in the suppression of this cult. The Chinese might accuse them of undermining the whole social order which was founded on respect for the family. Unable to suppress ancestor worship, the Jesuits attempted to prove that veneration of the dead was not idolatrous but spiritual. They maintained that Chinese Christians should be allowed to take part in ancestor worship, whereas other missionaries strenuously opposed the practice. It was around this problem that the quarrel over the Chinese Rites raged in the seventeenth and in the first half of the next century.

The Jesuits, contending that the ceremonies connected with Confucianism and ancestor worship were purely civil, tried to convince the Pope and the European public of the justice of their views through their writings. The controversy was ended definitively in 1742 when the Pope decided absolutely against the Jesuits.

Although the Jesuits had failed to get control of missions

in China, they obtained a monopoly on missionary publications until almost the end of the eighteenth century. Such a circumstance is not surprising because the Jesuits on the whole were renowned scholars, carefully selected to convert the highly civilized Chinese. Other missionaries were warned by their superiors to steer clear of purely intellectual matters.[3]

The Jesuits through their researches, therefore, gave an impetus to Sinological studies in Europe. The earlier missionaries, Álvaro de Semedo (1585-1658), author of *Histoire universelle du grand royaume de la Chine* (1667) which was first published in 1642, Nicolas Trigault (1577-1628), Lazare Cattaneo (1560-1640), and Gaspar Ferreira (1571-1647 or 49) compiled dictionaries, but they were not published.[4]

Martini (1614-1661), who was sent to Europe from China in 1651 in connection with the Rites controversy, especially influenced the progress of Chinese studies in the West. His great *Chinese Atlas,* originally published in Amsterdam by the well-known publisher, Blaeu and translated into almost all of the languages of Europe, was the first important geographical work on the "Celestial Empire." This author also wrote a serious historical work parts of which Du Halde used in his *Description de la Chine.* Because of these works, Martini is important, but he also had a more direct influence upon the advance of Sinology in the West. While he was in Amsterdam busy with the publication of his atlas, Golius (1596-1667), who was Professor of Arabic and later, also of mathematics in the University of Leyden and had a fair collection of Chinese books but no knowledge of Chinese, was eager to meet him. Golius obtained a short interview in Leyden and subsequent conferences at Antwerp before Martini hastened to Rome. During these interviews, Golius, who had become interested in Chinese chronology through his Arabic studies, was able to establish for the first time the complete identity of the medieval Persian list of

---

[3] Pinot, *op. cit.,* 73 *et seq.*

[4] Cordier, "Études chinoises en Europe," *op. cit.,* 426; Pfister, *op. cit.,* I, 51-56, 78-80, 111-20, 143-46.

"Catayan" words, published by Graevius, with the Chinese cycles and chronological series and therefore the identity of "Catay" and "China." At this time, Martini also gave Golius several Chinese books and manuscripts. After his return to Leyden, Golius wrote *De Regno Catayo Additamentum* as an appendix to Martini's *Atlas*. In this work, Golius gives the circumstances of his conferences with Martini and makes use of the information he gained. This article is also significant because it contains the first printing from wood of Chinese characters in Holland and also the first properly printed Chinese characters in Europe.[5]

Still another seventeenth-century work, influential because of its popularity, is Athanasius Kircher's *China Illustrata* (1667) which contains many illustrations, representative of life in China. Kircher gives an explanation of the famous inscription of Hsi-an-fu of which he had already given a short account in his *Prodromus Coptus sive Aegyptiacus* (1636). For aid in the researches on this inscription, Kircher owed much to Boym (1612-1659), a Jesuit missionary. The former is indebted to the latter for the Latin translation and transliteration of the text and also for a book on the formation of Chinese characters.[6]

François de Rougemont (1624-1676), a Dutch Jesuit, Intorcetta (1625-1696), and Herdtricht (1624-1684) collaborated in a great work, *Confucius Sinarum Philosophus*, edited by Couplet (1623-1694). He carried many manuscripts to Europe when he returned in 1682 to give an account of missionary activities in the East, to present the Jesuits' point of view on the Rites question to the Pope, and to get new recruits for his mission. This work remained for a long time the principal source for the study of Chinese philosophy in the West. De

[5] Duyvendak, "Early Chinese Studies in Holland," *op. cit.*, 298 *et seq.*; Cordier, "Études chinoises en Europe," *op. cit.*, 400 *et seq.*; John Webb, *An Historical Essay Endeavoring a Probability That the Language of the Empire of China Is the Primitive Language* (London, 1669), p. 131. The first book printed in Europe in which Chinese characters appeared is Mendoza's *Historia del gran regno de la China* (1585).

[6] Duyvendak, "Early Chinese Studies in Holland," *op. cit.*, 324 *et seq.*; Cordier, "Études chinoises en Europe," *op. cit.*, 409 *et seq.*

Rougemont was the author of another significant book, *Historia Tartaro-Sinica* (1673).[7] The six missionaries, Guy Tachard, who remained in Siam, Joachim Bouvet, Louis Le Comte, Jean de Fontaney, Jean François Gerbillon, and Claude de Visdelou, who were sent to the Orient by Louis XIV, arrived in Peking, February 7, 1688. All of them acquired a fair knowledge of Chinese, but they left no treatises on the language to help Western scholars. Le Comte, upon his return to France, published his *Nouveaux mémoires sur l'état présent de la Chine*, noteworthy for its treatment of the Rites question. To this generation of missionaries belongs Noël who translated for the first time the *Hsiao Ching* or *Classic of Filial Piety*. His *Philosophia Sinica* (1711) played a very prominent role in the Rites controversy.[8]

Two extremely able missionaries whose knowledge of Chinese, Cordier wrote, was never surpassed and who had a profound influence upon the development of Sinological studies in Europe, through their extensive correspondence, were Prémare, the grammarian and philologist and Gaubil, the astronomer and historian. The latter's French translation of the *Shu Ching* or *Book of History*, which was not published until 1771, was more widely read than his astronomical treatises.[9]

Parrennin made extensive researches in the field of geography. In the course of his studies in connection with the atlases at the Imperial Library, he discovered many errors. The Emperor, K'ang Hsi, thereupon appointed a commission of Jesuits headed by Regis to correct the mistakes. The group completed the work in the years from 1708 to 1715. During this time Regis for the sake of accuracy made long journeys and collected much material on geography which Du Halde later incorporated in his *Description de la Chine*.[10] Other

[7] Duyvendak, "Les Études hollando-chinoises," *op. cit.*, 37; Pfister, *op. cit.*, I, 311, 321-28, 333-37, 363-66.

[8] Cordier, "Fragments d'une histoire des études chinoises," *op. cit.*, 225 *et seq.*

[9] *Ibid.*, p. 239; Ting Tchao-ts'ing, *Les Descriptions de la Chine par les Français (1650-1750)* (Paris, 1928), p. 41.

[10] "Le Développement des études sinologiques," *op. cit.*, no. IV, 1.

eighteenth-century missionaries of lesser importance were Florian
Bahr, compiler of dictionaries, Fourreau, author of a criticism
of Fourmont's *Grammatica Sinica,* Alexandre de La Charme,
translator of the *Shih Ching,* d'Incarville, de Ventavon, and a
few others who compiled dictionaries and made translations of
Chinese literature.[11]

The most important missionary Sinologue of the later eighteenth century was Amiot (1718-1793). His chief works are
*Art militaire des Chinois, De la musique des Chinois, tant
anciens que modernes, Vie de Confucius,* and *Dictionnaire tartar-
mandchou-français* (1789) which contemporaries commended.
With Amiot's death disappeared the last of the eminent missionaries in China who had distinguished themselves in the
study of Chinese language and literature.[12]

Other eighteenth-century publications of the Jesuits are the
Lettres édifiantes et curieuses, the *Description de l'empire de la
Chine,* a four volume work edited by Du Halde, *Mémoires
concernant les Chinois,* and De Mailla's *Histoire générale de
la Chine.* While native scholars were translating the *T'ung
Chien Kang Mu* into Manchu for the Emperor, De Mailla, who
was in Peking at the time, rendered extracts from the work into
French. In 1737 he sent the manuscript to France, and Fréret,
General Secretary of the *Académie des inscriptions et belles-
lettres,* who knew some Chinese, decided to have the translation
printed, but the project was dropped after Fréret's death. After
the dissolution of the Jesuit order in 1773, the work was published (1773-83) in twelve volumes by Grosier and Deshau-
terayes. Grosier, using Du Halde's work, added a thirteenth
volume in 1785 which gave a geographical description of the
provinces of China.[13]

The work which really sums up popular knowledge of China
in the West in the first half of the eighteenth century is Du

[11] *Ibid.,* 3; Cordier, "Fragments d'une histoire des études chinoises," *op.
cit.,* 285 *et. seq.*

[12] "Le Développement des études sinologiques," *op. cit.,* no. IV, 3, VI, 15;
Pfister, *op. cit.,* II, 837-60.

[13] Joseph-Anne-Marie de Moyriac de Mailla, *Histoire générale de la
Chine* (Paris, 1777), I, xxv *et seq.*; Pfister, *op. cit.,* II, 601; Cordier, "Fragments d'une histoire des études chinoises," *op. cit.,* 291.

Halde's *Description de l'empire de la Chine*. It had a great success, and before many years three editions in French and two in English appeared. The editor did not know the Chinese language and had never visited China. But he corresponded over a period of twenty-five years with missionaries stationed in the East. In this work and in other publications by Jesuit missionaries, such as the *Lettres édifiantes et curieuses*, the authors tried to prove that the Chinese were not superstitious and did not believe in magic, demons, or spirits. The public would thereby be convinced that the Chinese were spiritualists, believing since the earliest times in a personal God. Written for these definite purposes the works of Du Halde are unreliable and uncritical compilations.

It was but natural that these descriptions of China, conceived in a spirit of admiration for its civilization, exercised strong influence on the eighteenth-century French philosophers who were extremely critical of all existing European institutions. The China portrayed by the Jesuits seemed to furnish adequate proof that a civilization, based on entirely different principles from those upon which the Western nations were founded, could in addition to maintaining itself for centuries be superior to that of the West in many respects. The French philosophers, therefore, did much to popularize the favorable concepts of China.[14]

Several English writers, who were fairly familiar with Jesuit writings and travellers' accounts, also formed definite opinions in the seventeenth and eighteenth centuries about Chinese culture. Sir William Temple, Matthew Tindal, the English translator of Le Comte, Joseph Addison, and Alexander Pope, who had read much of the available literature on China, made many favorable statements about the Chinese and their great national sage, Confucius. Other writers, such as Daniel Defoe and Captain Dampier, criticized Chinese civilization severely.[15]

[14] Henri Cordier, *La Chine en France au XVIII siècle* (Paris, 1910), pp. 113-30; Ting Tchao-ts'ing, *op. cit.*, 99-104; A. H. Rowbotham, "China and the Age of Enlightenment in Europe," *CSPSR* (1935), 19, pp. 176-201.

[15] See Ch'en Shou-yi, "Daniel Defoe, China's Severe Critic," *NSEQ*

A few German scholars showed interest in the Orient. Leibniz early in his career began to read Chinese philosophy. In 1697 he published *Novissima Sinica* in which he praised Chinese culture and urged the interchange of knowledge between the East and the West. A. H. Francke, who was profoundly impressed by this work, founded in 1707 the *Collegium orientale theologicum*, a school for missionaries. "Sinic" was to be included in its curriculum. Another scholar, Christian Wolff, in an address which he gave in 1721 on Chinese philosophy tried to prove that the moral doctrine of Confucius in no way conflicted with Christian morality. This lecture based upon Noël's edition of the *Classics* contained the first full appreciation of Chinese scholasticism. Only a few German intellectuals, however, were interested in Chinese studies during the seventeenth and eighteenth ceuturies.[16]

The Jesuits at this time corresponded with the leading scholars of Europe, Bouvet and Grimaldi with Leibniz, Prémare with Fourmont and Fréret, Parrennin with Dortous de Mairon, and Gaubil with the astronomer, de l'Isle and Fréret. Because the bulk of this correspondence was not printed, a most significant portion of Jesuit scholarship remained unknown to the public which had at its disposal only those writings censured and edited by the Jesuits of Paris. The reason why all of the Jesuits' works were not published was because general readers were not interested in abstract studies of philosophy. They were intrigued by the *Lettres édifiantes et curieuses* which although giving much new material were writen in a fascinating style with all topics too heavy for contemporary taste omitted. The missionaries, modestly considering themselves transmitters

---

(1935), 8, pp. 511-50; "Sino-European Cultural Contacts since the Discovery of the Sea Route," *ibid.*, 44-74. As early as 1606, specimens of Chinese literature were brought to England. See W. D. Macray, *Annals of the Bodleian Library* (London, 1868), pp. 28, 60, 63, 91. On the general influence of China in England, see J. B. Botsford, *English Society in the Eighteenth Century* (New York, 1924), pp. 102-10; James E. Gillespie, *The Influence of Oversea Expansion on England to 1700* (New York, 1920).

[16] Reichwein, *op. cit.*, 79 *et seq.*; Pinot, *op. cit.*, 333-40; see Henri Bernard, "Chü Hsi's Philosophy and its Interpretation by Leibniz," *T'ien Hsia Monthly* (1937), 5, pp. 13-15.

of information, made no efforts to have their works printed. To avoid antagonizing their superiors at Rome and to escape losing their privileged positions at the court of Peking, the Jesuits did not present many of their more scholarly and critical researches on the various phases of Chinese civilization to the public.

A survey of Jesuit relations with European scholars reveals that eighteenth century intellectuals had more direct contacts with China and knew much more about its culture than the scholars of the following century. Some of the best Jesuit scholarship remained unpublished and was inaccessible to students in the nineteenth century. Fréret of the preceding century said Du Halde's works offered nothing new for the scholar.[17] In the nineteenth century, however, scarcely a work of any significance was published whose author did not use this work either directly or indirectly.

Jesuit influence in Europe began to wane as a result of the official dissolution of the order in France in 1762, and its complete abolition in 1773. Until 1760, when European admiration for China reached its height, the Jesuitical view of the Chinese predominated over the commercial point of view. The merchants had little chance to become acquainted with Chinese culture. Coming in contact chiefly with Chinese traders and the lower classes, they stressed the disagreeable features of Chinese civilization. When the Jesuit Order collapsed, the unfavorable opinions of the traders began to receive more and more attention after 1770. Then, economic considerations began to color all relations with the Orient.[18] Because of the strengthening of the unfavorable opinions of the commercial groups, the Jesuits' exaggerated praise of Chinese institutions and their excessive admiration for Chinese philosophy and literature tended to discredit their researches.[19] Yet their trans-

[17] Pinot, op. cit., 138 et seq.
[18] Reichwein, op. cit., 94, 149 et seq.; Adam Smith, An Inquiry into the Nature and Causes of the Wealth of Nations (London, 1908), pp. 55-56, 534-35.
[19] James Legge, The Chinese Classics (2nd ed., Oxford, 1865-95), IV, Part I, 114. (Vols. I, II were printed at the Clarendon Press, Oxford; vols.

lations and commentaries on various branches of Chinese knowledge continued to exert a powerful influence in the introduction of China's literature to the West through a large portion of the nineteenth century.[20]

During the seventeenth and eighteenth centuries knowledge of China also came into Europe through other channels as a result of a number of voyages especially of the Dutch to the East. Books by these travellers soon appeared. In 1592 was published at Leyden the first work, *Tresoor der Zeevaert* by Lucas Jansz Waghenaer, which gave first-hand material on China. The author received the information from Dirck Gerritz Pomp (1544-1604) who had been engaged in commerce with the Indies for twenty-four years and had made two voyages to China in the service of the Portuguese between the years 1568 and 1588. While at Goa and on the sea voyage home with him, Pomp supplied Jan Huygen van Linschoten with facts about the Orient which the latter doubtless incorporated in his *Description of the Navigation of the Portuguese in the Orient* (1595). Both of these books, containing much information on the East, remained for a long time the best guides for Dutch and foreign navigators. Other expeditions followed, such as those of van Neck (1601), van Waerwyck (1604), and Matelieff (1607), but these explorers had little direct contact with China itself.

Later in the seventeenth century, other travellers made many observations on China. For example Johan Nieuhoff's account of the embassy to China (1655-56) entitled *An Embassy from the East India Company of the United Provinces to the . . . Emperor of China* was published in Amsterdam in 1665 and was soon translated into French, German, English, and Latin. A few years later the story of the expedition of Bort on the coast of China and of the embassies at Foochow (1662)

III-V were printed at the London Missionary Society's printing office, Hong Kong).

[20] Several Jesuit works were published for the first time in the nineteenth century. Others were translated from the original Latin into modern European languages.

and Peking (1665) was published (1670); German and English translations followed shortly. The accounts of these voyages stimulated interest in the East. Nicholas Witsen published an important book, *Noord- en oost-Tartaryen* (1692). This work, while not devoted principally to China, gives many facts which its author had collected from numerous correspondents throughout the world. One of the greatest Dutch travellers of the eighteenth century was Samuel van de Putte (1690-1745) who succeeded in penetrating China overland from Tibet as far as Peking. Of his sojourn in the country, little is known because his journals and his other papers were destroyed in 1745 in obedience to his will.

The last great voyage of the Dutch to China was the expedition led by Isaac Titsingh. Van Braam took part in this embassy which the East India Company sent to China 1794-95. His account of the embassy was first published in French in Philadelphia 1797-98 by Moreau de Saint Méry. The illustrated descriptions of the Dutch embassies, which were usually translated into other languages, supplemented the work of the missionaries in making the reading public of the West familiar with Chinese life and customs and extended popular knowledge of the Orient among readers interested in tales of adventure.[21]

In the latter part of the eighteenth century when the French engrossed in the Revolution forgot about China, with the exception of a few intellectuals, the English, whose interest became more and more concerned with practical and commercial problems, tended to monopolize relations with the East. English literature on China became more limited to economic matters. After 1785 topographical descriptions and atlases were numerous.[22] At this time the Americans first began to trade with the Orient. Their interests remained primarily commercial and political throughout the following century.[23] The idea of the importance of China as a good market for the sale of surplus commodities was emerging by 1800.

---

[21] Duyvendak, "Les Études hollando-chinoises," *op. cit.*, 21-44; see Henri Cordier, *Bibliotheca Sinica* (Paris, 1904-08), cols. 2350-51.

[22] Reichwein, *op. cit.*, 150.

[23] Tyler Dennett, *Americans in Eastern Asia* (New York, 1922), p. 181.

When missionaries, travellers, and traders were making China known in Europe a few lay scholars were studying Chinese in the West. John Webb, an architect by profession, who became interested in the development of language, concluded that Chinese was probably the primitive language and wrote a curious octavo volume of two hundred and twelve pages entitled *An Historical Essay Endeavoring a Probability That the Language of the Empire of China Is the Primitive Language.* This book, which was originally published in 1669, is the first extensive treatment of the Chinese language by a European. Webb quoted in his *Essay* Mendoza's, Trigault's, Semedo's, Kircher's, and Martini's works and was also familiar with Nieuhoff's account in French translation of the Dutch embassy to China.[24]

Thomas Hyde of the Bodleian Library, who had acquired much information from an educated Chinese whom Couplet took from China to Europe in 1682, wrote a number of papers on Chinese subjects and by 1688 had learned to read Chinese.[25] Andreas Müller (1630-1694), a German scholar, who studied Chinese for a long time, edited the voyage of Marco Polo and wrote a few other works about China. His labors, however, produced few results, Cordier wrote.[26] Another German, Gottlieb Siegfried Bayer (1694-1738) was the last and at the same time the most remarkable of the earlier Sinologists. His best known work is *Museum Sinicum* (1730), the preface of which is valuable for its survey of Chinese studies.[27]

In the course of the eighteenth century, French scholars assume a very important role in the development of Sinology. The leadership of France began early because of the French Government's patronage from the days of Louis XIV, the facilities which the rich collection of Chinese books in the Bibliothèque Royale afforded for research,[28] and the interest of the

---

[24] Ch'en Shou-yi, "John Webb: a Forgotten Page in the Early History of Sinology in Europe," *CSPSR* (1935), 19, pp. 295-330.

[25] ———— "Thomas Percy and his Chinese Studies," *ibid.* (1936), 20, p. 211; Henri Cordier, *La Chine en France au XVIII siècle* (Paris, 1910), p. 131; Macray, *op. cit.*, p. 109.

[26] Bayer, *op. cit.*, 33 *et seq.*; Cordier, "Études chinoises en Europe," *op. cit.*, 420 *et seq.*   [27] *Ibid.*, 425 *et seq.*

[28] "Bazin's théâtre chinois," *C. Repos.* (1849), 18, p. 113.

French Government in the progress of French Jesuit missionaries whose influence on the intellectual life of France was very strong.[29] Fourmont (1683-1745), who taught Arabic languages in the Collège de France, became interested in Chinese through his associations with a Chinese Christian who went to Europe to take part in the debates on the Rites question and also through his correspondence with Prémare. In 1737 Fourmont published his *Meditationes Sinicae*, and his *Grammatica Sinica* which he had finished as early as 1728 appeared in 1742. This work was little more than a Latin translation of the grammar which the Dominican missionary, Varo, printed at Canton in 1703, but it was almost unknown in Europe. Since 1727 Prémare through his correspondence with Fourmont had given the latter much aid in his Chinese studies, and in 1728 he sent to Fourmont a manuscript of the *Notitia* which Fourmont utilized in the compilation of his grammar. He did not acknowledge his indebtedness to Prémare but wrote instead that the "essential points are correctly indicated in the two books, however that which I have written myself is better." Prémare's work was deposited in the Bibliothèque du Roi where it remained until parts of it were published (1831) by missionaries in Malacca. Both Fourmont's and Prémare's work aided Chinese studies in France and in Europe in the eighteenth and the nineteenth centuries.[30]

Joseph de Guignes (1721-1800), a student of Fourmont, was the last great Sinologue of the eighteenth century. His chief contribution was the collection, *Mémoires concernant l'histoire, les sciences et les arts, les mœurs, et les usages des Chinois . . .* (1775-1791) compiled in collaboration with Batteux and Bréquigny, and published in fifteen volumes to which a sixteenth volume, containing many articles by the Jesuits, Amiot and Cibot, was added in 1811.[31]

[29] James Legge, *Inaugural Lecture on the Constituting of a Chinese Chair in the University of Oxford; Delivered in the Sheldonian Theatre, October 27, 1876*, p. 5.
[30] Cordier, "Fragments d'une histoire," *op. cit.*, 233 *et seq.*
[31] "Le Développement des études sinologiques," *op. cit.*, no. IV, p. 4, VI, p. 15.

De Guignes's son was with Isaac Titsingh during the time the Dutch embassy was in China and was for some years French consul at Canton.[32] His chief contribution to Sinology was his *Dictionnaire chinois, français et latin* (1813).

European interest in Chinese language and literature lapsed somewhat during the last quarter of the eighteenth century and in the first part of the nineteenth when Romanticism took its place. It was not until the establishment of the new chair of Chinese in the Collège de France at the time of the Restoration that Chinese studies were established in the West. Abel Rémusat, for whom this professorship was created, wrote numerous practical treatises on the Chinese language and made translations of various pieces of Chinese literature.[33] Although an earlier Latin version had been made, Rémusat was in reality the first scholar to introduce the *Tao-Tê-Ching* to Europe.[34] He more than any of his contemporaries facilitated the acquisition of Chinese by Europeans. Stanislas Julien and other scholars, who gave attention to the drama, novel, and other kinds of colloquial literature, continued Rémusat's work.[35]

German scholars also took an important part in the development of Chinese studies in the nineteenth century. Julius Heinrich Klaproth (1783-1835) had a remarkable career. During the early part of the nineteenth century, when Oriental languages were very popular in Germany, he acquired for that time a fairly good knowledge of Chinese. In 1804 he was called to Russia and named a member of the academy of sciences as well as professor of Oriental languages. He went to France in 1815 where he published a number of works on China and on other countries of the East.[36]

A chair of Chinese and Tartar languages was established in

[32] C. L. J. de Guignes, *Voyages à Peking* (Paris, 1808), I, 255 *et seq.*

[33] "Huc's Christianity in China," *Dub. R.* (1857), 42, p. 439.

[34] J. J. L. Duyvendak, *Bird's-eye View of Sinology* (Published by the China Institute of America), p. 6.

[35] "Choix de contes et nouvelles par Théodore Pavie," *C. Repos.* (1851), 20, p. 225.

[36] "Le Développement des études sinologiques," *op. cit.*, no. VII, 13 *et seq.*

the University of Berlin in 1838 with Wilhelm Schott as professor extraordinary. Three years later, Schott received a similar appointment in the academy of sciences in the same city.[37] A little later Chinese professorships were created at Munich and at Vienna. A Sinologist of the former city, Johann Heinrich Plath, zealously studied all accessible materials, both Western and Chinese in Europe on early Chinese history.[38] Karl Friedrich Neumann, professor of Chinese history and language in the University of Munich made researches on Chinese history and foreign relations. Visiting the East early in his career, he made many acquaintances in the limited sphere of mercantile and missionary life in Canton. From Robert Morrison, missionary Sinologist and from original sources on the spot, he derived much material[39] to be incorporated later in his history of Eastern Asia.[40] Plath and Neumann were the only outstanding Orientalists at Munich. At Vienna August Pfizmaier made studies on a wide variety of subjects. His most important contribution was his research in ancient Chinese history. Neither his nor Plath's articles were for the general reader. Published by learned societies in their respective cities, they reached a limited number of scholars.[41]

At the University of Leyden, Johann Joseph Hoffmann, who was made a Professor of Japanese in 1855, also gave instruction in Chinese particularly for young men expecting to serve as interpreters in the Dutch East Indies. In 1877 a professorship in Chinese was given to Gustaaf Schlegel. For some years he had been associated with Hoffmann in the teaching of Oriental languages. Schlegel's interests were extremely varied. A four volume Dutch-Chinese dictionary is one of his contributions to

[37] Legge, *op. cit.*, 6.
[38] See *Sitz. d. bay. Ak. d. W.* and *Abh. d. bay. Ak. d. W.* for articles by Plath.
[39] "Literary Notices," *C. & J. Repos.* (1863), 1, p. 37.
[40] Karl Friedrich Neumann, *Geschichte des englisch-chinesischen Krieges* (Leipzig, 1855); *Ostasiatische Geschichte vom ersten chinesischen Krieg bis zu den Verträgen in Peking* (1840-1860) (Leipzig, 1861); "Die gegenwärtigen Zustände des chinesischen Reichs," *Unsere Zeit* (1857), 1, pp. 673-715.
[41] Pfizmaier's articles were published in *Sitz.* and *Denk. d. Ak. d. W. Wien.*

the study of Sinology,[42] and he with Cordier established the *T'oung Pao*.

The English lagged behind the Continent in the study of Chinese.[43] Robert Morrison, the first Protestant missionary to China, was a pioneer among English Sinologists in the nineteenth century. While in England in 1825 he in connection with a committee for the promotion of Chinese studies, of which Sir George Staunton, the Chinese scholar, was a member, recommended the introduction of Chinese into the Universities of Oxford and Cambridge. Although the group failed in their major purpose, a "Language Institute" was organized in London. There, Morrison taught Chinese several months to thirteen students. After his death in 1834, a committee purchased his Chinese library which in 1838 was presented to the University College on the condition that a professorship of Chinese language and literature to exist for at least five years be established. Samuel Kidd held the position until his retirement in 1842. It remained vacant until 1873. In a short time after that date the lack of students caused the post to remain unfilled for a while. In 1846 another Chinese chair was founded at King's College, London. James Summers and Robert K. Douglas occupied this position. Few students were attracted to the classes. The difficulties encountered in the introduction of Chinese into the universities of England prove that the British in general were not enthusiastic about the Chinese language.[44] There were, however, individual English scholars profoundly interested in Chinese literature. James Legge's translation of the *Chinese Classics* was a monumental piece of work, commended by contemporaries and by scholars of the present generation.

In the field of Sinology, the Americans were very backward. It is true that a few scholarly missionaries, such as Wells Williams, Bridgman, and others were interested in Chinese lan-

---

[42] Duyvendak, *op. cit.*, 10; Hendrik Kern, "Levensbericht van J. J. Hoffmann," *Verspreide Geschriften* (1928), XV, 235-47; "Dr. J. J. Hoffmann," *Ath.* Feb. 9, 1878, p. 189 *et seq.*

[43] "The Cochin-Chinese Language," *No. Amer. R.* (1841), 52, p. 406.

[44] Legge, *op. cit.*, 3 *et seq.*

guage and literature, but little real progress in Chinese studies in the colleges and universities is in evidence even as late as 1875.[45]

As the West particularly Great Britain and America desired extensive and varied information, the Pseudo-Sinologue had his opportunity. While a number of scholars were delving into Chinese literature and history, so-styled modern Sinologists with a contempt for detailed research and with a tendency toward ingenious speculation were making hasty and superficial generalizations on the entire field of Chinese civilization. Such a writer might live in one of the treaty ports, Peking, Hong Kong, London, Paris, Berlin, Munich, or San Francisco. Usually he had spent a few years in China and knew something of the Chinese language and the researches in Chinese literature. The chief sources of his material were a number of old French works, based on Jesuit accounts. Often such material published in periodicals or in book form was more widely read than were scholarly works which reached only a small number of intellectuals.[46]

Much of the information laid before the public in the nineteenth century was uncritical and incorrect. After 1842 with five of the largest maritime cities open to trade, travellers and foreign residents in China who had probably some knowledge of the language and greater opportunities for observation did write more accurately of various parts of the country, but long after 1842 the Western public entertained many curious notions about the Chinese.

[45] K. S. Latourette, "The Progress of Sinology in the United States," *NSEQ* (1935), 8, pp. 309-15.

[46] E. J. Eitel, "Amateur Sinology," *CR* (1873), 2, p. 1 *et seq.*; "Bazin's théâtre chinois," *op. cit.*

CHAPTER II

SURVEY OF SOURCES

THROUGH a cursory survey of the different categories of literature published in England, America, France, and Germany, an effort will be made to describe the scope and nature of European and American interest in China. This description of the literature is intended to show the types of books and articles written, to what extent they were read, and how far there was a definite demand for accurate information, particularly after 1840. It is a large and varied literature consisting of books, articles, and papers written by European residents and travellers in China. The mere existence of this literature is an illuminating commentary upon Western curiosity, for it indicates a wider interest than is commonly thought to have existed.

TRAVELLER'S ACCOUNTS

One of the best-known works of the middle of the nineteenth century is *The Chinese Empire* (1854) by the French Lazarist missionary, Huc. His objective was to make China known to everyone. Lacking all pretensions toward a polished literary style, he tried to relate, unaffectedly, the varied experiences and impressions of his tedious trips through the Chinese Empire.[1] On his journey through the very heart of the Empire from Tibet to Canton, he travelled in all the pride and pomp of a high government functionary, attended by mandarins and surrounded by a military escort. He had, therefore, close associations with persons of the highest rank. During a previous residence of no less than fourteen years in various parts of China, he carefully studied society in the Chinese Empire. With such unusual opportunities for close observation, Huc described the religion, manners, industries, and arts of the Chinese. He made no vague assertions for the whole of China, but spoke

[1] Evariste Régis Huc, *The Chinese Empire* (New ed., London, 1859), Preface.

only of those customs peculiar to the localities visited. Filled with amusing incidents and comical anecdotes, the narrative is entertaining as well as valuable. Portraying different types, such as the bonze, the mandarin, and the tea-porter, Huc attempted to analyze and to interpret Chinese character.[2] In a typical missionary fashion, the writer pictured China as a civilized nation removed from religious influence and rapidly falling into decay and ruin. As Huc's *Chinese Empire* was translated into English, it was probably as well known in England as in his own country. Many reviews of the work appeared in contemporary periodicals, and it was often the source of various articles published in English and American magazines.

Another work which had a wide vogue was Huc's *Christianity in China, Tartary and Thibet* (1857-1858). The activities of all the prominent Catholic missionaries, including François Xavier, Gaspard de la Croix, and Matteo Ricci, are sketched. The third and last volume, containing a single episode, the story of the famous K'ang Hsi's relations with the missionaries of the West, is in itself a unit. Through the struggles among the different groups of Catholic missionaries, the Pope and the Emperor were brought into conflict and the missionaries were driven out of the Empire. As it is the first formal and systematic history of Christianity in China and is written by a distinguished missionary, the work has a particular significance.

An amusing story of odd experiences is *Niphon and Pe-che-li* (1862) by the French traveller, De Fonblanque. He frankly admitted that his book did not pretend to be "either instructive, useful, or valuable." Those who looked for such merits he advised to read Huc.[3] His book is cited not for its special value but because it is quite typical of many travellers' accounts.

Merchants and business men were deeply interested in China,

[2] "Huc's Chinese Empire," *Dub. R.* (1855), 38, pp. 134-69; "Fortune and Huc," *Quar. R.* (1857), 102, pp. 126-65; "How to Travel in China," *Colburn* (1854), 102, pp. 379-94; "M. Huc's Travels in China," *Ed. R.* (1855), 101, pp. 415-42; *Liv. Age* (1855), 45, pp. 663-76; "Huc's China," *Fraser* (1855), 51, pp. 409-21.
[3] E. B. de Fonblanque, *Niphon and Pe-che-li; or, Two Years in Japan and Northern China* (London, 1862), Preface.

where many journeys were undertaken especially in the sixties and seventies to find new outlets for trade.[4]   After 1842, a considerable trade sprang up between Great Britain and the Orient, and Americans, French, and Germans had some commercial intercourse with China.   But the trade affected only a few of the seaports, and foreigners rarely visited the great inland provinces.   The jealous hostility of the Chinese educated and official classes toward Westerners was the first great obstacle in the way of increased contacts with the Chinese.   The great difficulty of the language, especially in the South where there are many dialects, prevented its acquisition by those who had long sojourns at the open ports.   Merchants had not the time for long and patient study.   As they were compelled to use interpreters in their business transactions, they were never brought into real contact with the large middle class, and were thus dèbarred from a thorough understanding of the more numerous and less prejudiced portion of the Chinese population.   Such an acquaintance, if it had been possible, might have led to a mutual appreciation between Westerners and Chinese.[5]

To learn something of the interior of China in general as well as for a definite commercial purpose, Cooper, an Englishman, in November, 1867, undertook an overland journey from Shanghai to Calcutta to discover a line of communication between China and India shorter and more direct than the route through the province of Szechwan and eastern Tibet, the only way open until 1871 or 1872.[6]   Cooper was primarily interested in the commercial prospects of England in China, but his narrative, *Travels of a Pioneer of Commerce in Pigtail and Petti-*

---

[4] A few explorations were made before 1871.   Raphael Pumpelly, sometime professor in Harvard University, was asked as early as 1863 by the Chinese Government upon the advice of Anson Burlingame and Sir Frederick Bruce to examine some of the principal coal fields of China.   The results of his explorations were not widely circulated as the Chinese Government soon lost interest in the expedition.   See Raphael Pumpelly, "A Journey in Northern China," *Galaxy* (1869), 8, pp. 467-76.

[5] T. T. Cooper, *Travels of a Pioneer of Commerce in Pigtail and Petticoats; or, an Overland Journey from China towards India* (London, 1871), p. 2.

[6] "An Englishman in China," *Cath. W.* (1871), 14, p. 322.

coats (1871), containing curious personal experiences, gives side lights on Chinese customs and some information on the natural resources of the country.

In 1869, European and American merchants, interested in the development of natural resources and in the investment of capital, obtained the services of Baron von Richthofen, and bore the cost of his explorations.[7] Letters written by the Baron to the Secretary of the General Chamber of Commerce at Shanghai, 1870-72, reveal an extraordinarily accurate picture of the geography, topography, products, and people of the parts of China which he visited. Careful attention was directed toward the lines of communication and places of trade. These letters and Richthofen's great work, *Ergebnisse eigener Reisen und darauf gegründeter Studien* (1877), furnish excellent examples of the tendency toward the acquisition of more specific information. They, like Cooper's *Travels*, are indicative of the augmented European interest in China for business and commercial reasons.

GENERAL DESCRIPTIVE WORKS

While many Westerners were making explorations and writing about the Chinese Empire, several Europeans and Americans had gone to that country as consular officials and missionaries. Perhaps the most significant and comprehensive work by a Western official is Sir John Francis Davis's *China* (1836). This account, partly a compilation from other authorities and partly material drawn from actual observation, contains a short history of European intercourse with China from the earliest times, a geographical sketch of the country, a summary of its history, a discussion of its government and legislation, a description of arts, inventions, science, natural history, agriculture, commerce, social customs, manners, and character of the Chinese, and a survey of the religions. This work was the source for numerous articles in English and American periodicals. It was also quoted by many subsequent writers on Chinese topics.

[7] J. R. Browne, "Under the Dragon's Footstool," *Overland* (1871), 6, p. 234.

G. T. Lay, aware of the quickened interest in China following the first Anglo-Chinese War, hoped to enlighten the West on the history, philosophy, literature, religion, social customs, arts, industry, and agriculture of the Chinese.[8]   In his book, *The Chinese as They Are* (1841), the author presents in a clear and concise style a fairly accurate picture of the Chinese and of their institutions.

T. T. Meadows, an English consular official in China, wrote two important books.   In his *Desultory Notes on the Government and People of China* (1847), he explained matters nearly or entirely new to the British public, such as civil divisions of the provinces, the duties and incomes of the mandarins and other agents of the government, and other things about which Europeans held erroneous ideas.[9]   His *Chinese and Their Rebellions* (1856) is a historical, descriptive, and interpretative work.   The author, devoting a section to the philosophy, morality, and polity of the Chinese people, gives an entirely new and unique view of the national fundamental beliefs and of the language used to express them in the Sacred Books; other divisions contain a general description of the geography, religion, and government of the Chinese.   Meadows's clear and able explanation of the salient points in the political administration was decidedly the best that had been written until the time that it was published[10] and is superior to much that has been written since.

Notable because the book was written by a merchant is John Scarth's *Twelve Years in China* (1860).   Keenly interested in China's commercial possibilities for Westerners, Scarth described such significant industries as the preparation of tea, silk, and sugar for the market.   Friendly toward the rebels, during the T'ai P'ing Rebellion, he stressed the corruption of the Imperial Government.   Scarth had a high regard for the Chinese people,

[8] G. T. Lay, *The Chinese as They Are* (Albany, 1843), Preface.

[9] T. T. Meadows, *Desultory Notes on the Government and People of China* (London, 1847), Preface.

[10] "China and the War," *Quar. R.* (1860), 107, p. 86; "China: Past and Present," *Westm. R.* (1858), 69, p. 371.

but he was bitterly hostile to the mandarins, whom he blamed for the untenable position of Westerners in China.

The writings of the missionaries, although sometimes inaccurate, biased, and prejudiced in their delineation of Chinese character and treatment of Chinese thought and civilization, in general form one of the most important and voluminous sources for an analysis of Occidental concepts of China and the Chinese from 1840 to 1876.[11]

An important descriptive account, *China; Its State and Prospects* (1838), was written by Medhurst, an agent of the London Missionary Society and also a distinguished Sinologist. Having kept a record of passing events during a journey along the northeast coast of China in 1835 to find out whether the country was open to Christianity, Medhurst contemplated the publication of his journal. In the course of a tour through England to plead the cause of missions, he found it necessary to explain more fully the political, moral, and spiritual condition of the people and to give a summary of the efforts made toward their conversion. Because these statements were received with considerable interest and because they awakened sympathy for the Chinese, the author decided to publish a work embracing the "general state of China, its state and prospects with special references to the diffusion of the Gospel."[12] Medhurst's book was regarded by contemporaries as one of the most valuable accounts of China. It threw much light on the strange customs of the East and made them unusually interesting to Europeans.

Widely read throughout the West were the writings of Charles Gutzlaff, a German missionary. Published in London, *China Opened* (1838), which was a description of the topography, history, customs, manners, arts, manufactures, commerce, literature, religion, and jurisprudence, ranked with Davis's *China* in importance and furnished much material for other writers on Chinese subjects.

Probably the most important single work on China by a

[11] Lay, *op. cit.*, Preface.

[12] W. H. Medhurst, *China; Its State and Prospects* (Boston, 1838), Introduction.

missionary is Wells Williams's *Middle Kingdom* (1848). It was widely reviewed and well received.[13] Its sources were personal observations, the study of native authorities, and the *Chinese Repository*. The Jesuit works of the eighteenth century were familiar to this writer, who used them with discrimination. After spending twelve years in contact with the Chinese people, speaking their language and studying their books, Williams felt himself competent to explain features of their polity and character and to give such views of their religious and social conditions as to encourage greater efforts toward their conversion. Upon his return from China to the United States, he found a demand for facts on the prospects for the extension of trade in the Chinese Empire. Others wished to find out the effect of the opening of China upon the introduction and diffusion of Christianity.[14]

The earlier chapters of the first volume contain an excellent geographical description. Other chapters discuss education and literary examinations, language, literature, architecture, dress, diet, social life, commerce, foreign relations, and the origin and progress of the first war with England. Describing all phases of Chinese life, the work is a good illustration of the range and diversity of subjects found in general accounts of the period. Williams presented his material in such a clear, systematic, and scholarly manner that his work today holds a respected place in American literature on China.[15]

A book somewhat similar in its aims and scope is Milne's *Life in China* (1857). Pledged to the cause of Protestant missions by his earliest associations, the author embarked for the Orient in the summer of 1839. With the exception of an absence of two years, he continued his missionary activities until about 1854 under the auspices of the London Missionary Society. In carrying on his work, it was his lot to visit various places, including Macao, Hong Kong, Canton, Chusan, Ningpo, and Shanghai. He travelled through the middle of the three prov-

---

[13] "Miscellaneous Notices," *Westm. R.* (1848), 49, pp. 241-43.
[14] S. W. Williams, *The Middle Kingdom* (New York, 1848), Preface.
[15] Revised ed., 1901.

inces of Chekiang, Kiangsi, and Kwangtung. During this long period, he recorded faithfully in his book his observations on the Chinese. Milne hoped to diffuse in England a fairer and more nearly correct knowledge of the Chinese and of their country and to rid Europeans of false and ridiculous notions and impressions. He also wished his book to further the cause of Christian missions in China.[16]

Lechler's book, *Acht Vorträge über China gehalten an verschiedenen Orten Deutschlands und der Schweiz* (1861), similar in content to the large number of books by English and American missionaries, has chapters on religion, language, literature, public instruction and examinations, the Chinese state, system of government, and family life. Like other missionary authors, Lechler tries to interest his compatriots in Chinese missions.

Lockhart's *Medical Missionary in China* (1861) is almost unique. His object is to show the importance of a medical missionary's work in a "heathen land" as aid in spreading the doctrines of Christianity.[17] Besides describing the activities of medical missionaries and the diseases common to the Chinese, the author summarizes the relations of England and the Orient and discusses the opium question. In this connection he advances the opinion that cotton should be raised in India instead of opium.

The most excellent and the most comprehensive work on social customs is Justus Doolittle's *Social Life of the Chinese* (1865). Even though the work is a simple treatment of Chinese life and manners especially in Foochow and vicinity, the descriptions of many of the customs are generally applicable to other parts of the Empire. These two volumes contain many details on betrothal and marriage, superstitious attitude toward disease, death, mourning and burial, religion, government, agriculture, competitive literary examinations, festivals, business and social customs, opium smoking, and a comparison of Chinese and scriptural quotations.

[16] W. C. Milne, *Life in China* (New ed., London, 1859), Preface.

[17] William Lockhart, *The Medical Missionary in China* (London, 1861), p. 117.

China and the Chinese (1869) by Nevius, another missionary, is more general than Doolittle's work. It contains much less detail on social customs. More space is devoted to the religious conditions of the people and the character and results of missionary work. Occasionally the author quotes other writers, but he relies for the most part on his own experiences over a period of ten years in all parts of the Chinese Empire.[18] Like many similar books, this one ends with an appeal for missions and deplores the neglect of missionary work.

After 1840, a scientific interest in the minerals and plant life of China is obvious. An English scientist whose works were widely read in England, in America, and also on the Continent was Robert Fortune. Although a botanist, he went to China originally in behalf of commerce. He was sent by the Board of Directors of the East India Company to obtain the finest varieties of the tea plant as well as native manufacturers' implements for the government tea plantations in the Himalayas. In 1843, the Horticultural Society of London sent Fortune to collect new plants for its garden at Chiswick. His report of this journey, *Three Years' Wanderings in the Northern Provinces of China* (1847), contains an account of his travels and adventures, with minute details on the cultivation of tea, cotton, and other plants. His sphere of observation was as varied as it was prolonged. Instead of confining himself to the districts to which foreigners were limited by treaty, he advanced boldly into the interior. On one of his journeys, travelling dressed like a native, he had rare opportunities for seeing Chinese life. Fortune was interested in the social rather than in the moral peculiarities and in the economic rather than in the spiritual conditions of the Chinese people. What he saw, he described without exaggeration.[19] A student of science and an accomplished botanist, he delineated clearly, in a fresh and simple style, the leading physical features of the districts and their different and often novel forms of vegetable life.[20]

[18] J. L. Nevius, *China and the Chinese* (New York, 1869), Preface, p. 6.
[19] "Fortune and Huc," *Quar. R.* (1857), 102, 127.
[20] "Interior China," *No. Brit. R.* (1857), 27, p. 89.

A Catholic missionary, Armand David, whose primary interest was natural science, was sent to organize a French college for the Chinese at Peking. While in the Orient he made several exploratory trips through different parts of China. The account of his third journey, *Journal de mon troisième voyage* (1875), written in the form of a diary, contains details on the weather, day by day, and specific information and observations on insects, birds, fossils, and other natural phenomena, but little material on the social usages and habits of the people.[21]

Whether Occidentals were missionaries or laymen, their books have a few characteristics in common. A trader, stressing the economic and social life, hoped to introduce Western machinery and products into China so that European countries might open up new markets for their manufactured goods. A missionary, emphasizing the unsatisfactory spiritual state of the people, desired aid in the Christianization of the Chinese. Practically every author gives some details on the manners and customs of the Chinese people. A feature of these books is the limitation of remarks to localities visited. Realizing that previous knowledge of China was sketchy and inaccurate, many writers definitely state their concern to clear up inexact ideas and to convey correct information.

In addition to the books by Western residents of China are a number of general treatises by Europeans some of whom never saw the Orient. *An Historical and Descriptive Account of China* (1836), which contributed largely toward the crystallization of European opinion of China, was written by Hugh Murray and five other authors who had never been there. After a preliminary survey of the natural features of the country, the compilers give an outline of China's history. They try to point out the advances made in civilization and the most memorable events that distinguished the successive dynasties together with a philosophical view of the causes of their rises and downfalls. They then refer to the knowledge of the Orient possessed by the Greeks and Romans. On that subject they hoped to throw

[21] Armand David, *Journal de mon troisième voyage d'exploration dans l'empire chinois* (Paris, 1875), Preface.

additional light by tracing an early maritime route to Canton, thereby proving the existence of an ancient trade in tea. The remainder of the first volume is concerned with the efforts of modern European nations to open commercial intercourse and the reception of Westerners at the Imperial court. The second volume is devoted to the literature, religion, government, industry, manners, and social life. In the final volume the authors give a superficial description of the interior of the empire, with a sketch of its foreign commerce, particularly with England. Because of its comprehensiveness, this work was often used as a reference, but it had many defects. Its authors' failure to use the work of the contemporary Sinologists, such as Klaproth and Rémusat, suggests that the Sinological researches of continental Europe were largely independent of and remote from the popular interest which gathered momentum through and following the decade of the forties. On the contrary, the authors quote copiously De Mailla, Mendoza, Purchas, and similar authorities. This book is an excellent example of the tendency to generalize and to draw information from the seventeenth-century and eighteenth-century writers. For some years after 1840, the older methods continue with the development of the newer and more scientific means of collecting information about the Chinese Empire.

A work favorably received was Samuel Kidd's *China* (1841). Kidd was, however, a missionary at Malacca for seven years. He returned to England in 1832, and afterwards became professor of Chinese in University College, London.[22] The object of his book was "to excite an interest on behalf of the Chinese in those who are seeking comparatively unexplored fields of research where they may acquire extended views of man, in his moral and intellectual state, in his social connections and in relation to the Supreme Power from which he believes himself to have emanated."[23] Kidd's work is a scholastic rather than a practical study. Instead of describing the obvious characteristics

---

[22] "List of Works on China," *C. Repos.* (1849), 18, p. 419.

[23] Samuel Kidd, *China, or, Illustrations of the Symbols, Philosophy, Antiquities, Customs, Superstitions, Laws, Government, Education and Literature of the Chinese* (London, 1841), Preface.

of a particular custom, he tried to fathom the state of mind underlying a specific practice.

THE ANGLO-CHINESE WARS OF 1839-42 AND 1856-60

Special problems connected with the opening of China absorbed the attention of many Westerners. The war of 1840 naturally brought the opium question to the front. The European press poured forth works on China. Pamphlet upon pamphlet was laid before the public, and column after column and page after page, in periodicals and in newspapers, were filled with remarks on China. Apathy was no longer the order of the day. "Have you heard the latest news from China?" "Has war been declared?" "Is foreign commerce likely to be reëstablished?" Such questions were asked with concern in England upon the arrival of each successive mail from the East.[24] Many of the pamphlets were unimportant in content, but the large number which was printed proves that the subjects discussed, commercial mainly, were very important, especially to the people of England and America.

Many officers and others connected with the expedition to China during the first Anglo-Chinese War wrote accounts of the conflict. The most complete treatment of the earlier stages of the war is Bingham's *Narrative of the Expedition to China* (1842). Besides being a preliminary survey of the opium question and a systematic arrangement of the important facts of the expedition, the story is enlivened by personal experiences and readable sketches of Chinese character and customs. Loch's account, *The Closing Events of the Campaign in China* (1843), which supplements Bingham's, is equally well arranged. It gives a good survey of the later events of the war with some details on the topography of the country and on Chinese character. Still another book is *The Chinese War* (1844), by John Ouchterlony. Recording events more or less as they happened, he approaches his subject objectively. Toward the end of the work, he devotes some space to a description of the country and various places of peculiar interest. Some of the books by sol-

---

[24] "Pamphlets on China," *C. Repos.* (1840), 9, p. 156 *et seq.*

diers on the Chinese situation in the decade of the forties give interesting glimpses of society, but because of the circumstances of their authors' sojourns in the East and the nature of their interests, the works are filled with much purely military detail.

One of the best accounts of the earlier part of the second Anglo-Chinese War (1856-60) is by Wingrove Cooke, a newspaper correspondent. *China* (1858) by this author was popular, and wielded a wide influence on public opinion in France as well as in England. A French writer on Chinese affairs observed that Cooke's correspondence retraced faithfully not only the events of the campaign that was ended by the fall of Canton, but also gave an accurate description of Chinese ports at the beginning of the war.[25] It is not merely a history of the war, but contains much material on China and its inhabitants which Cooke thought would be useful to the British for commercial reasons. He says that it was "by slow gradations that a full conception of the enormous future which this eastern Asia could open to the commercial thousands and to the laboring millions of his own countrymen" became fixed in his own mind and was allowed to appear in his correspondence.[26] The entire book has a certain levity of style which makes it very readable.

The German work, *Ostasiatische Geschichte vom ersten chinesischen Krieg bis zu den Verträgen in Peking* (1861) by Neumann surveys the twenty years of Chinese history from 1840 to 1860. In the first chapter, Neumann notes the remarkable geographical position of China and its peculiar name, the "Middle Kingdom." The origin of the use of opium, the gradual increase of trade in that article, the enormous profits arising from the trade, the various qualities of opium, the kinds preferred by the Chinese, the laws against its importation into China, and the evasion of such laws are discussed as a preliminary to the second chapter which explains the conditions at the outbreak of the first Anglo-Chinese War. The events of this conflict and the treaties ending it are fully explained. After summarizing in a few pages the causes and progress of the

---

[25] Charles Lavollée, *La Chine contemporaine* (Paris, 1860), p. 220.
[26] G. W. Cooke, *China* (London, 1858), Preface p. xxxiii.

rebellion, the author gives a fairly full account of the expeditions of England and France against China and of the treaties closing the second European war against China and their results. Neumann's position as professor of history and of the Chinese language in the University of Munich gave his writings considerable weight and prestige.[27]

After the second war with China, a number of accounts of the expedition of 1860 were published. Robert Swinhoe's *Narrative of the North China Campaign of 1860* (1861) is probably the best known. His sole object was to write a complete history of the campaign, but he includes minor occurrences because they often make clear the chief events and give a continuity to the whole. He inserts many anecdotes to make the subject matter entertaining.[28] The history of the campaign is interspersed with side lights on the manners and customs in the localities he passed through. Another book dealing with the same period is Fisher's *Three Years' Service in China* (1863), essentially a narrative of the personal experiences of an engineer-officer, with some interesting observations on Chinese character, art, agriculture, and other phases of their culture. As the book touches on collateral events only when it is necessary to preserve the thread of the narrative, the author claims that it should not be considered history.[29] Being well-written, the book is readable and entertaining.

FOREIGN RELATIONS

With the steady development of commercial and diplomatic intercourse between the East and the West, it was natural for students to investigate the history of relations between China and the Occident. Probably the most important book on that subject is *Histoire des relations politiques de la Chine avec les puissances occidentales . . .* (1859), by Pauthier. Its purpose was simply to survey the various efforts of Western powers to

---

[27] "Literary Notices," *C. & J. Repos.* (1863), 1, p. 38.

[28] Robert Swinhoe, *Narrative of the North China Campaign of 1860* (London, 1861), Preface.

[29] Arthur Fisher, *Personal Narrative of Three Years' Service in China* (London, 1863), p. 1.

establish political and commercial relations with China. The greatest obstacle to such attempts was the etiquette of the court of China, described fully by Pauthier. This history, written by one of the prominent French Sinologists, was fairly authoritative.

A history of foreign relations different from Pauthier's was Baron de Meriten's *Sketch of Our Relations with China during Three and a Half Centuries, 1517-1869* (1871). He had been Chinese secretary to the French Legation at Peking and commissioner of Chinese customs at Foochow. His purpose was "to instruct Western nations on the subject of the relations between China and the West," so that Occidentals could draw correct conclusions from the facts laid before them. He pointed out that the policy of conciliation and forbearance advocated by many of his contemporaries was tried chiefly between 1517 and 1839 and even until 1856. During these three centuries, its unvarying results had been humiliation, conflicts, and massacres. Baron de Meritens, a practical man of affairs located in China for many years, based his conclusions on his own observations and experiences while Pauthier conducted his researches in Europe. The latter is undoubtedly more objective in his point of view than the former.

THE T'AI P'ING REBELLION

In the summer of 1850 when Europeans were concerned about the questions of trade and diplomatic contacts with China, they began to hear rumors of an upheaval in the interior. This movement came to be known as the T'ai P'ing Rebellion, the most important event of the time and one of the greatest revolutions that the world had ever seen.[30] Several histories of the movement were published.

Charles Macfarlane, in *The Chinese Revolution* (1853), traces the history of the uprising with special emphasis on the conditions which made such a revolt possible. The author was particularly concerned in clarifying the Chinese situation for Western readers whom he considered totally ignorant of the

---

[30] "The Revolution in China," *Ecl. M.* (1854), 31, p. 91; "The Past and Future of China," *Blackw.* (1854), 75, p. 54; "The Chinese Revolution," *Colburn* (1853), 99, p. 180.

actual conditions of the Empire. *A History of the Insurrection in China* (1853) by two Frenchmen, Callery and Yvan, originally printed in French and later translated into German and English, had a large circulation.[31] It is essentially a narrative of the Rebellion, but the authors interspersed their account with descriptions of certain localities and with instructive pictures of Chinese life and manners.

Certainly the most discerning and fairest discussion of the Rebellion to 1856 is Meadow's *Chinese and Their Rebellions* (1856). Dispensing with a tedious enumeration of dates and minute detail, through intelligent observation and a skillful use of contemporary material he drew his conclusions on the causes and progress of the Rebellion. Although he opposed intervention either in behalf of or against the rebels, he hoped for their success. Under their regime, the position of foreigners would certainly be no worse. At the same time, the T'ai P'ings would provide a basis for the growth of national feeling and unity and for an extension of diplomatic intercourse and commercial privileges.[32]

Lindsay Brine's book, *The Taeping Rebellion in China* (1862), permeated with a friendly spirit toward the Chinese, was popular; at the time of its publication it was considered one of the most valuable accounts of the Rebellion.[33]

A story of the revolt quite different in tone is Lindley's *Ti-Ping Tien-Kwoh; the History of the Ti-Ping Revolution* (1866). It is not only a narrative of the author's personal adventures and experiences during four years of military service with the T'ai P'ings, but it contains, according to the author, a complete history of the Rebellion, its political, military, and social organization, and accurate descriptions of its extraordinary leader, Hung Hsiu-ch'üan, and his principal chiefs. It also traces the rise, progress, and circumstances of the movement together with its bearing on the people of China and of Great Britain.

[31] "Contemporary Literature of France," *Westm. R.* (1853), 60, p. 631.
[32] T. T. Meadows, *The Chinese and Their Rebellions* (London, 1856), pp. 74-325.
[33] "The Yang-tsze River, and the Taepings in China," *Ecl. M.* (1863), 58, p. 334.

As the book is really a defense of the T'ai P'ings and their principles, British policy in China during the Rebellion receives a severe indictment.

COMMERCIAL EXPEDITIONS

After the opening of China and the establishment of diplomatic relations between the East and the West, commercial matters became of paramount importance. Martin was sent to examine the financial and political interests of Great Britain in China. After extensive investigations, he published two books, *Reports, Minutes and Despatches, on the British Position and Prospects in China* (1846) and *China, Political, Commercial and Social* (1847), in which he reaches the conclusion that peaceable and profitable trade with the whole of the Chinese Empire would be of great advantage to both countries.[34]

Reinhold Werner's book, *Die preussische Expedition* (1863), on the expedition to China in the years 1860, 1861, and 1862, indicates German interest in the development of commercial intercourse with the Orient. The chief purpose of the expedition was the conclusion of commercial treaties with China, Japan, and Siam. The author, in writing the account of the enterprise, hoped not only to make the German public acquainted with China but to call attention to the great opportunities for the development of economic interest in the Far East. Certainly the contents of this book reached many readers, for the material first appeared in the *Deutsche allgemeine Zeitung* and later went through at least two editions in book form.[35]

The Austrians, sensing the importance of trade relations with China, sent an expedition headed by Karl von Scherzer to the East in the interest of trade. The account of this enterprise, *Fachmännische Berichte über die österreichisch-ungarische Expedition nach Siam, China und Japan (1868-1871)* (1872), sketching the economic conditions in the Chinese Empire, gives

[34] R. M. Martin, *Reports, Minutes and Despatches on the British Position and Prospects in China* (London, 1847), Preface.

[35] Reinhold Werner, *Die preussische Expedition nach China* (2nd ed., Leipzig, 1873). See prefaces to the first and second editions.

general information on commerce, money, banking and credit conditions, currency, imports, exports, agriculture, industry, and mineral resources.

IMMIGRATION

The question of Chinese immigration became a vital problem between 1840 and 1876 especially in America, to which many Chinese were coming. No book, it seems, was devoted exclusively to the subject, but *The Oldest and the Newest Empire: China and the United States* (1870), by William Speer, a missionary to China and later to the Chinese in California, is largely concerned with the problem of immigration to that state. In the first place, the author pictures the Chinese in their native land, summarizes the history of the Empire, and describes the manners, customs, arts, and industries of the Chinese, all of which is to serve as a groundwork for the discussion of their contacts with the people of the United States. The earlier part of the book is based upon material drawn largely from other writers, such as Davis, Williams, and Gutzlaff.[36] The second part of the volume bears directly upon the subject of Chinese immigration, and is the most interesting portion of the work.

TRANSLATIONS OF CHINESE LITERATURE

The sources discussed in the preceding pages consist of books or pamphlets written by Westerners, mostly in English, about China in general or on some particular problem connected with that country. Another kind of material consists of translations, largely French, of various examples of Chinese literature. Stanislas Julien, reputed to be one of the greatest Orientalists of his day, made translations of many specimens of novels and short stories. Julien's purpose arose from his realization that, with China opened in such a definitive manner, no literary help in any form existed for studying the modern Chinese language without an instructor. Julien's versions of the novels *P'ing Shan Leng Yen, les deux jeunes filles lettrées* (1860), and

[36] William Speer, *The Oldest and the Newest Empire: China and the United States* (Hartford, Connecticut), Preface, p. 3 *et seq.*

Yü Chiao Li, les deux cousines (1864, second edition) were received in France and in other countries most favorably.[37]

Another French scholar, the Marquis d'Hervey-Saint-Denys, in *Poésies de l'époque des Thang* (1862), rendered into French some of the masterpieces of Chinese poetry.[38] Sir John Francis Davis also translated examples of poetry in *Poeseos Sinicae Commentarii* (1829), of which a new and augmented edition appeared in 1870. A few translations of novels were also published in English. Davis, for example, in *Chinese Novels* (1822) translated in an abridged form three Chinese tales. A new edition of this book appeared in 1843. Such translations were made for various reasons. In the first place, novels give a complete and intimate picture of the Chinese.[39] Again, as savants were studying Chinese literature for its own sake, it was natural for them to introduce it to their countrymen through the medium of translation. Lastly, with the increasing contacts between the East and the West, it was important to familiarize the Occident with China through its literature. Although in Germany interest in Chinese literature was limited to a small number of Sinologists, a few Chinese novels were translated[40] and part of the *Classics* was put into German. For instance, Von Plaenckner translated the *Ta Hsüeh* (1875), accompanied by commentaries.

Medhurst, an English missionary, translated the *Shu Ching* with the title of *Ancient China, the Shoo King, or the Historical Classic* (1846). This book had already been put into French by Gaubil and corrected by De Guignes. Because that version was too free, in many respects faulty, and unknown in

[37] Stanislas Julien, *Yu-Kiao-Li; ou, les deux cousines* (2nd ed., Paris, 1864), Preface, p. xv *et seq.* Translated by Abel Rémusat in 1826 but unknown to the generation after that date. See T. F. Wade, . . . *A Progressive Course, Designed to Assist the Student of Colloquial Chinese* (London, 1867), Preface, p. xiv *et seq.*

[38] M. J. L. Hervey-Saint-Denys, *Poésies de l'époque des Thang* (Paris, 1842), lxv *et seq.*

[39] J. F. Davis, *Chinese Novels* (London, 1822), p. 9 *et seq.* (New ed. 1843).

[40] Chuan Chen, *Die chinesische schöne Literatur im deutschen Schrifttum* (1933), pp. 20, 28, 84, Bibliographie.

England, Medhurst made a new translation.[41] The first complete translation of the *Chinese Classics* into a European language is that of James Legge, an English missionary, who landed in the East towards the end of 1839, and was stationed at Malacca for three or four years. Before leaving England, he had studied for a few months under Kidd at the University of London. Legge, to fit himself for his position, began to study the *Classics*, in which are found the bases of the moral, social, and political life of the Chinese people. In 1856 he first discussed his project for the translation of the *Classics* with friends. Finally the matter was brought before Joseph Jardine, a merchant, who expressed himself favorably toward the plan as follows: "I know the liberality of the merchants in China, and that many of them would give their help to such an undertaking, but you need not have the trouble of canvassing the community. If you are prepared for the toil of the publication, I will bear the expense of it. We make our money in China, and we would be glad to assist in whatever promises to be of benefit to it."[42] After receiving Jardine's offer, Legge, hoping that the series would be of real value to missionaries and to students of Chinese literature, set to work on his translation of *The Chinese Classics* (1861-85).[43]

In San Francisco, Loomis published a small volume of selections from the *Classics*, entitled *Confucius and the Chinese Classics* (1867). This work, probably the first anthology of its kind, is unique. Almost all other translations were for missionaries and for students of Chinese literature and only incidentally for the general reader. The growing commerce between the United States and China created an American interest in Chinese character, customs, and literature. To meet the demands for information about Oriental culture, a book firm in San Francisco intended to publish a work in fourteen volumes which would

[41] W. H. Medhurst, *Ancient China. The Shoo King or the Historical Classic* (Shanghai, 1846), Preface p. viii *et seq.*
[42] James Legge, *The Chinese Classics* (Oxford, 1893), Preface.
[43] These translations were partly published in F. Max Müller's series, *The Sacred Books of the East* (Oxford, 1879-85), Vols. III, XVI, XXVII, XXVIII.

include all the *Chinese Classics* and other specimens of their literature, but this work, apparently, never materialized.[44]

The prefaces, introductions, and notes to translations are important. The scholars in explaining their motives usually point out the merits and value of the works which they translate. As the foremost Sinologists, familiar with the original Chinese, made the translations, any opinions expressed in connection with such works carry more weight than the ideas given in general surveys. European scholars of Chinese were responsible, directly or indirectly, for the introduction of many examples of Chinese literature to the West.

TRANSLATION OF THE BIBLE INTO CHINESE

While Western Sinologists, such as Julien, Davis, and others were chiefly confronted with the problem of putting masterpieces of Chinese literature into European languages, the missionaries had a still more difficult task of rendering the Bible and various tracts on Christianity into Chinese. Because the missionaries hoped to translate the Bible sufficiently well to command the respect of the literati, it was necessary to obtain the collaboration of the best missionary Sinologists in China.

In 1843, representatives of the British and American societies met in Hong Kong and decided upon a plan of coöperation according to which the missionaries of Hong Kong and the Five Ports were assigned certain portions of the Bible to translate. Finally, the various translations were to undergo revision in a committee selected by the Protestant missionaries stationed in China. Medhurst, J. Stronach, Milne, Bridgman, Boone, Shuck, Lowrie, and Culbertson served at some time on this committee. A serious disagreement arose in this group over the question of the proper Chinese terms for God and the Holy Spirit, especially for the former. Many terms were proposed, but, in time, *Shen* and *Shang Ti* were preferred. The Americans favored the former, while the British chose the latter.[45]

[44] A. W. Loomis, *Confucius and the Chinese Classics* (San Francisco, 1867), Preface.
[45] See K. S. Latourette, *A History of Christian Missions in China* (New York, 1929), p. 261 *et seq.*

The Terms controversy brought forth many pamphlets and articles by Boone, Legge, Malan, Medhurst, and other missionaries.[46] In the end two versions of the Bible were completed. Medhurst's, Stronach's, and Milne's translation, completed in 1852 or 1853, had more literary grace but less accuracy than Bridgman's and Culbertson's version which was finished in 1862. Bridgman with the aid of other missionaries completed an edition of the New Testament. Although the plan for a "Union Bible" was not quite successful, it was responsible for a much better translation than any earlier Chinese versions of the Bible.

MONOGRAPHS ON CHINESE LITERATURE

Wylie's *Notes on Chinese Literature* (1867) is still the most comprehensive work on the subject, although it is rather a catalogue than a history. The book was written primarily to serve as a guide for Europeans beginning their study of Oriental literature.[47] A monograph, somewhat similar in scope and purpose, is Schott's *Entwurf einer Beschreibung der chinesischen Litteratur* (1853).[48] He surveys the entire field and gives a short summary of each class of literature. This concise study was considered very useful by contemporaries.[49] These works were the only efforts made before 1876 to give a survey of the

[46] *A Few Thoughts on the Question, What Term Can Be Christianized for God in Chinese?* (1864), 3 pp.; James Legge, *Letters on the Rendering of the Name God in the Chinese Language* (Hong Kong, 1850), 73 pp.; Legge, *The Notions of the Chinese Concerning God and Spirits: with an Examination of the Defense of an Essay, on the Proper Rendering of the Words Elohim and Theos, into the Chinese Language, by William Boone* (Hong Kong, 1852), vii, 166 pp.; S. C. Malan, *Who Is God in China? Shin or Shang-Te?* (London, 1855), vii, 310 pp.; W. H. Medhurst, *A Dissertation on the Theology of the Chinese, with a View to the Elucidation of the Most Appropriate Term for Expressing the Deity, in the Chinese Language* (Shanghai, 1847), 280 pp.; W. H. Medhurst, *An Inquiry into the Proper Mode of Rendering the Word God in Translating the Sacred Scriptures into the Chinese Language* (Shanghai, 1848), 170 pp.

[47] Alexander Wylie, *Notes on Chinese Literature* (Shanghai, 1867), Preface.

[48] Wilhelm Schott, "Entwurf einer Beschreibung der chinesischen Litteratur," *Philo. u. hist. Abh. d. Ak. d. W.* (1853), pp. 293-418.

[49] James Summers, *A Handbook of the Chinese Language* (Oxford, 1863), Preface, p. x.

entire field of Chinese literature in European languages, although monographs on different phases of the subject were published within the period. Davis wrote a book on Chinese poetry, *Poesos Sinicae Commentarii* (1870), and Bazin published a series of articles on the drama, *Le Siècle des Youên* (1850-52).[50]

DICTIONARIES AND GRAMMARS

As contacts with China increased along many different lines, Westerners began to compile dictionaries and grammars to aid in their immediate acquisition of the language and to make China's history and literature more accessible to Occidentals. Prémare's grammar, *Notitia Linguae Sinica,* written in the eighteenth century and not published until 1831, was a very important book at this time. In 1856, Bazin's grammar was published.[51]   A new edition of Abel Rémusat's grammar appeared in 1857.[52]   The most important publication on the Chinese language was Julien's work, *Syntaxe nouvelle de la langue chinoise* (1869-1870) which attracted much attention among European Sinologists.[53]   The Chinese grammars compiled by French Orientalists are more erudite, but the English and Americans, because of their practical interests, prepared many useful aids for Chinese study.

A book by Charles Rudy, *The Chinese Mandarin Language after Ollendorf's Method* (1874), is cited not for its intrinsic value but because it indicates a trend toward the popularization of Chinese studies in Europe. He had about five establishments in Paris for the speedy acquisition of languages largely for practical purposes, and Chinese was added at this time to the course of study. It seemed to be the general consensus of opinion that the English had done comparatively little in the

[50] Antoine Bazin, "Le Siècle des Youên, ou tableau historique de la littérature chinoise," *JA* (1850), 15, pp. 5-48, 101-48, 16, pp. 428-75, (1851), 17, pp. 5-51, 163-211, 309-77, 479-533, 18, pp. 247-89, 517-52, (1852), 19, pp. 435-519.

[51] Antoine Bazin, *Grammaire mandarine* (Paris, 1865).

[52] Abel Rémusat, *Élémens de la grammaire chinoise* (Paris, 1857).

[53] See Stanislas Julien, *Syntaxe nouvelle de la langue chinoise* (Paris, 1869-70), II, 409-35 for reviews of the first volume by various scholars.

realm of grammar and lexicography, but Pfizmaier, the Viennese Sinologist, in 1867, commended the work of English missionaries in the field.[54]

Two or three German Orientalists prepared treatises on the Chinese language. Stephan Endlicher published in Vienna quite a comprehensive grammar, *Anfangsgründe der chinesischen Grammatik* (1845). A few years later Schott's *Chinesische Sprachlehre* (1857) appeared in Berlin. This work was well known and was considered an important guide for students of Chinese.[55]

Many dictionaries and vocabularies were compiled after 1840. Medhurst's two-volume *Chinese and English Dictionary* (1842) was designed to comprise within as small a compass as possible, all the characters with a few exceptions in the Imperial Dictionary, *K'ang Hsi Tzu Tien*. Medhurst maintained that a uniform and comprehensive dictionary was imperative for missionaries and for consular officials in China. By 1874 the dictionaries of Medhurst and others were almost forgotten. The only lexicons available for the use of English speaking students, besides the reprint of Morrison's *Syllabic Dictionary* (1865), were small vocabularies for the different dialects. The need for a good dictionary prompted Wells Williams to compile his *Syllabic Dictionary of the Chinese Language* (1874) which surpassed all earlier compilations.[56]

Although French Sinologists introduced the study of Chinese into Europe, they were very slow in printing a French-Chinese dictionary. A few dictionaries in manuscript form and other aids for the study of Chinese had been arranged, but they had disappeared by 1840.[57] The first dictionary to be published was Paul Perny's *Dictionnaire français-latin-chinois de la langue mandarine parlée* (1869, 1872). By this compilation the author hoped to be of service to missionaries, diplomats, merchants, and

---

[54] A. Pfizmaier, "Die neuesten Leistungen der englischen Missionäre auf dem Gebiete der chinesischen Grammatik und Lexicographie," *Sitz. d. Ak. d. W. Wien* (1867), 56, pp. 72, 80.   [55] James Summers, *op. cit.*, Preface   [56] "Dr. Williams' Dictionary," *CR* (1874-75), 3, p. 226.   [57] "Nouvelles littéraires," *J. Savants* (1867), pp. 325-26.

scholars.[58] The Germans produced no dictionary of importance from 1840 until 1876. While both the French and Germans were backward in this field of Sinology, the English and American missionaries published the most important dictionaries and vocabularies of the Chinese language.

STATE PAPERS

Another kind of material which reveals Western interest in China consists of *State Papers*. Any opinions on China found in such sources were usually expressed by statesmen or politicians who collected their information from standard works on China or from popular, contemporary accounts. During the time of such crises as the wars between England and China, the diplomatic relations of the British with that country were thoroughly discussed. Many contributors to current periodicals used *Parliamentary Papers* as source material for their articles on British policy. The French and Germans also made wide use of British *State Papers*.[59] Although the speeches in Parliament gave very little first-hand information on Chinese culture, they extended knowledge of China and aroused interest among the British not only in diplomatic connections with China but in the customs of the country.

Another illustration of the use of *State Papers* as a source for Western opinion are the documents of the California Legislature during the fifties, sixties, and seventies when the problem of Chinese immigration was an absorbing question in the United

[58] Paul Perny, *Dictionnaire français-latin-chinois de la langue mandarine parlée* (Paris, 1869-72), Preface.

[59] *RDM* See articles on China (1840-76). K. F. Neumann, *Geschichte des englisch-chinesischen Krieges* (Leipzig, 1855); *Ostasiatische Geschichte vom ersten chinesischen Krieg bis zu den Verträgen in Peking (1840-1860)* (Leipzig, 1861); "Das Chinesenthum, die Jesuiten und die evangelischen Sendboten," *ZDMG* (1853), 7, pp. 141-55; "Ostasien und Westamerika," *Z. allg. Erdk.* (1864), 16, pp. 305-30; "China," *J. d. Lit.* (1840), 89, pp. 190-236; "Eine chinesische Parabel," *Westermann Mh.* (1858), 4, pp. 598-99; "Die gegenwärtigen Zustände des chinesischen Reichs," *Unsere Zeit* (1857), 1, pp. 673-715; "Die Sängerin," *Westermann Mh.* (1857), 3, pp. 482-95; "Wie die Chinesen, ihre Gong, ihre Tomtam, und Symbeln machen," *ibid.* (1852), 2, p. 158.

States especially in California. These papers reveal clearly the attitude of various groups of citizens toward the Chinese.[60]

IMAGINATIVE LITERATURE

At the present fairly accurate interpretations of various phases of Oriental life may be gleaned from imaginative literature with Chinese themes, but within the period from 1840 until the end of 1875, Occidental notions of China were gathered almost entirely from other sources. No important novels were written in English or German during those years with China as a setting and with Chinese characters. In France the translation of novels, plays, and poetry from the Chinese stirred the imagination of a few novelists and poets. The first European to make use of Chinese materials in creative literature was the seventeenth-century Dutch poet, Vondel, who derived his information from Martini's *De Bello Tartarico Historia* and wrote a drama called *Zungchin*. In the eighteenth century, Voltaire wrote his well known drama, *L'Orphelin de la Chine*. Théophile Gautier, interested in China as early as 1830, was perhaps the first of his generation to discover the artistic possibilities of Chinese material in translation. He in turn was somewhat instrumental in creating in his associates and admirers an interest in the Far East. Gautier's appreciation of China had a greater influence upon his daughter, Judith, than upon any other writer. For many years the French public regarded her as the leading literary interpreter of the Orient. Never visiting China, she knew that country only through books and conversations with Chinese in Europe. Her studies with Ting Tun-ling, who was originally taken to France to aid Callery in the compilation of his dictionary, began in 1863. Four years later she published the *Livre de Jade*, imitations in rhythmical prose of ancient and modern Chinese poetry. This book must have increased French interest in China especially in literary circles, although copies have always been rare.

In 1868, Judith Gautier published an original novel, entitled *Le Dragon Impérial* as a serial in *La Liberté*. This is probably

[60] *Cal. Leg., Jols. of Sen. and Ass.*

46 WESTERN CONCEPTS OF CHINA AND THE CHINESE

the first French novel with a Chinese setting, a plausible Chinese plot, and Chinese characters. The popularity of Chinese themes and art among nineteenth-century French writers such as the Gautiers, Sardou, Mérimée, Hugo, Méry, Flaubert, and the Goncourts indicates a fairly general interest in China among literary groups. The careful use of Chinese sources by Théophile Gautier and by his daughter, Judith, in her earlier writings especially, make their works fairly important interpretations of Chinese life.[61]

American contacts with the people of China were extremely limited before the first group of Chinese immigrants landed in California in 1848. Chang-Fong, a juggler, had given an exhibition of his art as early as 1842, and in 1847 a Chinese woman, eating with chopsticks and talking Chinese, was shown on Broadway in New York. But the appearance of the Chinese on the Pacific coast furnished much local color for imaginative literature. While literary figures in the Eastern states ignored the Orientals, writers in the West introduced them into fiction. Bret Harte and others were aroused by the unfair treatment of the Orientals and by the prejudice of the Americans. Harte's poem, *Plain Language from Truthful James*, published in the *Overland Monthly* in 1870, was reprinted many times. Two illustrated editions appeared shortly and two musical versions of the poem and a *Heathen Chinee Songster* were published. *Plain Language from Truthful James* was also reprinted in two English periodicals, *The Piccadilly Annual* and *The Spectator*. The publication of this satirical poem on the treatment of the Chinese in America inspired most of the verses on similar themes written during the seventies.

Harte was also interested in the Chinese as a source of local color. As a picturesque portion of the population, they figured in a few of his short stories. But he portrayed only their more obvious qualities, their placidity, their secretiveness, their dex-

[61] W. L. Schwartz, *The Imaginative Interpretation of the Far East in Modern French Literature* (Paris, 1927), pp. 13-64; Hung Cheng Fu, *Un Siècle d'influence chinoise sur la littérature française (1815-1930)* (Paris, 1934), Chap. II.

terity, and their odd style of dress. He showed little understanding of the Orientals and their culture.[62]

LETTERS

Another kind of material, which should not be overlooked,
consists of letters written during the years from 1840 to 1876
by foreign merchants stationed in China. Very few traders
wrote books, and they left few commentaries on Chinese civilization. But their letters convey the impression that their knowledge and their understanding of Chinese customs and institutions
were extremely limited. Their interests in China seem to have
been only in so far as its conditions affected the supply and
demand of commodities and trade prospects in general. Frequent references, for example, are made on the progress of the
rebels and on the extent of their interference with the trading
activities of the various foreign mercantile houses of China.[63]
From no other sources, perhaps, can more accurate and detailed
information be obtained on the economic effects of the T'ai
P'ing Rebellion. From these letters trade fluctuations can be
traced from year to year and even from month to month. But
this correspondence also indicates that foreigners, especially the
traders living in the ports, formed social groups which stood
rather apart from the Chinese and had comparatively little social
contact with them. Because they knew the Orientals only
through business relations, the Western merchants had little
opportunity to acquire accurate and definite notions on Chinese
character and civilization.

GENERAL PERIODICALS

Perhaps the most effective means of determining the degree
of European and American interest in China and Occidental

[62] W. P. Fenn, *Ah Sinn and His Brethren in American Literature* (Peiping,
1933), pp. 1-131.
[63] Frank Groom, Letters, September 1, 1860, March 5, 1861, July 20,
1862 (Wason Collection, Cornell); R. P. Dana, Letters to Samuel Dana,
May 2 and August 16, 1863; John Heard, Letters to Parents, April 19 and
May 18, 1861; A. F. Heard, Letter, September 4, 1860 (Baker Library,
Harvard).

opinions of that country and its people is a survey of the articles published from 1840 to 1876, in the magazines of England, America, France, and Germany. These articles prove that the English and the Americans on the whole were more curious about things Chinese than was the general public on the Continent. Some thirty or forty English and American magazines published a thousand or more articles of varying length on a great number of subjects from 1840 to 1876. As the former date marks the outbreak of the first Anglo-Chinese War and the beginning of closer contacts with China, many articles dealt with European and Chinese diplomatic relations. Several papers discussed literature. Usually excerpts were quoted to give the general reader some idea of Chinese plays and novels.[64] Two or three articles listed proverbs.[65] About a dozen papers described the various religious groups. Reviews and notices of the more important books on China or subjects connected with that Empire were published. Just as many books of a descriptive nature were written during this period, twenty-five or more papers entitled *China and the Chinese* were printed in the leading English and American periodicals. Including material on character, social customs, religion, and other institutions in their papers, the writers attempted to give the public a concise and clear account of Chinese civilization, based on a number of books by travellers and by residents in China. These articles were significant in focusing attention on China and the Chinese. The comparatively short summaries of Chinese culture published in magazines with wide circulations were read by more persons than books of three to five hundred pages. They were composed by fairly critical and discriminating writers who had read rather extensively and had arrived at their own conclusions through a comparison of authorities. This type of article represents not the opinions of one observer but often the composite ideas of a number of authoritative writers.

[64] "The Literature of the Chinese," *Chamb. J.* (1844), 2, pp. 250-53, 280-82, 290-93.

[65] A. W. Loomis, "Chinese Proverbs," *Overland* (1873), 10, pp. 82-85; "Chinese Proverbs," *All the Year* (1874), 32, pp. 498-500.

Despite the alertness of the English and the Americans to the possibilities of trade, not many articles on purely commercial questions were written during the period for general periodicals. *Hunt's Merchants' Magazine* (1839-1870), published in New York and limited to information on trade and allied subjects, contains much material on the progress and the scope of the China trade. The files of this periodical are probably the best published source for a careful study of the American trade with China from 1839 until 1870. Other papers were written about specific localities, coast lines, industries, agriculture, coins, and many other subjects.

From the number and contents of articles, published during each of the thirty-six years, the conclusion may be drawn that, during the year 1840, Westerners were not particularly interested in China itself. The articles of that year were concerned primarily with the opium problem and the war. In 1841 approximately the same number of articles were published, but they dealt more with social customs, agriculture, literature, and all phases of Chinese culture. During the late forties interest in China seemed to lapse, but again in 1853 the T'ai P'ing Rebellion turned European attention toward the East. In the fifties and sixties, many articles appeared on the Rebellion, English policy in China, and immigration. When England was at war with China or when Americans were struggling with the immigration problem, the people of both countries became more interested in Chinese institutions. A decrease in the number of magazine articles indicates a lessening interest in China about 1865. A writer in the *Chinese and Japanese Repository* remarked in 1865 that Parliament showed no signs of interest in Chinese affairs.[66] The abatement of curiosity about the Chinese continued for a year or two, but in the late sixties and seventies interest was again quickened and diversified. Social, intellectual, and commercial matters began to attract the West.

In contrast to the English periodical literature, the French journals do not contain as many articles or are they as diver-

[66] "Parliamentary Debates," *C. & J. Repos.* (1865), 3, p. 300.

sified as to subject matter. Reviews of books, published in France, England, and other countries appeared in the *Bibliographie Catholique* and other periodicals. Not many articles of an interpretative and a descriptive character were published, but two fairly complete papers of this kind were printed in the *Revue des Deux Mondes.*[67] Both describe the Chinese Empire, its inhabitants, their character, their manners, and their customs. While American, English, and even German periodicals inserted short descriptions of curious landmarks and odd customs, few such articles were found in the French reviews.[68] Even though the French had not developed commercial relations with China to the extent that the English and Americans had, they were concerned about their trade prospects there. Two or three long, carefully written articles on foreign commerce in China were published in one of the leading French periodicals.[69] In the forties, the French were somewhat interested in Anglo-Chinese relations and in the relations of other countries, especially their own, with the Orient.[70]

During the early sixties, the T'ai P'ing Rebellion was the subject of two long articles.[71] As the question of immigration did not vitally concern the French, few wrote on it. A fairly comprehensive article, however, discussed the Chinese in the different parts of the world.[72] But with Paris and its rich col-

[67] L. M. de Carné, "Exploration de Mékong," *RDM* (1870), 85, pp. 316-49, 886-917, 86, pp. 651-84; J. P. E. Jurien de la Gravière, "Souvenirs d'une station dans les mers de l'Indo-Chine," *RDM* (1853), 2, pp. 502-34, 3, pp. 5-47.
[68] Léo de Bernard, "Macao," *Monde illus.* (1857), no. 28, p. 13; Maréchal de Lunéville, "La Rue Zu-Phaï-Léou à Pekin," *ibid.*, no. 7, pp. 11-13.
[69] Auguste Haussman, "Canton et le commerce européen en Chine," *RDM* (1846), 16, pp. 298-340; Rodolphe Lindau, "Le Commerce étranger en Chine," *RDM* (1861), 35, pp. 769-74.
[70] Prosper Giquel, "La Politique française en Chine," *RDM* (1872), 99, pp. 5-34; Charles Lavollée, "La Diplomatie anglaise et les affaires de Chine," *RDM* (1859), 24, pp. 580-623.
[71] René de Courcy, "L'Insurrection chinoise," *RDM* (1861), 34, pp. 5-35, 312-60; Léon Renard, "L'Insurrection chinoise," *Corres.* (1863), 59, pp. 246-79.
[72] Ed. du Hailly, "Souvenirs d'une Campagne dans l'Extrême Orient," *RDM* (1866), 66, pp. 396-420.

lections of Chinese literature the center of European Sinology and French commerce with the Orient largely undeveloped, the French devoted their energies to the intellectual aspects of Chinese culture.[73]

Studies on the poetry, drama, and novel were published in the more important French periodicals. Most of the articles on philology, literature, and related subjects were writen by persons who had not been in China but had studied the works of Rémusat, Julien and others. Although a few papers appeared on religion, the French were not deeply interested in that subject.[74] While a very large number of short articles were printed in British and American periodicals on social customs, weddings, funerals, houses, and opium smoking, the number of such articles in the French reviews is very small.[75] The French, evidently, had very little interest in the more superficial aspects of Chinese society.

The number of articles published from year to year in France did not vary greatly. Yet, because of France's part in the expedition of 1860 against China a slight increase in the number of articles occurred in the sixties.

A survey of the German periodical literature, in comparison with the English, American, and French, is interesting. Approximately the same number of articles were found in German periodicals as in the French publications, but while the French were chiefly interested in the intellectual, the German articles were almost as diversified in subject matter as the English. Besides book reviews, a number of fairly long articles, describing Chinese culture, was published. A paper by Neumann summarizes Gutzlaff's career in China and analyzes one of his books as a source of information on that country.[76] The Germans like

[73] Léon Renard, "L'Insurrection chinoise," *Corres.* (1863), 59, p. 278.
[74] Th. Pavie, "Les trois religions de la Chine," *RDM* (1845), 9, pp. 451-76; J. J. Ampère, "La troisième religion de la Chine, Lao-tseu," *RDM* (1842), 31, pp. 521-39.
[75] Léo de Bernard, "Mœurs chinoises," *Monde illus.* (1857), no. 27, p. 14.
[76] K. F. Neumann, "China," *J. d. Lit.* (1840), 89, pp. 190-236; W. Reinhold, "China und die Chinesen," *Westermann Mh.* (1862), 12, pp. 167-80, 251-67, 365-80, 512-23.

the English were concerned about the political future of China. Neumann, long interested in European diplomacy in the Orient, wrote an important paper on that subject.[77] Other German writers discussed the opium question and the first Anglo-Chinese War.[78] A few short articles, on the T'ai P'ing Rebellion, appeared from 1852 to 1863.[79] Even though their commerce with the East was relatively unimportant, the Germans were interested in trade with China.[80] After the conclusion of peace between England and China in 1842, the foothold gained by German merchants in Hong Kong and Canton was largely responsible for German interest in the China trade,[81] in a railroad connection between China and Europe,[82] and in railroad building in China.[83] The immigration problem did not affect the Germans directly, but because the question was widely discussed especially in the United States and Australia, a few short papers on the subject were printed.[84] The Germans were curious about social customs, such as those connected with dinners, banquets, marriage, and foot-binding.[85] They, apparently, had not studied Chinese literature as much as the French, but some treatises on that subject were written. In a periodical a series of short

[77] K. F. Neumann, "Die gegenwärtigen Zustände des chinesischen Reichs," *Unsere Zeit* (1857), 1, pp. 673-715; "Der Krieg der Westmächte gegen China," *ibid.* (1864), 8, pp. 165-202, 372-85.
[78] A. Wulfert, "Der Opiumkrieg," *Illustrirtes Familienbuch* (1858), 8, pp. 344-48; Röbbelen, "Ueber das Opiumessen und Opiumrauchen," *Unterhaltungen* (1857), 2, pp. 792-95, 811-14.
[79] "Eine Geschichte der Taipings," *Westermann Mh.* (1863), 13, pp. 567-68; "Der chinesische Bürgerkrieg," *Europa* (1853), pp. 518-20; "Chinesische Zustände," *Didaskalia* (1855), 2, no. 199.
[80] "Politische und commerzielle Uebersicht," *D. Monatsschrift* (1843), pp. 68, 413, 571.
[81] "Die Deutschen in China," *Neue Europa* (1846), 2, p. 144.
[82] "Die Eisenbahnverbindung zwischen China und Europa," *Westermann Mh.* (1874), 36, pp. 445-47.
[83] "Eisenbahnen in China," *ibid.* (1865), 17, p. 668.
[84] "Die Chinesen in Australien," *Daheim* (1869), pp. 623-24.
[85] "Ein chinesisches Gastmahl," *Europa* (1857), pp. 1467-72 (1858), pp. 739-46; A. Ecker, "Die künstlichen Missstaltungen der Körperform," *Westermann Mh.* (1862), 12, p. 633; C. König, "Eine chinesische Hochzeit," *ibid.* (1869), 25, pp. 169-72; "Besuche in China," *Land u. Meer* (1873), 30, p. 571.

papers was published on the dramatic poetry of the Chinese. These articles seem to be based on secondary works and the translations of the French Sinologists and Sir John Francis Davis. After a short general introduction on Chinese drama, summaries of the most famous examples follow with a description of the stage where the plays were acted.[86] Another article contains a translation of the play, *Die Sängerin* with explanations and comments.[87] A comparatively short paper treats the main classes of Chinese novels and summarizes the more celebrated examples of each class.[88]

The number of articles does not vary greatly from year to year. More were published during the years 1857, 1858, and 1859; the reason seems to have been the keen interest in the diplomatic relations of China and the West.

A survey of the English, French, and German periodical literature reveals the more diverstified and more extensive interests of the English and the Americans and their greater concern about diplomatic and commercial matters. Their direct contacts with China led to a desire to know about the customs, and character of the Chinese people. The French, because they did not have as many direct connections with the East, were not so varied in their interests as the English. The French public was less curious about bizarre social customs than were the English and the Americans but more interested in Chinese literature. German interest was not as keen and as diversified as the British and the American but more varied than the French.

PUBLICATIONS ON CHINA AND THE FAR EAST

The periodicals limited to China or to the East as a whole are a very important source for information about the Chinese and their country. The journals were in almost every instance

---

[86] "Die dramatische Poesie der Chinesen," *Morgenbl.* (1844), 38, pp. 5-6, 10-11, 13-14, 18-19, 21-22, 26-27, 37-38, 42-43, 45-46, 50-51, 53-55, 58-60.

[87] K. F. Neumann, "Die Sängerin," *Westermann Mh.* (1857), 3, pp. 482-95.

[88] "Der chinesische Roman," *Europa* (1864), pp. 1127-32.

published by missionaries either in China or England. The purpose of *Notes and Queries on China and Japan* (1867-1870) was to make available facts, collected from time to time by foreigners in the Far East who had not time to write books. As many statements still rested upon the authority of the Jesuit missionaries of the eighteenth century or upon the work of a single and, perhaps, biased or ill-informed observer, this publication through its "Queries and Replies" features, was designed to correct many old misconceptions. This periodical also included papers on society, geology, ethnology, philology, and other subjects. The magazine, published for only a short time in China, was not well known. Much of its material, however, supplied sources for articles published in England, and its contributors also wrote for English periodicals.[89]

A magazine somewhat similar in its scope and its aims to *Notes and Queries* is the *Chinese Recorder and Missionary Journal* (1868). Although its main object was to serve as a medium of communication for Protestant missionaries, it printed a number of valuable papers on history, literature, philosophy, social usages, and government.[90] Because the journal was published in China, it is difficult to gauge its influence on Western opinion. Some of the more important articles, however, were reprinted by English magazines.

The China Review (1872-1901), in some respects a successor to the two periodicals already mentioned, was a very important publication. Its editors, hoping to make the journal a repository of information, published some excellent papers on the arts, science, literature, religion, manners, and customs of China and of the Far East by such scholars as Mayers, Eitel, and Edkins. It also contains reprints of some of the more valuable articles of the *Chinese Repository*.[91] The department known as "Literary Intelligence" is useful. It announced new publications, and often critically summarized their contents. This magazine, although launched by the same editor as *Notes*

---

[89] "Introductory Notice," *N. & Q. on C. & J.* (1867), 1, p. 1.
[90] "Close of the First Half Volume," *C. Recorder* (1868), 1, p. 115.
[91] "Foreword," *CR* (1872), 1, p. 1.

and Queries on China and Japan, is more literary. Less space is given to the more obvious features of Chinese society. This change suggests that the English were examining Chinese civilization more seriously and critically. Their interests no longer centered on the external aspects of Chinese society but on Chinese thought.

Two compendia of data, the *Chinese Repository* (1832-1851) and the *Chinese and Japanese Repository* (1863-1865), were published. The former, consisting of twenty volumes, is one of the most valuable publications of its period on China. Bridgman and Williams, both American missionaries, were largely responsible for the early volumes of the series. Excellent papers were contributed by students of the history, language, and literature of China. The objects of the editors were to review books on China, to notice changes that had occurred in the "Middle Kingdom," and to distinguish between what was true and what was false. Such subjects as natural history, geography, commerce, social relations, morals, literature, arts, sciences, religion, and foreign relations were discussed. By a careful analysis of successive volumes, various trends of interest may be traced. As few copies were to be found in England even as early as 1863,[92] this publication was probably not directly responsible for a diffusion of knowledge about the East in Europe. Important Western authorities, however, were familiar with the *Repository* and valued it as a compendium of accurate information. Indirectly it contributed toward a better knowledge of China and of its people.

In 1863 the *Chinese and Japanese Repository* was launched in London by James Summers whose main object was to increase European knowledge of China and Japan. Various groups should know conditions in the Orient. The merchant and business man needed many particulars on the physical features, climate, and population of China. The missionary should be acquainted with the language, customs, manners, superstitions, and the physical features of the country. Scientists and other

---

[92] "Introductory Essay," *C. & J. Repos.* (1863), 1, p. 2; R. S. Britton, *The Chinese Periodical Press 1800-1912* (Shanghai, 1933), p. 28.

scholars had a tremendous interest in this quarter of the globe. To satisfy the needs of these groups, the *Chinese and Japanese Repository* hoped to include in its pages pictures of Chinese life, stories from their histories, tales from their novels, ballads and ancient songs, portraits of their philosophers, statesmen, and patriots, journals of tours through the provinces, accounts of visits to cities and remarkable places, and notes on monuments, pagodas, and all objects of curiosity in nature and art.[93] Because the publication was discontinued in 1865, it did not have time to carry out its aims.

JOURNALS OF LEARNED SOCIETIES

The publications of societies contain much material on China. Wherever educated Englishmen gathered, they collected material to enlighten themselves and their compatriots and to improve their position in the land of their sojourn. An early organization, established for these purposes, was the *North China Branch of the Royal Asiatic Society*.[94] Its objects were outlined in the inaugural address by Bridgman in which he emphasized the need for more thorough study of Chinese philology and grammar and carefully written essays on the history of Chinese literature.[95]

The president's address delivered before the *North China Branch of the Royal Asiatic Society*, February 18, 1874, summarized the progress of the organization and noted the more important articles published in its journal. The largest number of articles were on the geography of China. Edkins published in an early number of the *Journal* (1858+) a discussion of the historical evidence to show that the Yangtze River once flowed to the sea through three channels. Ward also contributed the first sailing directions for the voyages between Woosung and Hankow. Itineraries of journeys through different provinces were

[93] "Introductory Essay," *op. cit.*, p. 1 *et seq.*
[94] After the publication of the first number of the *Journal of the Shanghai Literary and Scientific Society* the organization was affiliated with the *Royal Asiatic Society.*
[95] *Journal of the Shanghai Literary and Scientific Society* (1858), 1, p. 1 *et seq.*; *JNCBRAS* (1865), 2, Preface.

published. In the department of history and antiquities, Frederick Mayers submitted a series of chronological tables. Wylie's catalogue on coins was significant for the numismatist. Other scholars translated and discussed Chinese inscriptions. Medhurst prepared a paper on the celebrated tablet of Yü which was supposedly a contemporary record of the efforts to subdue a flood four thousand years ago. French members contributed fairly exhaustive articles on natural history. Eugène Simon wrote *Notes on an Agricultural Chart of China.* Armand David prepared an elaborate paper on the natural history of Northern and Western China. The life and customs of the people yielded material for several papers. Simon carefully described the operation of the small mutual loan societies and the banking system of China. Other articles were on the literary examinations, the Chinese game of chess, and many other subjects.[96] Information for practical purposes holds first place, although material on many phases of Chinese civilization is found in this periodical.

The Journal of the Royal Asiatic Society (1834+) published some twenty articles, during the period, on various aspects of Chinese life and thought. Two papers dealt with the Triad Society. Buddhism, literature, trade, and the physical features of the country were subjects for other papers.

The Journal of the American Oriental Society (1843+), concerned with Oriental literature in general, printed before 1876 about a dozen articles on subjects related to China. They were often reprints from publications in Europe or China.

The Journal Asiatique (1822+), a publication for the Orient as a whole, shows French interest in ancient Chinese works. The French compared the philosophy, religion, and philology of the Chinese with that of other peoples. Few papers were written by business men on such subjects as trade, communications, or industry, and little interest was taken in missions. The journal was published by and for savants.

The German learned societies published a number of articles on different phases of Chinese culture. Plath wrote many papers

[96] "The President's Address," *ibid.* (1874), 9, p. xxv *et seq.*

33835464

from 1861 to 1874 for the *Royal Society of Munich*.[97] They include information on the language, religion, law, literature, and domestic life of the people of ancient China. His writings, based on extensive although uncritical research among Chinese sources, were familiar to the Sinologists not only on the Continent but in England and among the missionary scholars of China. *The Academy of Berlin* printed a few important treatises on the language and literature of China by Wilhelm Schott.[98] Less than a dozen articles on Chinese subjects were published from 1840 to 1876, and these with only one or two exceptions were by Schott. *The German Oriental Society* also printed three or four fairly long articles on the religion, literature, and philosophy of the Orient.[99] *The Imperial Academy of Vienna*[100] published from 1850 to 1875 about sixty articles by Pfizmaier. He was interested mainly in ancient Chinese history, but he prepared a few treatises on language, trees, and natural science. Pfizmaier's work, which is detailed and pedantic with many translations of excerpts from Chinese sources, is not considered of great value at the present.

The Germans, pioneers in the development of geographical knowledge, inserted much material on China in their publications on geography. In the fifties and sixties, the *Geographical Society of Berlin*[101] printed papers, which usually summarized the results of British travellers' explorations in different parts of China. Frequently the material was drawn from the *Journal of the North China Branch of the Royal Asiatic Society* and other English publications. After 1870, the travels of Baron von Richthofen aroused considerable interest in the natural resources of China and the possibilities for trade; the Germans then began to depend upon their own researches and explorations for material on the East.

[97] *Sitz. d. bay. Ak. d. W.* (1860-74).

[98] Wilhelm Schott, "Entwurf einer Beschreibung der chinesischen Literatur," *Philo. u. hist. Abh. d. Ak. d. W.* (1853), pp. 293-418.

[99] See ZDMG (1847-76).

[100] *Denk. d. Ak. d. W. Wien* (1850-75); *Sitz. d. Ak. d. W. Wien* (1848-75).

[101] *Z. allg. Erdk.* (1853-65); *Z. Ges. Erdk.* (1866-75); *Verh. Ges. Erdk.* (1873-75).

The Journal of the Royal Geographical Society (1830-1880) published several papers on the natural resources of various localities, the navigability of rivers, and expeditions to discover feasible trade routes especially between India and China. Even though the *American Geographical and Statistical Society* was incorporated as early as 1852, the Americans by the end of 1875 had made only slight progress in the field of geography. The study being new, attention was focused on the Western hemisphere rather than Asia. The *Bulletin of the Geographical Society of Paris*,[102] during the period from 1840 to 1876, published a number of papers on Chinese subjects. This group was interested in such topics as agriculture, trade, natural resources, Chinese geographical knowledge, and progress in map making. The French, in contrast to the English and Germans, showed their preference for researches on the relations of China and other countries in ancient times and on the geographical literature of the Chinese.

Annual letters and reports of missionaries constitute an unusually important collection of material. Probably the most significant and fullest series is the *Annales de la Propagation de la Foi* (1823+), which consists of letters from missionaries in all parts of the world. Certain sections of each volume of the *Annales* deal with Catholic missions in China. The letters, written by missionaries who were stationed in China, contain many details on the life and social customs in the different provinces. The missionaries, corresponding with their superiors, members of their respective families or with friends, confined their observations to the localities in which they lived. Often to illustrate the problems peculiar to his province, a missionary gave minute details on the topography and resources of his district.[103] Probably no other single collection of material gives as much specific information on the topography, natural

---

[102] *BSG* (1840-76).
[103] "Extrait de deux lettres de M. Delamare, missionnaire apostolique au Su-Tchuen," *Annales de la Propagation de la Foi* (1840), 12, pp. 479-83.

resources, products, social life, and occupations of the people in such a large number of provinces.

The *Missionary Register*, London (1813-55) and the *Missionary Herald* (Boston, 1805+) contain many extracts from the letters and journals of Protestant missionaries and are another important source for reliable information on political conditions, details on customs and social institutions, descriptions of various provinces, and the progress of Christian missions in China.

MUSEUM COLLECTIONS

Besides written material, museum collections and the articles and products displayed in the international exhibitions, beginning about the middle of the nineteenth century, helped to give Westerners a more definite and concrete notion of Chinese life. Nathan Dunn, an American merchant of China, assembled a collection of articles in common use and took it to England and America.[104] The *Chinese Repository* quotes the *Morning Post*, June 21, 1842, in describing the royal visit to the Chinese Museum. The Queen was impressed with the gorgeous appearance of the apartment which was a miniature representation of China. Her Majesty in commenting upon various objects displayed her knowledge of Chinese customs.[105] A contemporary said that "Mr. Dunn has exhibited a taste and a spirit in this matter worthy of high commendation. His benefaction to the world is great and his memory will live. He has brought China to Europe and introduced the people of the Central Kingdom to the West." Such museums of Chinese articles contributed toward the popular interest of England and the United States in China because a large number of people in England and in the eastern cities of America saw Dunn's collection.[106]

---

[104] W. B. Langdon, *Descriptive Catalogue of the Chinese Collection* (London, 1844); J. R. Peters, *Descriptive Catalogue of the Chinese Museum in the Marlboro Chapel* (Boston, 1845); Peters, *Miscellaneous Remarks upon the Government . . . As Suggested by an Examination of the Articles Comprising the Chinese Museum* (Philadelphia, 1847).

[105] "Dunn's Chinese Collection," *C. Repos.* (1843), 12, p. 562.

[106] Bonacossi visited the collection in London. Very much impressed by it, he wrote that Dunn's collection was one of the most beautiful ornaments

INTERNATIONAL EXHIBITIONS

The international exhibitions introduced the Western public to certain kinds of Chinese art and various commercial products. The first exposition, which was held in London in 1851, exhibited specimens of Chineses produce and industry. They were collected by Rutherford Alcock, consul at Shanghai, and sent to the Board of Trade for the exhibition. This collection was by no means complete and inadequately represented the resources of the Empire. In the Chinese section were a number of objects of art in bronze, inlaid wood, porcelain, soapstone, and enamels. Colors used by the Chinese for dyeing, silks, brocades, and other products of the Chinese looms were on display together with hemp, indigo, and other agricultural products.[107]

At the exhibitions in London in 1862 and Paris in 1867, travellers, army officers, and scholars who happened to have Chinese articles, such as vases, incense burners, bits of carved ivory, screens, water-color paintings, and sundry specimens of Chinese art and craftsmanship put them on display.[108]

An attraction of the Paris exposition was a Chinese café-restaurant-theatre which was constructed like one of the kiosks of the Summer Palace. The first room, although filled with all

---

of the city and had received general admiration. See A. Bonacossi, *La Chine et les Chinois* (Paris, 1847), Preface. "It [the Chinese Museum at Philadelphia] is preëminently the most extensive, elegant, and tasteful collection in America. The *coup d'œil* is gorgeous and imposing, and in the detail, it will satisfy the most fastidious observer . . ." *Knicker.* (1839), 13, p. 88. Libraries and museums exhibited Chinese objects of interest, such as clay figures representing all degrees of rank, portraits, drawings, carvings, and manuscripts. See W. D. Macray, *Annals of the Bodleian Library* (London, 1868), p. 338. See also articles in the Peabody Museum, Salem, Massachusetts.

[107] Alexander Michie, *The Englishman in China* (Edinburgh, 1900), I, 200 *et seq.; Great Exhibition of the Works of Industry of All Nations, 1851. Official . . . Catalogue* (London, 1851), III, pp. 1418-25.

[108] *International Exhibition, London, 1862. Illustrated Catalogue of the Industrial Department*, III, Foreign Division, pp. 43-44; *Official Catalogue of the Industrial Department*, p. 168; *International Exhibition, 1876. Official Catalogue*, Part I, pp. 241-43; J. B. Waring, *Masterpieces of Industrial Art and Sculpture at the International Exhibition* (London, 1862), Vols. I, II, III; *Paris Universal Exposition, 1867, Complete Official Catalogue* (2nd ed., London, 1867). See Tabular Index.

kinds of Chinese objects, did not arrest the public eye very long because it had already seen many of these and similar objects in the Parisian curio shops. Nor did visitors tarry very long at the restaurant where savory Chinese dishes were served. They went almost immediately to the pavilion where two young Chinese girls, brought to Paris expressly for the exposition, were established in an apartment similar to their own in China. Probably not knowing what to do with themselves, they decided to converse, smoke, eat, and drink as if they were unobserved.[109]

Not until 1873 at the exhibition in Vienna was a well ordered and systematic collection of samples and specimens of minerals, agriculture, horticulture, forestry, chemistry, textiles, metal, wood, earthenware, paper, musical instruments, and architectural models from the important provinces exhibited.[110] The Chinese section was one of the most attractive features in the Philadelphia exposition of 1876. The division owed much of its importance and its value to Hu Kuang-yung,[111] of Shanghai, an "eminent Chinese mandarin" said to be the wealthiest banker in the Empire. He had a reputation, both throughout Asia and Europe, as a collector of ancient and valuable specimens of art. At the exposition he was represented by his nephew, Hu Ying-ding, a young mandarin of the fourth class who spoke English fluently.

The enamelled and cloisonné ware and the bronzes, some of which were supposed to have been from two hundred to five hundred years old, were very fine examples of Chinese craftsmanship. The collection of furniture intrigued Westerners. Carved and ornamented with inlaid work in ivory and in rare woods in the most beautiful and artistic manner, this furniture

[109] Hippolyte Gautier, *Les Curiosités de l'exposition universelle de 1867* (Paris, 1867), p. 21.

[110] *Austro-Hungarian Universal Exposition, Vienna, 1873, Port Catalogues of the Chinese Customs' Collection.*

[111] Hu Kuang-yung bought his official title after the pacification of Turkestan by Tso Tsung-tang which he financed. He was presented with the Yellow Jacket. Later, however, his goods were confiscated on the charge of embezzlement. See *Chinese Biographical Dictionary* [in Chinese] p. 689.

was much admired. A masterpiece of delicate carving was the series of twenty-one ivory balls carved one within the other. Examples of metals, chemicals, textiles, and other products of China were also displayed.[112] The Chinese exhibits at the expositions of 1873 and of 1876, in Vienna and in Philadelphia, respectively, were much larger than those of the earlier exhibitions. It is significant to note, however, that although Westerners were extremely appreciative of Chinese craftsmanship as shown in the enamel and cloisonné ware and in the antique bronzes, no paintings were mentioned in the discussions of the merits of Chinese art displayed at the exhibitions, and only a few water-colors seem to have been exhibited at any of the expositions.

[112] *Frank Leslie's Historical Register of the United States Centennial Exposition 1876*, Frank H. Norton, ed. (New York, 1877), p. 244 *et seq.*

CHAPTER III

WESTERN NOTIONS OF THE CHINESE EMPIRE

OCCIDENTALS as early as the seventeenth century developed a few definite concepts which they always associated with China. They were profoundly impressed by the antiquity, enormous extent, and the vast population of the country. A territory, stretching fourteen hundred miles from east to west and as many from north to south, had more than three hundred million inhabitants living under the rule of one sovereign and supposedly preserving their customs from a period prior to the beginning of authentic records elsewhere.[1] The history of the human race presented no similar phenomenon to that of China which had maintained its national unity and independence for more than four thousand years without any serious changes either in its theories of government or in its fundamental institutions.[2]

Although many European and American writers made extravagant statements about the antiquity of China, some pursued a middle course. They admitted that the country had attained a very great age.[3] The most reliable native historians, however, conceded that its long duration had been exaggerated. The truth was that the Chinese like other nations had a legendary period, and Westerners gave too much credence to the statements of earlier authors who did not distinguish between what was considered mythical even in China and what was substantiated by authentic historical records.[4]

Occidentals realized that, even though they could not tell

[1] J. F. Davis, *China: A General Description* (New ed., London, 1857), II, 407 *et seq.*; S. W. Williams, *The Middle Kingdom* (New York, 1848), I, 1; "Early History of China," *Westm. R.* (1840), 34, p. 261; "Chinese History," *C. Repos.* (1841), 10, p. 2.

[2] Andrew Wilson, *The "Ever Victorious Army"* (Edinburgh, 1868), p. 4.

[3] J. H. Plath, *Ueber die lange Dauer und die Entwickelung des chinesischen Reiches* (München, 1861), p. 3.

[4] Davis, *op. cit.*, I, 217; Williams, *op. cit.*, II, 193; "Early History of China," *op. cit.*, 261 *et seq.*

how long China had been an independent country, it had maintained a separate existence for a long period of time and had developed certain characteristics that accounted for its longevity.[5] Few writers seem to have been able to give satisfactory explanations for its long life. Sir George Staunton and the early Jesuit missionaries attributed its stability to the influence of the doctrine of filial piety and parental authority which was universally accepted by the people.

Meadows, an ardent admirer of Chinese civilization, ascribed the long duration of China to the principle that good government consisted in the elevation of able and talented men to public office. The basis of this principle was men's desire to distinguish themselves among their countrymen. The doctrine of filial piety, which demanded an extreme devotion not only to parents but to the sovereign as father of the nation, Meadows believed, was also an important factor in the long life of the Empire.[6]

Patterson in his essay, *The National Life of China*, stressed the geographical isolation of the Empire, bounded on the north by vast deserts, on the west by mountains, and on the south and east by a rough sea. To these explanations for the continuous existence of China was added still another—namely, the peculiar character of the written language which served as a powerful bond of union. Because the characters of that language represented not sounds but things or ideas in the widest sense of the term, it stood superior to and unaffected by the fluctuation of sound and dialect. The speech and thought of the Chinese were, therefore, kept within certain rigid limits. Over the spoken language with its frequent changes and interruptions, the written language stood supreme. A native of Shantung might be unable to understand the spoken words of a Cantonese, but they used identical characters to express the same meaning.[7]

[5] Plath, *op. cit.*, 3.

[6] T. T. Meadows, *Desultory Notes on the Government and People of China* (London, 1847), pp. 124 *et seq.*, 152, 189; T. T. Meadows, *The Chinese and Their Rebellions* (London, 1856), p. 578; V. de Mars, "La Question chinoise," *RDM* (1857), 9, p. 484; Plath, *op. cit.*, 23.

[7] R. H. Patterson, *Essays in History and Art* (Edinburgh, 1862), pp. 235-318.

Wilson believed that a deeper influence than filial piety, the choice of able officials, or the character of the language was responsible for the preservation of Chinese nationality. An examination of the *Shu Ching* or the *Historical Classic* showed the belief of the Chinese in a fundamental principle upon which was based their whole system of political and social organization. This first principle consisted in the presence of a divine harmony in the universe which affected all existing objects with which men came in contact. Especially in the *Shu Ching* but in all of the *Classics*, harmony is the fundamental and ruling idea that governs the actions of the Chinese.

Wilson thought the ideal state of the Chinese sages was similar in its principles, although not in all of its details, to that which Plato depicted in his *Republic*, to the organization which Fichte deduced in his *Geschlossene Handelsstaat* and to Carlyle's ideas on the perfect state. But the early sages, Wilson pointed out, succeeded in establishing their state so that however short it may have fallen in practice, it always aspired towards and was theoretically guided by the ideas on which it was founded. The Chinese views on parental authority and the choice of able men for official positions were, Wilson said, only subdivisions of the great idea of harmonious unity. In all relationships and in all combined action, a symmetrical unity was necessary. The Chinese regarded all existence in its normal condition, from the lowest to the highest, as moving sphere within sphere. Among no other people was organization and centralization as highly developed. Their idea was to have an organic unity in which the lower naturally and willingly submitted to the higher. Yet neither in theory or in practice were the Emperor and his subordinates free to enforce their decrees. Passages from the *Classics* and from the promulgations of the Government itself illustrate the great doctrine of harmony. All ideal relationships consisted in an adaptation of the higher existence to the lower as well as in submission of the lower to the higher.[8]

[8] Wilson, *op. cit.*, 7 *et seq.*

A reason for the order and harmonious relationship, prevailing in China, may be the laws of that country which received much praise from Staunton, who translated the primary provisions of the penal code of China into English in 1810. Westerners, though critical of certain features of the code, especially the frequency of corporal punishment, in general, commended it. In an article published in the *Edinburgh Review* in 1810, the reviewer of Staunton's work said:

. . . the most remarkable thing in this code appeared to us to be its great reasonableness, clearness and consistency—the business-like brevity and directness of the various provisions, and the plainness and moderation of the language in which they are expressed. . . . [It is] a calm, concise and distinct series of enactments, savouring throughout of practical judgment and European good sense. . . . When we pass, indeed, from the ravings of the Zendavesta of the Puranas, to the tone of sense and of business of this Chinese collection, we seem to be passing from darkness to light,—from the drivellings of dotage to the exercises of an improved understanding: And, redundant and absurdly minute as these laws are, in many particulars, we scarcely know any European code that is at once so copious and so consistent, or that is nearly so free from intricacy, bigotry and fiction. In everything relating to political freedom or individual independence, it is indeed wofully defective; but, for the repression of disorder, and the gentle coercion of a vast population, it appears to us to be, in general, equally mild and efficacious. The state of society for which it was formed, appears incidentally to be a low and a wretched state of society; but we do not know that wiser means could have been devised for maintaining it in peace and tranquillity.[9]

The strangeness of China, which differed entirely from all other countries, stirred Westerners' imagination.[10] Whether

[9] "The Penal Code of China," *Ed. R.* (1810), 16, p. 431 *et seq.* This article was quoted in the following books: G. T. Staunton, *Miscellaneous Notices Relating to China* (2nd ed., London, 1822-50), Appendix, p. 389 *et seq.*; W. B. Langdon, *Descriptive Catalogue of the Chinese Collection* (London, 1844), p. 161 *et seq.*; Williams, *op. cit.*, I, 306; J. L. Nevius, *China and the Chinese* (New York, 1869), p. 72; R. S. Maclay, *Life among the Chinese* (New York, 1861), p. 77.

[10] "The Chinese Puzzle," *Chamb. J.* (1863), 40, p. 94; George Mogridge, *The Celestial Empire* (London, 1844), p. 141.

the significant features of the language different from all others
or whether the more trivial and superficial characteristics, man-
ifested in its social customs, were examined, Europeans and
Americans were amazed at the curious and unusual features of
Chinese civilization.[11] A striking peculiarity of this singular
nation, which is supposed to be another proof of its unlikeness
to the rest of the world, was the contrast of the progress of
China with the development of other countries.

Although historians and antiquarians believed that China
had developed very early a superior civilization, they thought
that Chinese culture had remained stationary for centuries. The
Chinese possessed in a simple form, long before Europeans were
even in the infancy of civilization, some of the greatest inventions, such as the compass, printing, and gunpowder, but they
never developed them sufficiently for adequate use from the
European point of view. Their intricate compass made possible
neither navigation nor commerce on a large scale. Their printing, which was after all rudimentary, did not lead to the development of a literature worthy of the great invention. Occidentals
often reproached the Chinese because they never developed
their block printing into printing by movable types. Westerners
seemed to have a contempt for the use of gunpowder exclusively
for fireworks. They admitted, however, that the Chinese had
improved several of their arts and manufactures such as porcelain and silk, but they criticized the Chinese for their lack of
progress in general.[12]

Closely related to and probably responsible for the stationary
condition of the Chinese Empire was the tenacity with which
the Chinese mind clung to its own ideas and impressions. Laws,
customs, manners, and the rules of social life were not affected
by changes in dynasties. The culture of the conquerors themselves was usually absorbed by the Chinese form of civilization
so that in the end the invaders took over Chinese customs and
dropped their own.[13]

[11] "Huc's Travels in China," *Liv. Age* (1855), 45, p. 666 *et seq.*
[12] *Ibid.*, 667; *Hegel's Philosophy of the State and of History*, G. S.
Morris, ed. (Chicago, 1887), p. 139 *et seq.*
[13] E. R. Huc, *The Chinese Empire* (New ed., London, 1859), Preface,
p. xv *et seq.*

Of all the national characteristics, immobility or unchangeability was, perhaps, the strongest and most unique.[14] A notion prevailed in Europe and America that the Chinese were in 1840 as they had been at the time of Confucius. The same code of laws which ruled their remote ancestors governed them in the nineteenth century, and their dress, habits, manners, and mode of life were said to be precisely the same as their ancestors'.[15] China was supposed to be the only country in the world where fashion was not synonymous with change.[16] The Chinese in practice illustrated their favorite maxim—"All that is old is valuable, all that is new is valueless."[17] Many Europeans regarded the Chinese as a conservative, stationary, and fossilized people. An English writer said that they were in 1860 exactly what they were when England sent its first embassy to China in 1793 with the sole difference that Lord Macartney found them amiable whereas they were the reverse in 1860.[18]

Du Halde and the Jesuit missionaries were undoubtedly responsible for the dissemination of such notions about China's unchangeability and stationary conditions. In the *Description of the Empire of China*, Du Halde makes the following comments:

. . . for more than four thousand Years, it [China] has been almost constantly governed by its own Princes; and has continued the same with regard to the Attire, Morals, Customs and Manners of the Inhabitants, without deviating in the least from the wise Institutions of its ancient Legislators.

As the Inhabitants find within themselves everything that is necessary for the Conveniences and Pleasures of Life; so judging their native Soil sufficient to supply all their Wants, they have ever

[14] "China and the Chinese," *Liv. Age* (1853), 39, p. 639. "The Yang-Tsze River, and the Taepings in China," *Ecl. M.* (1863), 58, p. 334; Victor de Laprade, "Les Poètes classiques de la Chine," *Corres.* (1864), 62, p. 414; M. J. L. Hervey-Saint-Denys, *Poésies de l'époque des Thang* (Paris, 1842), p. xlix.

[15] "A Chinese Garden of the Eleventh Century," *Chamb. J.* (1855), 24, p. 140; "China," *Dub. R.* (1844), 16, p. 451 *et seq.*; H. Hensler, "Chinesische Novellen," *Unterhaltungen* (1859), 4, p. 209.

[16] "Quaint Customs in Kwei-chow," *Ecl. M.* (1872), 78, p. 322.

[17] H. C. Sirr, *China and the Chinese* (London, 1849), II, 86.

[18] "Flaws in China," *All the Year* (1861), 4, p. 419.

affected to carry on no Commerce with the rest of Mankind. This Ignorance of distant Countries, led them into the ridiculous Persuasion that they were Masters of the whole World; that they inhabited the greater Part of it; and that all without the Bounds of *China* were Barbarians: Which aversion to foreign Trade, joined to the Solidity of the People, has not a little contributed to the constant Uniformity found in their Manners.[19]

Although the tendency to stress the antiquity of China and to hold that nothing had changed in it for centuries continued through the years from 1840 to 1876, there was a certain scepticism on the part of many Europeans because of their increasing contacts with the East. They came to realize that the Orient had been developing and progressing and the China of 1875 was not exactly like the country Marco Polo visited in the thirteenth century.[20] Contemporary China, they wrote, should be studied not from the ancient *Classics* or from the accounts of the Jesuits but by observation of the country itself. The immutability of the Asiatics was one of the established ideas based on an utter ignorance of their history, declared Huc.[21]

Another idea frequently expressed in Western literature especially after 1850 was the decadent condition of China. Probably the reason statements were often made after that date about the collapse of Chinese civilization was the outbreak of the T'ai P'ing Rebellion in the summer of 1850. The situation in China seemed to prove that the country had been stationary for a long time and of late had been actually retrograding.[22] The arts had declined. Neither silks nor porcelains equalled the quality of early times.[23] In the North, many cities once flourishing and alive with commerce had fallen into decay, and dilapidated buildings remained unrepaired.[24] Were the decline

[19] J. B. Du Halde, ed., *A Description of the Empire of China* (London, 1738), I, 237.
[20] "Feudal China," *Cornh.* (1874), 30, p. 549.
[21] Huc, *op. cit.*, 301; Pierre Laffitte, *Considérations générales sur l'ensemble de la civilisation chinoise* (Paris, 1861), p. 48.
[22] V. de Mars, "La Question chinoise," *RDM* (1857), 9, p. 483; John Scarth, *Twelve Years in China* (Edinburgh, 1860), p. 230.
[23] "The National Life of China," *Blackw.* (1854), 75, p. 607.
[24] Sirr, *op. cit.*, II, 393.

visible only in the temples, it might be explained by the increasing apathy or scepticism of the people in regard to religion. But these signs of decay extended into almost every department of state.[25] The most frightful corruption penetrated the whole mass of society. Magistrates sold justice to the highest bidder. Mandarins instead of protecting the people oppressed and pillaged them by every means in their power.[26]

The general disorganization, which had penetrated into every part of Chinese society, lay partly in a very important modification of the ancient system of government, introduced by the Manchus. They permitted no mandarin to stay in the same place for more than three years and no official to be appointed in his own province. The motives for such a measure are obvious. The Manchu Tartars, terrified at their small number in the midst of the Chinese, took steps to maintain their supremacy and prevent counter-revolution. But Huc pointed out another element which contributed towards disintegration. The great Chinese mandarins, wandering from province to province without becoming attached to a particular locality, had not time to make themselves all powerful with the people so that they could lead a rebellion. Their policy, perhaps judicious for the consolidation of Tartar power, only made for disorder in the end. Magistrates and public officials who remained only a few years in a post lived like strangers. Their chief interest was the accumulation of wealth which would make it possible for them to retire in luxury. The fundamental principle of the Chinese monarchy was thereby destroyed, for the magistrate no longer felt a personal responsibility for the people under his jurisdiction.[27]

While Occidentals considered China a decadent nation they thought it could survive the period of retrogression.[28] Again and again, it had reformed itself after a period of chaos and convulsion. Its periodic revolutions tended to throw off the corruption

[25] "The National Life of China," op. cit.
[26] Huc, op. cit., 66. [27] Ibid., 232 et seq.
[28] John Thomson, The Straits of Malacca, Indo-China, and China (New York, 1875), p. 347; W. J. Hail, Tsêng Kuo-fan and the Taiping Rebellion (New Haven, 1927), Chap. I.

which ease and apathy had produced. Occidentals believed China would endure forever because of its vast homogeneous population.[29]

Chinese national traits, stressed by Europeans since the beginning of contacts with the Orient, were their conceit and their pride. Separated from the rest of the world, they viewed with contempt all other countries. China assumed the title "Celestial Empire" and also styled itself the "Middle Kingdom." Other nations were barbarians, doomed to live at the extremity of the "square cornered earth" or upon the small islands in the four seas surrounding the "Middle Kingdom."[30]

A few Westerners drew a distinction between the Government's and the people's attitude toward foreigners. The people, in general, were not hostile to outsiders.[31] The ancient philosophers did not recommend ill-treatment for foreigners, and Confucius urged sovereigns to receive strangers cordially. Sinibaldo de Mas maintained that the Manchus and not the Chinese closed the country.[32] Davis also said that the natural aversion of the people to strangers was encouraged by the mandarins.[33] The point was also made that the chief cause of the unpopularity of Occidentals in China was the Emperor's assumption of universal supremacy. The natives maintained that foreigners rightfully owed the same allegiance to the Emperor as they themselves did. Nothing irritated the upper classes more than to see Westerners living in the country with exemption from its laws and in defiance of the local authorities.[34]

The Chinese were not supposed to be interested in Occidentals or in their civilization. They simply ignored their intellectual progress, their institutions, and their industries.[35] They

---

[29] "The National Life of China," op. cit., 607 et seq.

[30] Mogridge, op. cit., 212 et seq.; Williams, op. cit., II, 595.

[31] Baron von Richthofen, Letters, 1870-72 (Shanghai), p. 77; G. W. Cooke, China (London, 1858), p. 112.

[32] Sinibaldo de Mas, La Chine et les puissances chrétiennes (Paris, 1861), I, 358.

[33] Davis, op. cit., I, 301.

[34] "The Present Condition of China," Ecl. M. (1871), 76, p. 26.

[35] Huc, op. cit., p. 200 (Quoted from Abel Rémusat); J. F. Davis, Sketches of China (London, 1841), I, 109.

boasted of their sages' superior wisdom and profound erudition. Proud of their ancient literature and ignorant of the customs of Western nations, they regarded foreigners as unfitted for intellectual matters. On the contrary they readily admitted the superiority of the West in the fields of science, inventions, and commerce. But from the Chinese point of view as it was interpreted by Europeans, these accomplishments were nothing in comparison with the wisdom in their ancient writings.[36]

After the first Anglo-Chinese War and the T'ai P'ing Rebellion, Occidentals were convinced that the Chinese could not maintain their policy of exclusion and thereby protect their institutions from all foreign influence. The advances which diplomats, merchants, and missionaries made especially after 1840 in influencing the opinions of the classes of people with whom they came in contact, the increased facilities for communication, and the rapid progress of Japan after 1850 were exerting a strong and peculiar pressure on China.[37] An important result of the isolation of China, Westerners said, was a serious check in its development. The civilization of Europe was the product of the interfusion of diverse types of culture from Judea, Greece, Rome, Egypt, and the remote countries of Western Asia. The civilization of China was indigenous.[38]

Closely associated with the idea of the evolution of China as a great nation, working out its fate slowly and gradually in seclusion, was the notion of a certain peacefulness and repose which had always permeated the "Celestial Empire." Since the seventeenth and eighteenth centuries when Jesuit missionaries had drawn delightful pictures of the tranquillity and stately repose of China,[39] Westerners had regarded it as the most peaceful country in the world.[40] Davis said that the Chinese had lived so much in peace that they had a horror of all kinds of

[36] Justus Doolittle, Social Life of the Chinese (New York, 1865), II, 422.
[37] R. K. Douglas, The Language and Literature of China (London, 1875), p. 1 et seq.
[38] "Feudal China," Cornh. (1874), 30, p. 549.
[39] Athanasius Kircher, La Chine illustrée . . . , Traduit par F. S. Dalquié (Amsterdam, 1670), pp. 155, 223 et seq.
[40] Charles Macfarlane, The Chinese Revolution (London, 1853), p. 1.

political disorders. "Better be a dog in peace than a man in anarchy" was a common maxim.[41]   The Chinese Empire was a stupendous example of a consistently peaceful policy, remarked Williams.[42]   He thought the reasons for this tranquil condition were to be found partly in the diffusion of political education among the people and partly in their plodding, peaceful, and industrious character.[43]

Other writers challenged the notion that peace had always prevailed in China.   Macfarlane emphasized the exaggeration in the Jesuits' description of the tranquillity of the Chinese Empire.   Such a condition of perpetual calm never existed among the Chinese, he contended, but the world had continued to receive the fiction of China's perpetual peace as an undoubted truth.[44]

The majority of Westerners probably accepted these stereotyped notions as late as 1840, but the outbreak of hostilities between England and China in that year contributed toward the gradual breakdown of old conventional concepts.   Many Europeans who wrote after the war declared that China was no longer an unknown region, enveloped in secrecy and mystery. After 1842 the European and American public was not dependent for information upon the colored and exaggerated reports of the few travellers and missionaries who were allowed inside the borders of China.[45]

[41] J. F. Davis, *China* . . . (London, 1857), I, 259.
[42] Williams, *op. cit.*, II, 162.   [43] *Ibid.*, I, 299.
[44] Macfarlane, *op. cit.*, 1; Frederick von Schlegel, *The Philosophy of History*, Translated from the German . . . by James Burton Robinson (5th ed., London, 1847), p. 124.
[45] "The Present Condition of the Chinese Empire," *C. Repos.* (1843), 12, p. 1 *et seq.*

CHAPTER IV

THE BREAKDOWN OF SECLUSION

THE CHINESE, having pursued a policy of almost absolute seclusion for a long period of time because they regarded their country as the foremost empire in all the world and the doctrines taught by their sages superior to all other systems of philosophy, maintained that everything foreign was barbarian and not worthy of their attention. After the discovery of new trade routes to the East toward the end of the fifteenth century and the opening of European commerce with the Orient in the following century, the Chinese engaged in a limited trade with the Western powers. But during the sixteenth, seventeenth, and eighteenth centuries the foreign merchant was confined to a few ports, little diplomatic intercourse was carried on, and the only foreigners allowed in the interior were a relatively small number of Roman Catholic missionaries.[1]

The partial opening of the country after the first Anglo-Chinese War naturally aroused great expectations and hopes among many Europeans and Americans. Western traders and merchants had visions of a thriving and lucrative trade carried eventually into the very heart of the Chinese Empire. Ambitious capitalists hoped to develop the natural resources of China by introducing modern methods of mining, building railroads, and improving methods of water transportation through the use of steamboats on the great rivers of China. The missionaries redoubled their efforts after the war to introduce Christianity and Occidental civilization into all parts of the Empire. But these groups were disappointed because the first Anglo-Chinese War served only as an opening wedge in the wall with which China had enclosed itself. By the terms of the treaty of Nan-

---

[1] K. S. Latourette, *A History of Christian Missions in China* (New York, 1929), p. 79; T. W. Knox, "The Chinese Embassy to the Foreign Powers," *Harper* (1868), 37, p. 592 *et seq.*; Alexander Michie, *The Englishman in China* (Edinburgh, 1900), I, 111.

king (1842), foreigners were allowed to trade in only four ports besides Canton.[2]

After that date, however, China was making more and more contacts with the Western world, and changes very gradually began to take place especially in the purely material aspects of Chinese civilization. It was not until after the second war with England that foreigners were permitted to go into the interior. By the decade of the seventies, Western business men were discussing prospects for trade and the possibilities for the investment of capital throughout China. Although Western financiers were investing their money in China during the latter part of the nineteenth century, it was not until the second decade of the twentieth century, when on a much larger scale roads and railways were constructed, factories equipped with modern machinery were built, projects for land reclamation through drainage and irrigation were launched, and schemes for water supply and electric power were put into effect, that the old policy of exclusion was broken down.[3]

The West referred to the first Anglo-Chinese War as a major crisis in the history of China. It was supposedly the point of departure for the change from old things, which had existed for some twenty centuries, to the newer Western ideas, which would revolutionize all phases of national life.[4] Some writers who maintained that China had been adhering for ages to old institutions and accepting nothing new or different thought the war made the Chinese realize that their country must accept a few innovations or else cease to be a great empire. To this group the importance of the war lay in its effect upon Chinese thought. Others emphasized more the effect of the War of 1840 upon European opinion of China. Westerners at last concluded that the "Middle Kingdom" was not as immobile, stationary, changeless, and lethargic as they had believed it to be. Probably European opinion of China rather than

[2] H. B. Morse and H. F. MacNair, *Far Eastern International Relations* (Boston, 1931), p. 127 *et seq.*

[3] "Editorial Note," *Changing China* April, 1933, p. 3.

[4] "Der Bürgerkrieg in China," *Europa* (1853), p. 367.

China itself was vastly changed by the first war between that country and England.

Politically, the war was of immense importance to China. The clash gave an immense shock to the Empire. It did much to shake the stability of the Tartar dynasty because the military prestige of the ruling powers was destroyed and the treasury was exhausted. Money had to be extorted from the people, and offices which had hitherto been reserved as rewards for merit were openly sold to the highest bidder.[5] The general discontent which followed the War of 1840 tended to discredit the Government with the people, and made possible open rebellion in 1850.[6] Shortly after the close of the first Anglo-Chinese War, Westerners, familiar with the internal situation in China, predicted a revolution. Underlying the quiet and seemingly prosperous state of the country was an undercurrent of dissatisfaction.[7] Williams emphasized the quick recuperation of China after the war. The cities and provinces most affected by the conflict were rapidly regaining their prosperity. The Government was re-establishing its authority, and the people were returning to peaceful occupations. But elements of discontent, which at any moment might flare into open revolt, were present.[8]

It was not until the month of August 1850 that the *Peking Gazette*[9] began to refer to the insurrection.[10] Europeans from that date were deeply interested in the movement. More than one writer referred to the rebellion as one of the most important events of modern times.[11] Westerners held various theories

[5] "The China Question," *Liv. Age* (1857), 54, p. 319.

[6] *Annual Register* (1863), p. 120; Andrew Wilson, *The "Ever Victorious Army"* (Edinburgh, 1868), p. 57; "Review of Far Eastern News," *Asiat. J.* (1840), 33, p. 145.

[7] "Journal of Occurrences," *C. Repos.* (1844), 13, p. 560.

[8] S. W. Williams, *The Middle Kingdom* (New York, 1848), II, 594 *et seq.*

[9] A private printing of official edicts, memorials, and proclamations.

[10] Charles Macfarlane, *The Chinese Revolution* (London, 1853), p. 46.

[11] Joseph Marie Callery and Melchior Yvan, *History of the Insurrection in China* (New York, 1853), p. 9; "The Chinese Revolution," *Liv. Age*

on the origin of the movement.   The oldest and most generally accepted notion was that the insurrection was purely political in its first objects, and grew chiefly out of Chinese hatred for the Tartars, the weakness of the Government, and the arbitrary oppression of the official classes.[12]   Secret societies had for more than two hundred years played an important role in the history of the Chinese Empire in spite of the Government's efforts to suppress them.   The most famous organization was the Triad Society which was not only powerful in the various provinces of the Chinese Empire but also among the Chinese of Singapore, Siam, and Malacca.   This group, an integral and permanent factor in Chinese society, scattered the seeds of revolt against the Manchus throughout the entire country.[13]

Other forces which hastened the outbreak of the Chinese rebellion were at work.   The revolt at the same time had a decidedly religious tinge.   Many saw in the insurrection a religious revolution, accidentally political, brought about in the name of the doctrines expounded by Protestant missionaries.[14]   Hung Hsiu-ch'üan, the leader of the rebellion, was a native of Kwangsi.   In 1836 while in Canton for the examinations he acquired a set of Christian books, but he did not examine them until some years later.   Meanwhile, he had a serious illness during which he had several visions. Afterwards he pronounced them revelations from God.   He believed himself carried to Heaven where a venerable man on a throne addressed him as follows:

All human beings in the whole world are produced and sustained by me; they eat my food and wear my clothing, but not a single one among them has a heart to remember and venerate me.

(1853), 39, p. 235; *Colburn* (1853), 99, p. 180; "Der Krieg der Westmächte gegen China," *Unsere Zeit* (1864), 8, p. 373.

[12] *Ibid.*

[13] René de Courcy, "L'Insurrection chinoise," *RDM* (1861), 34, p. 9 *et seq.*; Lindesay Brine, *The Taeping Rebellion in China* (London, 1862), p. 113; Williams, *op. cit.*, I, 394, II, 284; W. T. Power, *Recollections of Three Years' Residence in China* (London, 1853), p. 198.

[14] K. F. Neumann, *Geschichte des englisch-chinesischen Krieges* (Leipzig, 1855), p. 358.

What is, however, still worse, they take of my gifts, and therewith worship demons; they purposely rebel against me and arouse my anger. Do not thou imitate them.[15]

The elderly man then gave Hung a sword to destroy the demons and a seal with power to overcome spirits. Next he led Hung to the parapet of Heaven to gaze upon the earth. Its evil and depravity made a great impression upon the latter. In other visions Hung met a middle-aged man whom he called his elder brother. From these trances Hung always emerged filled with wrath and indignation because of evil practices of men around him. The memories of these visions seemed to have faded completely after his recovery, but about six years later he read the Christian tracts which came into his possession in 1836. They explained conclusively to Hung Hsiu-ch'üan the meaning of the various visions which he had almost forgotten. He immediately began to preach his doctrine, but because the people of his native village opposed him, he finally went to the Kwei district in Kwangsi.

About 1846 or 1847 Hung Hsiu-ch'üan and his cousin, Hung Jin, went to Canton where they studied the Bible under the direction of Issachar Roberts, a Protestant missionary. About 1847 Hung Hsiu-ch'üan went back to Kwangsi. His activities together with those of his neighbor, Feng Yun-shan, who had been particularly successful in establishing religious communities known as the God-worshippers in eastern Kwangsi, greatly alarmed the authorities, and Feng was imprisoned. The troubles of 1846 and 1847 afforded an occasion for turning the new religious brotherhoods into armed bands. As early as 1848 they had some skirmishes but no serious clashes with the Imperial soldiers. Hung Hsiu-ch'üan at this time emerged as leader of the rebellion.[16]

The leader of the movement was invested with a grandeur which overawed his compatriots and perplexed foreigners. But

[15] W. J. Hail, *Tsêng Kuo-fan and the Taiping Rebellion* (New Haven, 1927), p. 34.
[16] *Ibid.*, Chap. II; "Religion of the Chinese Rebels," *Quar. R.* (1854), 94, p. 176 *et seq.*; René de Courcy, *op. cit.*, 18 *et seq.*

Wilson found no reason to suspect the man's sincerity. According to this author, he was not a political adventurer or imposter.[17] Perhaps the strongest argument in favor of the rebels' religious sincerity was the fact that Westerners who came in contact with them believed them to be serious and earnest. Their public orders were scrupulously enforced in camp, and they repeated their acts of worship two or three times each day.[18]

The accounts of visions, revelations, and personal interventions of the Deity were told mainly in the *Book of Celestial Decrees* and in the *Revelations of the Heavenly Father*. The latter according to Christian standards was gross and profane. The Almighty appeared of his own accord to convict a traitor in the insurgent camp. The conversation and manner in which the culprit's evasions were detected sank to coarseness. The *Book of Celestial Decrees,* which attested the leader's commission, was less offensive. It recited divine proclamations, which urged the insurgents to be brave, and to believe in the Supreme God. A publication of a very different stamp was the *Trimetrical Classic* which tells about the writer having been taken up to Heaven and Jesus having come down to instruct and encourage Hung Siu-ch'üan in his arduous enterprises. All of these writings have a trace of biblical thought and language which caused much discussion among missionaries and other foreigners. Yet in the reference to national history, the appeal to antiquity, the unconscious prominence given to parental authority and family relationships, and the peculiar and specific exhortations to virtue, the works were thoroughly Chinese.

The distinctive features of Christianity, enumerated in the creed of the insurgents, however, stand out unmistakably in a simple, forceful way. Errors from the Christian point of view were found, but such were expected. The practices of the converts revealed imperfections. Much was written about the so-called sacrifices. The ceremony consisted of offerings of such things as animals, flowers, and food. The practice came from

[17] "Religion of the Chinese Rebels," *op. cit.,* 177; Wilson, *op. cit.,* 35 *et seq.;* Charles Taylor, *Five Years in China* (New York, 1860), p. 370.
[18] *Ibid.,* 350 *et seq.*

the old Confucian form of worship. It was not unusual for the T'ai P'ings to cling to this custom; pagan peoples, when first converted to Christianity, retained many of their old heathen rites. Their cruelty, although no greater than that observed in the religious wars of Europe, shows that the precepts of Christianity, in practice, had not been embraced by its Chinese adherents. Again, fanaticism was clearly intermingled with the pretensions of their spiritual and political leader in whom, according to the Chinese constitution, the two offices were united.[19] Some great truths were unrecognized; others were obscured. The religion of these insurgents was not pure Christianity, but it was a step towards it. During the entire history of the human race very few nations, at one single stride, had made greater changes in their religious system than the Chinese rebels. Although imperfect at the time of their introduction, these ideas, some believed, would eventually produce a great and lasting effect upon the Chinese national mind.[20] Others like Huc did not give much credit to the Christianity of the insurgents. Their religion and mystical sentiments, Huc thought, inspired no great confidence. It was difficult for him to see in the T'ai P'ing leader any more than a Chinese Mohammed, who tried to establish his power by force.[21]

Still another theory on the origin of the T'ai P'ing Rebellion was held by those who attributed its beginning to an uprising of the Miao Tsu, mountain folk, of the province of Kwangsi. When the Manchu dynasty came into power the southern provinces refused to recognize the new rulers and set up a rival Emperor in 1647. Tartar troops finally put an end to the

---

[19] "Religion of the Chinese Rebels," *op. cit.*, 171 *et seq.*

[20] J. M. Mackie, *Life of Tai-ping-wang, Chief of the Chinese Insurrection* (New York, 1857), p. 3; Brine, *op. cit.*, 77; "Fishbourne's Impressions of China," *Liv. Age* (1855), 45, p. 398; "American Diplomacy in China," *No. Amer. R.* (1859), 89, p. 499; J. E. Johnson, "Tai-ping-wang and the Chinese Rebellion," *New Eng.* (1871), 30, p. 389 *et seq.*; Wilson, *op. cit.*, 59; W. L. G. Smith, *Observations on China and the Chinese* (New York, 1863), p. 104 *et seq.*

[21] E. R. Huc, *The Chinese Empire* (New ed., London, 1859), Preface, p. xiii *et seq.*; J. F. Davis, *China* (New ed., London, 1857), I, 176.

power in the south, but the remnants of the army fled to the mountains of Kwangsi, the home of the Miao Tsu, an aboriginal race. Never recognizing the authority of the Manchus, these people under various pretenders kept up a continual resistance against the Imperial authorities. In their loyalty to the dethroned dynasty, their national independence, their deep hatred of the Tartars, and their friendliness toward Christianity because of their early ruler's associations with the Jesuits and Christian converts, some missionaries believed to find an explanation of the political and religious movement known as the T'ai P'ing Rebellion. A leader having been necessary, the Miao Tsu chose Hung Hsiu-ch'üan to command them. This explanation of the rebellion seemed more plausible to de Courcy than the Protestant version. The natural hatred of the Miao Tsu against the Tartars, their attachment to the Ming dynasty, and the confidence and boldness, which they had shown in their numerous victories over the Imperial armies, certainly contained elements of revolt and success more powerful, he contended, than the desire for personal defense which had led a small band of recent converts to take up arms to protect themselves from persecution by the Imperial authorities. But this theory was refuted. The first symptoms of the revolt appeared in the districts of Kwangsi far from the mountains where the Miao Tsu lived. Even though the Christian ideas of the T'ai P'ings could have come from Catholic as well as other sources, the majority of the principles were drawn from the writings of Protestant missionaries.[22]

Besides political and religious causes, the T'ai P'ing Rebellion was also attributed by contemporaries to the extreme impoverishment of the peasantry in the southern provinces. One of the most renowned of the T'ai P'ing rebels said that the sole idea of most of the men who joined the revolt was to obtain food.[23] Later writers have emphasized the social and economic aspects of the rebellion which was from their point of view an uprising of peasants, agricultural laborers, handworkers, and

---

[22] René de Courcy, "L'Insurrection chinoise," op. cit., 21 et seq.
[23] "The Present Condition of China," Ecl. M. (1871), 13, p. 16.

poorer landowners against the landlords, rich peasants, and wealthy gentry.[24]

Other Westerners maintained that another contributing cause was the latent infiltration of European political ideas into the open ports. These principles were carried by the missionaries into the innermost parts of the Empire.[25] Gutzlaff, besides teaching the Christian faith, supposedly introduced the Chinese to Western political theories and encouraged them to demand better government. Speaking many dialects fluently, Gutzlaff, during his long and slow voyages on junks with talkative Chinese, might have instilled in them his own political ideas. The rebellion probably did not originate with this missionary, but Westerners believed him to have contributed indirectly toward the movement by the infusion of both political and religious elements.[26]

The revolt, which actually began in 1848, did not become serious until about 1850. In 1852 the rebels moved north into Hunan by way of the Hsiang River. Early in 1853 they captured Wuchang and Nanking. Because of the weakness of the Ch'ing dynasty which was at the same time harassed by the French and the English, the T'ai P'ings were able to extend their sway through the Yangtze Valley. Not until 1865 were the Imperial forces able to defeat them. Because of the fanaticism and ravages of the rebels, which interfered with Western trade especially in the Yangtze Valley, Occidental powers turned against the T'ai P'ings and helped to expel them from the territory around Shanghai.[27] The effective operations against the rebels in this area were initiated by Frederick Townsend Ward, an American adventurer and soldier of fortune who was born in Salem, Massachusetts.[28] He began his work under crushing

[24] K. S. Latourette, *The Chinese Their History and Culture* (New York, 1934), I, 376 *et seq.;* John Thomson, *The Straits of Malacca, Indo-China, and China* (New York, 1875), p. 45.

[25] "The Rebellion in China," *Liv. Age* (1853), 38, p. 655.

[26] Macfarlane, *op. cit.,* 81 *et seq.*   [27] Latourette, *op. cit.,* I, 376 *et seq.*

[28] Ward was born in 1831 after Salem's foreign trade began to decline. The traditions of its Oriental commerce remained. The sea captain of the earlier days had retired, but the "dust and cobwebs under the eaves of his attic concealed camphor-trunks and cedar-trunks stuffed with . . . pongee

difficulties. Even his own countrymen among the merchants of Shanghai gave him little encouragement. The English actually obstructed and abused him. But in time the foreign residents in the Orient came to respect and admire him.[29]

By 1860 rebel forces, who were not really T'ai P'ings but bands only loosely affiliated with them, were ready to undertake the capture of Shanghai. It was of vast importance because it controlled the mouth of the Yangtze-Kiang. At the time of this crisis, Ward was acting as first officer on the Chinese armed steamer, the *Confucius*. While serving in this capacity, he received an introduction to Yang Tze-tang, head of the Taki banking firm and chairman of a committee of patriotic Chinese merchants in Shanghai.[30] Ward thereupon made an offer to this official to capture Sungkiang, a rebel stronghold and the capital city of the Shanghai district for a definite sum of money. Once in possession of Sungkiang Ward proposed to establish headquarters there for operations by land and water for the ultimate relief of Shanghai. He soon obtained sufficient funds to begin operations. At first he recruited deserters from foreign ships and Filipinos who were always available at Shanghai. After trouble with the British authorities over the use of their

---

silks . . . with now and then a bit of bronze or Nanking ware or silver filigree or lacquer, and unbroached casks of Canton ware might lie in hiding behind the wood-pile in his cellar . . . , when a family returned from residence abroad, it was not unusual to bring with them Chinese cooks and nurse-maids and house servants, so that the garb of the Oriental was almost as familiar then as laundry work has made it since. . . ." It was in this atmosphere that Ward spent his early years, and after he failed to get a cadetship at West Point, he temporarily gave up a military career. In 1847 he sailed to China in the clipper ship, *Hamilton*. During this trip, Ward probably learned something of the conditions in China which made him eager to try his fortune in that country. After adventures in Central America, in Mexico, and supposedly with the French army in the Crimean War, he returned to China about 1859. See Robert S. Rantoul, "Frederick Townsend Ward," *Historical Collections of the Essex Institute* (1908), 44, p. 1 *et seq.*; Holger Cahill, *A Yankee Adventurer* (New York, 1930), p. 11 *et seq.*; Wilson, *op. cit.*, 62 *et seq.*

[29] Cahill, *op. cit.*, 114 *et seq.*; A. A. Hayes, "An American Soldier in China," *Atlan.* (1886), 57, p. 193 *et seq.*

[30] H. B. Morse, *The International Relations of the Chinese Empire* (London, 1910-18), II, 70; Wilson, *op. cit.*, 63 *et seq.*

seamen in his army and reverses because of insufficient numbers, Ward recruited native Chinese to be commanded by Western officers and carefully drilled in Western military tactics.

By the second week of January 1862 the T'ai P'ing advance guards were at Shanghai, and the rebel army was on the march toward the coast. During the first week of February Ward with a thousand of his Chinese troops and two hundred Filipinos, supported by two thousand soldiers under Li Ai-tang, defeated a T'ai P'ing force at Kwanfuling, west of Shanghai. This victory immediately established Ward's reputation and from this time his force was associated with Admiral Sir James Hope and the French Admiral, Protet. After the capture of Hsiaotang, a strongly fortified city, the governor of Kwangsi, in a memorial to the throne, praised the bravery of Ward and his troops. The Emperor conferred upon the American the title of "General" and upon his force the name of the "Ever Victorious Army." Ward also became a mandarin of the fourth class with an opaque blue button and a tiger embroidered on his badge of official rank. Later he became a major general and was finally raised to the third class of mandarins and entitled to wear the peacock's feather for distinguished military achievement.[31]

After the capture of Ningpo in May 1862 by the French and the British, Ward was ordered by Li Hung-chang, governor of Kwangsi, to Ningpo to help the Imperialists expel the rebel force of twenty thousand men from the city of Yu-Yao on the Hangchow Bay opposite Ningpo. During the campaign in this region Ward was mortally wounded at Tsz'ki. His body was taken to Shanghai for an elaborate funeral. Many civil and military authorities then accompanied his remains to Sungkiang where they were interred with great ceremony in the Confucian temple.[32] Later in 1877 a memorial temple was dedicated with impressive religious rites.

[31] Rantoul, *op. cit.*, 1 *et seq.*; Cahill, *op. cit.*, 114 *et seq.*; Wilson, *op. cit.*, 65 *et seq.*

[32] Edward Forester, "Personal Recollections of the Tai-Ping Rebellion," *Cosmo.* (1896), 22, p. 216; Wilson, *op. cit.*, 90.

After Ward's death two of his officers, first Forester who resigned his command shortly because of ill-health and afterwards Burgevine had control of the "Ever Victorious Army."[33] Ill-feeling between Burgevine and Li Hung-chang led to the former's dismissal, and Sir John Holland of the Royal Marines was put in charge of the force until Major Charles George Gordon of the British Royal Engineers could take over the command of the "Ever Victorious Army" in March 1863.[34]

Gordon found the troops demoralized and on the verge of mutiny because of arrears in their pay and because of their loyalty to Burgevine. Almost the whole province of Kiangsu and a large part of Chekiang were overrun by the T'ai P'ings who were obtaining arms from Shanghai and Ningpo and engaging foreign adventurers. The Chinese authorities caused him considerable annoyance because of their laxness in forwarding funds for the payment of troops. The country was extremely unfavorable to military operations. It had few roads, and the network of canals, streams, and rivers made the swift movement of an army almost impossible. This region had also been plundered so that adequate supplies were not available. In spite of these disadvantages, Gordon, who was unfamiliar with the country, fought for more than a year with great success. He soon gained the respect of his officers and his soldiers because of his bravery, fairness, and humanity.[35]

Because the "Ever Victorious Army" under Ward and later under Gordon included many of their nationals, Europeans and Americans watched with unusual interest its part in crushing the rebellion. Wilson, a contemporary, and Hail, a more recent student of the movement, however, stressed the role of Tsêng Kuo-fan in the rebels' defeat. The latter wrote that "foreign observers were so dazzled by the fame of the valuable little force of foreign trained soldiers organized by Frederick Townsend Ward and eventually led by 'Chinese Gordon,' that they have immortalized the 'Ever Victorious Army' of three thousand men, almost canonized Gordon, and relegated the real

---

[33] Forester, op. cit.   [34] Cahill, op. cit., 245 et seq.
[35] Wilson, op. cit., 144, 254 et seq.; Cahill, op. cit., 268 et seq.

hero of the T'ai P'ing Rebellion [Tsêng Kuo-fan] to oblivion."[36] The Imperialist victories of Tsêng Kuo-fan and his generals drove the T'ai P'ings into the seaboard districts of Kiangsu and Chekiang. Foreign residents seemed to think that the presence of the rebels in these provinces indicated a general triumph of the T'ai P'ing cause. Wilson did not think so. If the T'ai P'ings had succeeded in taking Shanghai and Ningpo, they might have caused the Chinese authorities much trouble, but the latter speculated that the British would not ignore treaty obligations or go counter to their own interests by allowing the rebels to capture these two consular ports. The advance of the T'ai P'ings, Wilson argued, did not prove that Tsêng Kuo-fan and his generals could not have ended the rebellion in their own way.[37]

Although such a movement as the T'ai P'ing Rebellion was nothing new to the Chinese, the conditions surrounding the uprising were vastly different. According to precedent some powerful Tartar or Chinese prince would have quelled the revolt and have put himself on the throne. Again the Empire might have been divided between two independent dynasties. Occidentals from 1850 to 1860 predicted the dissolution of the country into a number of loosely federated states. They were convinced that the Empire had become too large and too unwieldy to remain intact.[38] At the same time foreign factors complicated the situation in China. If the other European powers had been out of the way, Michie believed Russia could have taken control of China. The latter was sufficiently protected by the jealousies of rival European powers.[39]

Although the rebels were largely destructive in their effects upon China, they were reformers and constituted the first movement to "save" China through the introduction of Western

---

[36] Hail, *op. cit.*, Introduction, p. xiv.

[37] Wilson, *op. cit.*, 258 *et seq.*

[38] W. C. Milne, *Life in China* (New ed., London, 1859), p. 434.

[39] Alexander Michie, *The Siberian Overland Route from Peking to Petersburg* (London, 1864), p. 370; Macfarlane, *op. cit.*, 168 *et seq.*; "Der Krieg der Westmächte," *Unsere Zeit* (1864), 8, p. 385; "Celestial Intelligence," *Chamb. J.* (1850), 14, p. 172.

ideas and innovations. They probably retarded reform along Western lines because their excesses made intelligent and influential Chinese abhor any changes in the established order. Doubtless, some of the principles of the T'ai P'ings influenced later reformers, but it is difficult to trace any definite connection between the T'ai P'ing Rebellion and the radical twentieth-century movement which was also along anti-Manchu lines and began in the South where feeling against the Manchus was strongest. The later movement owed much of its strength and support to over seas Chinese who through their contacts with the West were more progressive than the Chinese who had remained at home. Some of the enthusiasm of these immigrants can possibly be traced to the T'ai P'ings, who, escaping from China after the collapse of the rebellion, agitated abroad for reform. Biographers of Sun Yat-sen have pointed out that in his youth he had contacts with groups of T'ai P'ing origin.[40]

Regardless of the actual changes which the rebellion made in the organization of the Empire and in national thought, the first Anglo-Chinese War and the T'ai P'ing Rebellion made Westerners believe that China was in a state of transition after centuries of immobility. By 1855 a revolutionary spirit prevailed and activity was the order of the day after a long period of stagnation.[41] During the revolt and afterwards, occasional references to the "awakening" of China are found. Macfarlane insisted that, as a result of the revolution, China had an "awakening."[42] Another contemporary wrote in 1854: "It is truly a great and wonderful thing to see a mighty nation thus awakening, after the sleep of untold ages."[43] Again in 1871 Browne said that "the ancient empire of China had risen from its dead sleep of ages, brushed away the cobwebs from its eyes,

---

[40] Leonard S. Hsü, *Sun Yat-sen, His Political and Social Ideals* (Los Angeles, 1929), 3 *et seq.*; Lyon Sharman, *Sun Yat-sen, His Life and Its Meaning* (New York, 1934), pp. 17, 62, 85 *passim*.

[41] "China," *Liv. Age* (1858), 56, p. 472; J. E. Bingham, *Narrative of the Expedition to China* (London, 1842), I, Preface, p. xii; R. S. Maclay, *Life among the Chinese* (New York, 1861), p. 347.

[42] Macfarlane, *op. cit.*, 137.

[43] "The Revolution in China," *Ecl. M.* (1854), 31, p. 109.

yawned in dreary wonder at the mushroom growth of nations around it. . . ."[44] Although a few Westerners referred to the "awakening" of China usually as a direct consequence of the T'ai P'ing Rebellion, the Western concept of China's "awakening" belongs to a period after 1876. Europeans and Americans believed, however, that the country had begun to stir from within, and these signs of life made them more hopeful of its future.

[44] J. R. Browne, "Under the Dragon's Footstool," *Overland* (1871), 6, p. 155.

CHAPTER V

IMMIGRATION

WESTERNERS, especially the Americans and the British, were gradually becoming more and more interested in the Chinese after 1840 primarily because of increased contacts through trade. But two important problems forcibly centered attention on the Chinese. Capitalists, observing the excellent qualities of the industrious Orientals, became aware of the possibilities for their employment in undeveloped areas and places where labor was dear and scarce. Only the lower classes with rare exceptions could be induced to leave their native land.[1] They were said to have emigrated because of their oppressive government and because of the extremely low wages at home where the population was very dense.[2] Oftentimes the emigrants had not enough money for their passage to the new country. They became bondsmen to any person who paid the sum and were a prey to extortioners and swindlers. The vessels transporting the Asiatics were similar to those used for African slaves, and because of their crowded conditions these ships were called "floating hells" in the books and official reports of the period.[3]

Despite these obstacles many Chinese settled in the United States, Canada, Australia, South America, and the West Indies. In the United States, Canada, and Australia, the problem which arose from immigration and the arguments for and against the movement were essentially the same. The number of Chinese

[1] S. W. Williams, *The Middle Kingdom* (New York, 1848), I, 223.

[2] R. H. Conwell, *Why and How. Why the Chinese Emigrate* (Boston, 1871); F. H. Norton, "Our Labor-System and the Chinese," *Scrib.* (1871), 2, p. 65.

[3] H. B. Morse and H. F. MacNair, *Far Eastern International Relations* (Boston, 1931), p. 263; J. E. Bingham, *Narrative of the Expedition to China* (London, 1842), I, 24, *et seq.*; "Emigration and the Coolie Trade in China," *Westm. R.* (1873), 100, p. 75; Edmond Plauchut, "La Traite des coulies," *RDM* (1873), 106, pp. 178-93; Anatole Langlois, "La Traite des coulies chinois," *Corres.* (1872), 89, pp. 133-58.

in California, where the majority who came to the United States settled, was placed approximately at fifty thousand in 1862. These figures, taken from the *Report of the Joint Select Committee of the Legislature of California*, were obtained from the leading Chinese merchants of San Francisco, who had kept an accurate account of the arrivals, the deaths, and the departures of their countrymen.[4] About thirty thousand were engaged in mining; the twelve hundred connected with agriculture were hired chiefly as laborers. About two hundred worked in the cigar factories of San Francisco. Two thousand more or less were traders. A large number found work as domestic servants and in the laundry business.[5] Although the Chinese did not engage in this occupation at home because their native costume did not require the kind of laundry work necessary for American dress, they immediately set up laundry establishments in San Francisco and reduced the price for such work one half.[6] The shortage of cooks, waiters, and domestic servants on the West coast gave the Chinese a chance to take over these occupations.[7] The decade following the year 1850 marked an enormous expansion in railroad construction, and many Chinese came to the United States to work on these projects. Many other kinds of employment were opened to the Chinese in California because capitalists rushed to San Francisco with money, energy, and manufacturing experience. Native labor was scarce, but Chinese labor proved satisfactory. The Asiatic immigrants were unusually adaptable; they quickly learned different kinds of factory work. They were also quiet, patient, courteous, honest, conscientious, and persevering.[8]

Certain groups in Australia and the United States, partic-

[4] *Cal. Leg., App. to Jols., 13th sess.* (1862), Doc. 23, p. 3.
[5] *Ibid.*
[6] H. C. Bennett, *Chinese Labor* (San Francisco, 1870), p. 28 *et seq.*
[7] William Speer, *The Oldest and the Newest Empire: China and the United States* (Hartford, Connecticut, 1870), p. 499.
[8] A. W. Loomis, "How Our Chinamen Are Employed," *Overland* (1869), 2, p. 231 *et seq.*; "John Chinaman in Australia," *House. W.* (1858), 17, p. 417; H. N. Day, "The Chinese Migration," *New Eng.* (1870), 29, p. 6; "The Chinese Immigration and Education in Jamaica," *Liv. Age* (1854), 43, p. 230.

ularly the merchants of San Francisco and of Melbourne and even the up country storekeepers of Australia, opposed a positive restriction on immigration.[9] Such limitations, the merchants of California argued, would sooner or later be detrimental to the interests of the state not only in depriving it of many consumers but in debarring the treasury of a large amount of revenue from the various licenses required of Chinese immigrants.[10] A fair and enlightened policy toward China and its citizens was therefore necessary. By extending and strengthening contacts with the Orient, and thereby increasing commercial intercourse, San Francisco's wealth and prestige could be greatly enhanced.[11] The Chinese, some argued, would aid the development of the state of California by the reclamation of its tule lands and by the cultivation of rice and other crops.[12]

In America labor was comparatively scarce and dear. Because of this situation, manufacturers were compelled to sell their commodities at a higher price than European manufacturers who had plenty of cheap labor. Capitalists in the United States naturally welcomed the Chinese who would work for lower wages than the native Americans or European immigrants. Through the use of Asiatic labor, American traders hoped to compete favorably in the world market with the manufactured products of all other countries.[13]

Although the main arguments in favor of Chinese immigration into the United States and into the British colonies were based on economic considerations, some stressed the duty of Christian peoples toward the Orientals. The United States had an immense unsettled domain, and its citizens who enjoyed the "blessings of freedom" should share them with the millions of oppressed and "unenlightened" Chinese.[14] Ministers of the Christian religion were deeply interested in the immigration movement because Chinese, converted in their new homes,

[9] "John Chinaman in Australia," op. cit., p. 416; "Die Chinesen in Australien," Daheim (1869), 5, pp. 623-24.

[10] Cal. Leg., App. to Jols., 7th sess., Sen. (1856), Doc. 16.

[11] Ibid.

[12] Ibid., 6th sess., Sen. (1855), Doc. 19, p. 5.

[13] Bennett, op. cit., 40.

[14] Cal. Leg., App. to Jols., 6th sess., Sen. (1855), Doc. 19, p. 13.

would carry Christianity throughout the Chinese Empire when they returned to their native country.[15] They would also introduce some of the rudiments of Western civilization into China.[16] Having developed a preference for many American commodities, they would make them known to their compatriots and thereby increase the exports of many American merchants.

Many people in the United States and Australia were strenuously opposed to the admission of large numbers of Chinese into their territories. For social reasons various objections were raised. The Chinese differed greatly from the Americans or the British colonists in race, language, religion, and customs. They would, consequently, be incapable of assimilation.[17] The Californians would become Chinese before the latter became Californians.[18] The Orientals made no efforts to learn the English language. They showed no desire to adopt Occidental customs.

The Chinese associated together in the mining districts of the Western States, and took possession of and worked out many sections of mineral lands. Exhausted of their wealth, these districts were left without a vestige of improvement upon which the revenue officers could collect taxes. In cities the Chinese also congregated and took possession of entire streets. It was impossible for Americans to reside in the neighborhood because of the loathsome living conditions of the Chinese.[19]

A ground for serious objection to immigration was the presence in California about 1870 of nearly three thousand Chinese women of objectionable character. Many of them had been

[15] C. W. Brooks, "The Chinese Labor Problem," *Overland* (1869), 3, p. 419; "John Chinaman in Australia," *op. cit.;* E. Jenkins, *The Coolie, His Rights and Wrongs* (New York, 1871), p. 298; "Chinese Immigrants," *Mission Field* (1868), 13, p. 67.
[16] John Scarth, *Twelve Years in China* (Edinburgh, 1860), p. 254.
[17] A. G. Thurman, *Speech at Cincinnati, September 10, 1870*, p. 8; *Cal. Leg., App. to Jols., 6th sess., Sen.* (1855), Doc. 19, p. 3; "John Chinaman in Australia," *op. cit.;* "Die Chinesen in Australien," *op. cit.*
[18] Eugene Casserly, *Speech on the Fifteenth Amendment and the Labor Question, Delivered in San Franscisco, California, July 28, 1869*, p. 11.
[19] *Cal. Leg., App. to Jols., 6th sess., Sen.* (1855), Doc. 16, p. 4; "Chinese American Citizens," *Liv. Age* (1854), 43, p. 125; "Emigration of Chinamen to India and America," *ibid.* (1869), 102, p. 822.

abducted from their homes and were supposedly bartered or sold in America.[20]   Bennett, a friend of the immigrants, admitted that many just complaints had been made against the landing of these undesirables but that the Chinese were not responsible for their emigration.   Protests and petitions of respectable Chinese against the introduction of this element were frequently published in the newspapers of San Francisco, but the nefarious traffic was not stopped until the governments of China and the United States ended the practice.[21]

Few immigrants took their families with them or thought of making foreign countries their permanent homes.   They built no houses and cultivated very little land.   Only a few of the wealthier Orientals were engaged in mercantile business; they imported and sold articles needed by the Chinese.   Because only the very lowest strata of society left their homes, the Chinese were considered undesirable immigrants.   Many who were said to be vagabonds, criminals, and gamblers escaped punishment only by embarking for a foreign country.[22]

Opponents of Chinese immigration also argued that it was a kind of slave trade.   A large number of Chinese in California were supposed to be quasi-slaves working at half wages under the command of a task master.[23]   A system of serfdom was therefore imposed upon California in direct oppostion to all principles of equality.[24]

The unfitness of the Chinese for social assimilation gave rise to a rather serious political objection in the United States.   The Asiatics, it was maintained, were under a government as

[20] *Cal. Leg., App. to Jols., 18th sess., Sen. and Ass.* (1870), Vol. 2, Doc. 26.   [21] Bennett, *op. cit.,* 12 *et seq.*

[22] *Cal. Leg., App. to Jols., 17th sess., Sen.* (1867-68), Vol. 2, Doc. 27, p. 3 *et seq.*   [23] Thurman, *op. cit.,* 8.

[24] *Cal. Leg., App. to Jols., 3rd sess., Sen.* (1852), p. 733.   "The first recorded shipment of contract laborers to the American continent was from Amoy in 1847, in which year about eight hundred nominally free laborers were despatched to Cuba.   From that date emigration to the West Indies, and to Central and South America assumed entirely the form of contract labor.   That to California and Australia was free emigration; it was generally conceded that emigrants to both the last were comparatively well treated. . . ." H. B. Morse and H. F. MacNair, *Far Eastern International Relations* (Boston, 1931), p. 262 *et seq.*

absolute and as perfect as any that ever existed. Its whole organization was independent of the State or of the Federal Government. The Chinese Government functioned under the "Six Companies,"[25] and was in fact an *imperium in imperio*. It had its officers, its tribunals, and its law enforcement machinery and was a form of extraterritoriality. Contemporary police authorities of San Francisco said that persons had been flogged, imprisoned, beaten, and their property confiscated under the authority of and at the command of the Sino-California Government. The peculiar habits and customs of the Chinese, together with American ignorance of their mode of life, made it impossible, many contended, for the ordinary civil forces of the State to break up this extraordinary, tyrannical, and illegal organization.[26]

When much feeling against the Chinese prevailed in the United States particularly on the Pacific coast, the ratification of the Fifteenth Amendment was taking place. The Californians were very much alarmed because, with this amendment in force, they could not withhold the right of suffrage from the Chinese.[27] California and other states were, therefore, trying to discourage immigration by unfavorable legislation, much of which was declared unconstitutional. The Burlingame treaty, written by William H. Seward who favored the movement as a source of cheap labor for the completion of the Pacific railroad, contained clauses designed to remove the obstacles to Asiatic immigration. This treaty undertook to protect the Orientals by

[25] A W. Loomis, "The Six Chinese Companies," *Overland* (1868), 1, p. 221. "When the Chinese came to California and encountered the hostility that met them, they found it necessary to organize themselves into companies for mutual protection. There are six of these in San Francisco, directed by Chinese merchants of standing and influence. Each company represents a district in China, and emigrants join the company which covers the place from which they come. The companies procure labor for their members and take care of them in sickness and when unemployed. They advance money to bring out emigrants, and then take the stipulation of the emigrant for the speedy repayment of the sum advanced. This is briefly the system on which a false charge of peonage or slavery has been based." "The Coming Chinese," *Hunt* (1869), 61, p. 124.

[26] *Cal. Leg., App. to Jols., 6th sess., Sen.* (1855), Doc. 16, p. 4. Loomis, *op. cit.* [27] Casserly, *op. cit.*, 2.

guaranteeing to Chinese subjects "visiting or residing in the United States . . . the same privileges, immunities, and exemptions in respect to travel or residence as may there be enjoyed by the citizens or subjects of the most favored nation." The right of naturalization, however, was reserved, and the states were not forced to give the Chinese political rights.[28]

The most determined opposition to the immigration movement came from the working classes. Their objections were not very pronounced until some years after 1848 when the Chinese first appeared in large numbers on the Pacific coast. At first the Chinese were welcomed by the public. But after they began to compete with native labor by working for lower wages, sentiment turned against them.[29] It was said that many mechanics and laborers, previously employed in connection with land transportation or with steam navigation to and from the port of San Francisco, had been discharged to give place to the Chinese who worked for less money. Thousands of young women and girls could not find employment in factories because of the extensive use of Asiatic labor. Whatever benefit was derived from the employment of the Orientals was confined to a few capitalists, argued the working groups. To protect American labor from the inroads of Chinese workers, an "Anti-Coolie Association" was organized in California.[30] A petition of unemployed laborers to the Legislature of California complained that, because of the extremely low wages accepted by the Asiatics, the petitioners could not obtain work. Opportunities in every branch of industry were curtailed and diminished by the competition of the Chinese whose standard of living was far below that of native laborers.[31] Because the Chinese were regarded as a servile, inferior, and degraded race, their position was extremely low in the social scale. Native labor groups felt that this condition of a large proportion of

---

[28] Tyler Dennett, *Americans in Eastern Asia* (New York, 1922), p. 535 *et seq.*

[29] Speer, *op. cit.*, 471 *et seq.*

[30] *Cal. Leg., App. to Jols., 17th sess., Sen. and Ass.* (1867-68), Vol. 2, Doc. 36.

[31] *Ibid., 18th sess., Sen. and Ass.* (1870), Vol. 2, Doc. 23.

workers was derogatory to the character and the dignity of labor.[32]

An episode which caused much consternation among the workers throughout the Eastern and Middle States was the importation of about a hundred Chinese to work in a shoe factory in North Adams, Massachusetts. They were brought East in 1870 by a manufacturer whose employees were on strike against a drastic reduction in wages. The laborers then realized that the large manufacturers and capitalists had obtained a weapon which would make them absolute dictators of labor in America. Numerous agents of manufacturing establishments soon went to North Adams to observe the experiment.[33] From labor's point of view, it was not a question of a few Chinese here and there or of a large number of Asiatics in branches of labor relatively unimportant. But the problem was the existence of a systematized if not a concentrated movement to bring workers from China in such numbers as to supplant native labor throughout the country.[34]

While the Chinese were usually viewed with disfavor by many groups when they settled among people of European stock, as in the United States and Australia, impartial observers pointed out characteristics which made the Chinese superior colonists. Laurence Oliphant remarked that if the Chinese, the most active, the most industrious, and the most enterprising people in the world, were considered a source of weakness instead of a source of strength to a community, such a situation implied mismanagement. The Chinese who emigrated to Singapore, because of its freedom from commercial restraints and advantages of position, made the city what it was commercially and economically.[35] Another author called attention to the decided advantage which the superior civilization of the Chinese

---

[32] *Ibid.*, *7th sess.*, *Sen.* (1856), Doc. 13, p. 9.

[33] John Swinton, *The Chinese American Question* (New York, 1870), p. 3 *et seq.*

[34] Casserly, *op. cit.*, 7; *House Miscellaneous Documents, 42nd Congress, 3rd sess.* (1872-73), Doc. 81.

[35] Laurence Oliphant, *Narrative of the Earl of Elgin's Mission to China* (New York, 1860), p. 29.

gave them when they settled among a backward people. By their intelligence and their business capacity, they monopolized all the important and remunerative fields of work. Commerce passed into their hands; they became the leading business men of their communities.[36] Scarth believed that if the Chinese could be induced to become real colonists and take their families with them, they would prove invaluable to many undeveloped British possessions such as the West Indies, Ceylon, and Mauritius. In these colonies they would have opportunities to develop agriculture and industry.[37]

The British, interested in the development of the natural resources of British Guiana and Jamaica, favored systematic emigration from China.[38] Lobscheid, an English missionary, who was stationed in China for some years, was asked for advice on the subject. He declared the scheme to encourage Chinese immigration into these countries was practical. In 1859 he issued a notice to the Chinese in which he assured them of the honest and sincere intentions of the British Government to carry out the terms of the contracts with them. He induced a number of Orientals to embark with their families to Guiana. These earliest arrivals were sent to a lonely and secluded spot. Because the immigrants had lived in cities and densely populated places, they were depressed by their isolation. The settlers, therefore, became prejudiced against the colony and the whole project of emigration. They advised their compatriots to stay out of Guiana until they received more favorable news. The immigrants, however, made no complaints against the British for breach of contract. They were well cared for, and a few saved some money.[39]

The importation of Chinese laborers into Jamaica was also discussed during the fifties. In 1852 the Legislature of Jamaica

---

[36] R. S. Maclay, *Life among the Chinese* (New York, 1861), p. 123 *et seq.*

[37] John Scarth, *Twelve Years in China* (Edinburgh, 1860), p. 256; "Chinese Emigration," *Liv. Age* (1844), 2, p. 631.

[38] *Ibid.*

[39] William Lobscheid, *Chinese Emigration to the West Indies* (1862), pp. 1-42.

passed an act which created a fund of a hundred thousand pounds to defray the expenses of the importation of Chinese laborers into the island.[40] The British hoped that the Chinese would firmly establish themselves with their families and ultimately form an intelligent and an industrious middle class in both Jamaica and Guiana.[41]

Asiatic immigration to undeveloped and semi-tropical areas to which European colonists did not go in large numbers was apparently viewed with satisfaction by all classes of society. It was chiefly in regions where the Chinese had to compete with laborers of European stock that serious objections arose. Because of this opposition, the bad qualities and the inferiority of the Orientals were stressed particularly by the working classes and their sympathizers to prove that the Chinese were undesirable members of society.

[40] "The Chinese Immigration and Education in Jamaica," *Liv. Age* (1854), 43, p. 230.

[41] *Ibid.*; "Chinese Emigration to the West Indies," *Liv. Age* (1854), 40, p. 464; H. B. Auchincloss, "The Chinese in Cuba," *Hunt* (1865), 52, p. 187.

CHAPTER VI

OPIUM

ANOTHER problem which focused Western especially British attention on China was the opium trade. This question and the evils arising from it caused much agitation after 1834, when the monopoly of the East India Company was abolished. It had a tremendous influence upon all Anglo-Chinese relations in the nineteenth century, and the politicians, the merchants, the ministers, the moralists, and the philanthropists could find therein material for serious thought.[1] The British opium trade between India and China, which had been carried on for almost forty years before the outbreak of the first Anglo-Chinese War under a nominal if not an actual prohibition, became about 1836 or 1837 the object of very strenuous opposition. The Chinese weighed seriously toward the end of 1836 the proposal to legalize the trade. In 1837 and 1838 measures of increasing severity against the traffic were enforced. The general aspect of the question became more threatening every day, but no steps were actually taken against foreigners until December 12, 1838. On that date the Chinese made preparations to strangle a native opium dealer in the square in front of the factory at Canton.[2] This act, which led to a brief cessation of the trade, deeply offended foreigners particularly the English. March 10, 1839, Commissioner Lin, by order of the Emperor, appeared at Canton to suppress the traffic.[3] His drastic actions against the trade, the majority of the British Government considered a just cause for war. After many misunderstandings and the confiscation of some twenty

[1] "The Opium Trade with China," For. Quar. R. (1840), 24, p.114.
[2] Hansard (1840), 53, p. 669 et seq.; Report of the East India Committee of the Colonial Society on the Causes and Consequences of Military Operations in China (2nd ed., London, 1843).
[3] Samuel Warren, The Opium Question (London, 1840), p. 1 et seq.; Hansard (1840), 53, p. 711 et seq.

thousand chests of opium which belonged to British merchants, the so-called "Opium War" began in 1840.

Many Western writers argued that the war was not correctly described as an "Opium War," although the final breach was caused by the Chinese Government's energetic measures against smuggling in which English merchants with the connivance of the provincial authorities were engaged.[4] The attempt to end the opium trade was, therefore, merely an incident in a long train of circumstances. Tonnage dues, taxes on imports and exports, other fees on commerce, and arbitrary trade regulations irritated the British. After the middle of the eighteenth century the Chinese put trade exclusively under the control of a close corporation, the Hong merchants. On the side of the English, the East India Company controlled all British trade in China until 1834 when the Company's privileges were abolished and British Imperial officers were appointed to support British interests. A collision between the two governments whose views were totally different was inevitable. The war was also caused in part, other contemporaries argued, by many grievances arising from the refusal of the Chinese Government to receive on the basis of equality the representatives of foreign countries.[5]

Other commentators, who stressed the importance of the opium question in the origin of the war, cited the Chinese Government's attempts to prohibit the export of bullion which the Chinese believed to be injurious to their economic welfare. They issued edict after edict against the leakage of sycee and against the "oozing out" of dollars.[6] The Emperor's concern about the bad effects of opium on the health of his people was

---

[4] "New Works on China and the Late War," *Westm. R.* (1843), 40, p. 123 *et seq.*

[5] J. F. Davis, *China* (New ed., London, 1857), I, 146; T. T. Meadows, *The Chinese and Their Rebellions* (London, 1856), Preface, p. vi; J. Q. Adams, "Lecture on the War with China, Delivered before the Massachusetts Historical Society, November 22, 1841," *Proceedings* (1910), 43, pp. 295-325; see *C. Repos.* (1842), 11, p. 274 *et seq.; Memoirs of John Quincy Adams*, C. F. Adams, ed. (Philadelphia, 1876), XI, p. 30 *et seq.*

[6] J. E. Bingham, *Narrative of the Expedition to China* (London, 1842), I, 33; Warren, *op. cit.*, 73; *Hansard* (1840), 53, p. 716 *et seq.*

not genuine but was assumed to conceal his real wishes and purposes, the British argued. The Chinese, who were uneasy about the loss of specie which was paid for large quantities of opium brought from India, chiefly by British merchants, were making desperate efforts to correct the situation by the suppression of the opium traffic. Europeans criticized the Chinese position as ridiculous. They contended that rich silver mines of China contained an almost inexhaustible supply of metal.[7]

The author, emphasizing the misunderstandings between the Chinese and the British, maintained that all difficulties could have been overcome if judicious measures for the regulation of British intercourse with China had been adopted by the English Government before the rupture. The origin of the war lay in British ignorance of Chinese institutions, indifference toward the outbreak of the war, and failure to inform the Chinese Government of the change when the East India Company's monopoly was abolished in 1834. With this alteration in policy, the Company's officers, who were well acquainted with the Chinese people and had authority to enforce necessary regulations for British shipping, withdrew from the East; every British trader was free to buy and sell without restriction after 1834. The opium trade which had hitherto been held in check increased rapidly after 1840. The Chinese Government became alarmed. In the midst of these conditions, the British Government instructed Lord Napier to demand the right to set aside official etiquette and to communicate directly with the Emperor by letter. Such a peremptory request, unsupported by an embassy or a fleet, the Chinese mandarins regarded as an insult.[8] Many in England and America took the extreme view that all fault was on the side of the British and that the Chinese were blameless.[9]

Other groups, chiefly the merchants, attributed the war to Chinese pride and stupidity. They argued that the English always conducted themselves in China with moderation, upright-

[7] Warren, *op. cit.*, 68 *et seq.*
[8] "New Works on China and the Late War," *op. cit.*
[9] George Mogridge, *The Celestial Empire* (London, 1844), p. 74 *et seq.*; *Memoirs of John Quincy Adams, op. cit.*

ness, and honor. Lindsay, of the factory at Canton and later with the mercantile house in China, naturally sympathized with the British traders. He said that, notwithstanding the encouragement and even the support which the Chinese Government had previously given to the opium trade, its right to stop the traffic could not be disputed. But he severely criticized its method of procedure. If the Chinese had seized all opium vessels along the coast and confiscated their cargoes, foreign governments would have had no cause for complaint. The Chinese, however, held all foreigners indiscriminately in Canton and Macao many of whom had no connections with the trade and deprived them of their liberty and their property. Such high-handed treatment, Lindsay wrote, was not within the power of the Chinese.[10]

In a pamphlet which was published in 1840, Fry, the author, took a decisive stand against the trade and urged the government to end the traffic. To show the necessity for such a course, he tried to prove:

1. That the introduction of opium into China has been and is directly contrary to the laws of that Empire, and in open defiance of the Chinese Government, which never wanted the sincere desire, but the power to put it down.

2. That the British Indian Government, monopolizing the production of opium in our East-India possessions, cultivates, prepares, and sells it expressly for the Chinese market, without any respect to those laws and prohibitions.

3. That British subjects, under the sanction of the British Indian Government, persist in carrying that opium into China to be disposed of there, under circumstances of increasing and aggravated evil and atrocity.

4. That the properties of opium as a stimulus of luxury are morally and physically deleterious in the highest degree.

5. That the cultivation and monopoly of opium are attended with serious evils and oppressions in our East-Indian territories.

6. That this traffic has been, and is, highly injurious to the legitimate commerce of this country, and endangers a most important branch of our revenue.

[10] H. H. Lindsay, *Is the War with China a Just One?* (2nd ed., London, 1840), p. 16.

7. . . . that it [the opium trade] materially interferes with the progress in the East.[11]

Public opinion, directed by missionaries and humanitarians, was strongly opposed to the traffic. Medhurst, an agent of the London Missionary Society, denounced the opium trade as one of the greatest evils of the age because it demoralized the Chinese and served as a barrier to the introduction of Christianity. Widely quoted by Lord Shaftesbury and other opponents of the opium trade, Medhurst's writings contributed toward the formation of a definitive anti-opium movement in England even before 1840.[12]

The agitation against opium culminated in the Memorial presented to the Government in 1855 by the noted humanitarian, the Earl of Shaftesbury, chairman of the "Committee for relieving British intercourse with China from the baneful effects of a contraband in opium." This document emphasized the exclusively British character of the opium trade. Other Western countries either prohibited the traffic or were so unfriendly to the practice that their subjects engaged in the trade under the British flag.[13] The Memorial asserted that at least a million people were "annually sacrificed to enrich a few people and to save the Indian Government the trouble of finding a more legitimate means of obtaining revenue." The opium trade was also condemned in the Memorial because it hindered the progress of Christianity by paralyzing the efforts of missionaries.[14] Lastly, the traffic was attacked for its bad effects on British trade with China. The constant importation of opium

[11] W. S. Fry, *Facts and Evidence Relating to the Opium Trade with China* (London, 1840), p. 5 *et seq.*

[12] *Hansard* (1843), 68, p. 362 *et seq.*; Robert Alexander, *Rise and Progress of British Opium Smuggling* (3rd ed., London, 1856), p. 59; Charles Gutzlaff, *Journal of Three Voyages along the Coast of China in 1831, 1832, and 1833* (3rd ed., London, 1840), p. 57; S. W. Williams, *The Middle Kingdom* (New York, 1848), II, 496 *et seq.*

[13] "Papers Relating to the Opium Trade in China 1842-56," *Parliamentary Papers, Accounts and Papers* (1857), XLIII, 77-80.

[14] *Ibid.*; *Hansard* (1869), 198, p. 1194 *et seq.*; Nathan Allen, *An Essay on the Opium Trade* (Boston, 1850), p. 61.

impoverished the Chinese people by withdrawing the precious metals so that internal resources could not be developed.[15]

Refuting the arguments of the Memorialists, Sir John Bowring, in a letter to the Earl of Clarendon, declared that the opium trade was not a British monopoly. The Americans engaged in the trade on a large scale. The responsibility for the smuggling he placed upon the entire commercial community. The Memorialists' statistics on opium smokers and deaths caused from the use of the drug represented respectively a tenfold and a hundredfold exaggeration. The commercial figures, Sir John argued, were vague and inaccurate. No evidence, he said, existed to show that the amount of three million pounds which the Memorialists assumed to be the balance of trade in favor of China would have been used to purchase British manufactures, had it not been for the opium trade. The British merchants of China particularly stressed the unsound economic views of the Memorial. They maintained that the decrease of imports into China was due to other factors rather than to the opium trade.[16]

The attitude of the merchants in England, prompted largely by commercial considerations, is shown in a Memorial which was signed by two hundred and thirty-five merchants and manufacturers and presented to Sir Robert Peel as early as July, 1842. Apart from the moral issues they opposed the trade for economic reasons. They tried to prove that their commerce could not be conducted on a safe basis so long as the contraband trade in opium continued. Even if the drug trade were legalized, the traffic would inevitably undermine the commerce of Great Britain with China. The Chinese were paid for their manufactures chiefly in opium, the quantity of which, by 1842, had largely exceeded in value the commodities principally tea and silk that the English received from them. After about 1840, the Chinese did not import in large quantities British

[15] William Groser, *What Can Be Done to Suppress the Opium Trade?* (London, 1840); Robert Alexander, *Opium Revenue of India* (London, 1857), p. 6.

[16] *Parliamentary Papers, op. cit.*, p. 66, *passim.*

manufactures. The Memorialists supported their arguments by statistics. They said that the average Chinese demand from 1834 to 1839 for all British products was less by almost one hundred and fifty thousand pounds than it was for woollens alone from 1803 until 1808. During the interval from 1834 to 1839 the opium trade had increased from three thousand to thirty thousand chests.[17]

After 1840 the opium question, because of the efforts of different groups of anti-opium agitators, remained constantly before the English public. The Indian and British Governments, opium merchants, and others who were interested in the trade, were ever on the alert to meet the arguments of the opposition. Much material was also published on the subject. Many pamphlets were laid before the public.[18] The general works on China usually devoted a chapter or at least a few pages to the evils of opium smoking and to the "nefarious traffic" in the drug.[19] The most extensive account of the opium question is probably in Sirr's *China and the Chinese*. Strongly opposed to the trade, he wrote that the "horrors and evils of the traffic are such, as to render it unbecoming Great Britain as a Christian nation, to sanction, encourage, or permit its continuance, whatever may be the *apparent* profit to her merchants."[20] Lord Jocelyn emphasized the financial value of the opium trade to the Indian Government. He also opposed the suppression of the traffic because it would increase smuggling along the coast of India.[21] Another author, taking a midway position, com-

[17] "Journal of Occurrences," *C. Repos.* (1843), 12, p. 168; "Present State of the Opium Trade with China," extracted from the *Scottish Review*, January, 1860, p. 10.
[18] "Pamphlets on China," *C. Repos.* (1840), 9, p. 156 *et seq.;* H. W. Tyler, *Questions of the Day* (London, 1857), p. 10.
[19] Bingham, *op. cit.*, I, 29 *et seq.;* Williams, *op. cit.*, II, 382 *et seq.;* George Smith, *A Narrative of an Exploratory Visit to Each of the Consular Cities of China* (New York, 1847), p. 380 *et seq.;* H. C. Sirr, *China and the Chinese* (London, 1849), I, 251 *et seq.;* II, 282 *et seq.;* W. D. Bernard, *Narrative of the Voyages and Services of the Nemesis* (London, 1844), I, 174 *et seq.*
[20] Sirr, *op. cit.*, I, 251.
[21] Lord Jocelyn, *Six Months with the Chinese Expedition in China* (2nd ed., London, 1841), p. 142 *et seq.*

mented upon the exaggeration of the amount of smoking and smuggling. The merchants whom many writers represented as little better than buccaneers were respectable business men with immense capital. The trade in opium, although contraband, was so unlike what was usually understood by the term "smuggling" that people, unfamiliar with the trade, knew nothing of its nature. Fortune claimed that the Chinese Government made no serious attempts to stop the opium trade prior to the controversies which led to the war in 1840.[22]

The report of the debate in the British Parliament in April, 1840, on the Government's Chinese policy gives the opinions of the leading statesmen on the opium problem and the war. The debate was occasioned by the following resolution of Sir James Graham:

It appears to this House, on consideration of the papers relating to China, presented to this House, by command of her Majesty, that the interruption in our commercial and friendly intercourse with that country, and the hostilities which have since taken place, are mainly to be attributed to the want of foresight and precaution on the part of her Majesty's present advisers, in respect to our relations with China, and especially to their neglect to furnish the superintendent at Canton with powers and instructions calculated to provide against the growing evils connected with the contraband traffic in opium, and adapted to the novel and difficult situation in which the superintendent was placed.[23]

Denunciation of the opium trade and the war was the main theme of several speeches. Gladstone asserted that the British authorities, who were stationed in China, practically encouraged and protected the trade instead of co-operating with the Chinese for its abolition. He held that the opium trade could have been ended without any preventive service on the Chinese coast by stopping the sailing of opium vessels. It could have been crippled, if not extinguished, by the prohibition of the export of the drug from Bengal, by orders against its cultivation in Malwa, and by putting such a stigma on the traffic that no respectable

[22] Robert Fortune, *Two Visits to the Tea Countries of China* (3rd ed., London, 1853), I, 171 *et seq.*   [23] *Hansard* (1840), 53, p. 704.

merchant would engage in the trade.[24] Gladstone said "a war more unjust in its origin, a war more calculated in its progress to cover this country with permanent disgrace, I do not know, and have not read of."[25]

Those members of Parliament who defended the Government's policy cited the sanction of the opium trade by Chinese officials.[26] Their acquiescence, obviously, cleared the British smugglers of all blame.[27] The members who favored the Administration's policy based their arguments upon economic considerations. The opium trade, although contrary to the laws of China, had not been stopped by the British because it was profitable.[28] Lord Melbourne even said that because the English had large districts peculiarly fitted for opium production he could not pledge himself to give up the trade, but he did wish that the Government were not directly concerned in the opium business.[29]

The moral issues were raised by certain members of Parliament who denied Great Britain the right to foster and encourage for its own commercial advantage a trade which led to the destruction of hundreds of thousands of people.[30] Another speaker contended that the evils arising from the use of the drug were greatly exaggerated. If used in moderation, opium was not injurious. The gains from the trade were hardly more open to objections than the revenue from liquor sales was.[31]

Lord Palmerston challenged the Chinese Government's motives for the suppression of the traffic. Its purpose, according to Palmerston, was not the promotion of morality. It was a question of the protection of the agricultural interests. The poppy cultivation in China was becoming increasingly important; competition with Indian opium would curtail its development. Palmerston also mentioned the Chinese economists' desire to prevent the exportation of precious metals from China.[32]

---

[24] *Ibid.*, 812.

[25] *Ibid.*, 818.   [26] *Ibid.*, 741.

[27] *Ibid.*, 753.   [28] *Ibid.*, 752, 781, 782, 824.

[29] Williams, *op. cit.*, II, 526.   [30] *Hansard* (1840), 53, p. 856.

[31] *Ibid.*, 824.   [32] *Ibid.*, 940.

By the treaty of Nanking which closed the Anglo-Chinese War in 1842, Great Britain received an indemnity for the opium seized by the Chinese, but otherwise, no mention was made of the opium controversy.[33] The peace of 1842, however, did not end the discussion of the opium question either in Parliament or England at large.[34] In 1843 the matter was brought directly before the House of Commons by Lord Ashley, later the Earl of Shaftesbury, who presented three petitions from the Wesleyan, the Baptist, and the London Missionary Societies, asking the House of Commons to adopt effective measures to insure the abolition of the opium trade between India and China.[35] In his speech Lord Ashley tried to prove that so long as the opium trade was continued all British interests, both political and commercial, would be in a hazardous condition of uncertainty. Such conditions were injurious to commercial intercourse and might even lead to another war with China. The opium traffic was harmful to British trade because a pernicious drug was substituted for the manufactures of Great Britain.[36] Lord Ashley argued that the suppression of the opium trade would cause the Chinese to give their produce in exchange for British commodities.[37] The extension of England's commerce and the opening of new markets for British manufacturers would greatly benefit the English working classes and also the Chinese.[38] One serious objection to the abolition of the traffic in opium— namely, the loss of revenue, Lord Ashley attacked from the point of view of humanitarianism. He contended that if the profits could not be drawn from such an article as opium by any other means than by placing it within reach of the lower classes of China, no fiscal considerations could justify such a course of action.[39]

Depicting the frightful moral and physical effects of the drug, he asserted that the encouragement of the iniquitous traffic had retarded the progress of Christianity and impeded

[33] *Ibid.* (1843), 68, p. 368 *et seq.*
[34] *Ibid.*   [35] *Ibid.*, 362.
[36] *Ibid.*, 363 *et seq.*; (1870), 201, p. 497.
[37] *Ibid.* (1843), 68, p. 370 *et seq.*
[38] *Ibid.*, 375 *et seq.*   [39] *Ibid.* (1843), 68, p. 403.

the civilization of the Chinese because the opium policy of the British Government deeply antagonized the Orientals.[40] The Baptist Missionary Society decided in 1843 to work through American agencies because of Chinese hostility toward England.[41] Lord Ashley concluded his speech by moving:

> That it is the opinion of this House, that the continuance of the trade in opium, and the monopoly of its growth in the territories of British India, is destructive of all relations of amity between England and China, injurious to the manufacturing interests of the country by the very serious diminution of legitimate commerce, and utterly inconsistent with the honour and duties of a Christian kingdom; and that steps be taken, as soon as possible, with due regards to the rights of Government and individuals, to abolish the evil.[42]

Sir Robert Peel, spokesman for the Government, expressed fear that Lord Ashley's resolution would hinder the negotiations then in progress between the Chinese and British Governments. Lord Ashley thereupon withdrew his motion.[43] This debate of 1843 is significant because it was the first time that the question had been fully discussed in Parliament. The speeches for and against the trade and the comments upon them in the press put the question directly before the British public.

Although the opium trade was still prohibited by the Chinese after the treaty of Nanking, it continued to flourish. Chinese vessels, to carry the article, even registered under the British flag. October 8, 1856, the lorcha, *Arrow*, and its crew of twelve men were seized by the Chinese authorities in the Canton River. The vessel, owned by a Chinese, had previously been registered at Hong Kong and was entitled to fly the British flag until the expiration of its registration, September 27. The British consul at Canton demanded the sailors and an apology for the insult to the flag. The Chinese surrendered the twelve men with no apology, but the consul refused to receive them. This controversy, which was of course only one factor

[40] *Ibid.*, 377; (1857), 144, p. 2028; (1875), 225, p. 581, *passim.*
[41] *Ibid.* (1843), 68, p. 391; (1870), 201, p. 487.
[42] *Ibid.* (1843), 68, p. 405; (1857), 144, p. 2027 *et seq.*
[43] *Ibid.* (1843), 68, p. 469.

in the trouble between England and China, led directly to the
second Anglo-Chinese War. Many severely criticized this war
because it could not be justified on any grounds. Hostilities
ended finally when the conventions of Peking were signed, and
the ratifications of the treaty of Tientsin (1858) were exchanged
at the *Li Pu* or Hall of Ceremonies in 1860. The treaty of
Tientsin is a landmark in the history of the opium trade. By
this treaty the importation of opium was permitted upon the
payment of a moderate duty in spite of the strong protests of
the Chinese.[44] After 1860 the legal aspects of the traffic were
partially settled, but the moral phases of the question remained.[45]

In the debates in Parliament in 1870 and 1875[46] the speak-
ers for the Administration stressed the importance of the opium
trade from the economic point of view. Gladstone, who in
1843 severely criticized the previous policy of the Government
and the general state of affairs which led to the first Anglo-
Chinese War, contended in 1870 that the conditions producing
the earlier wars of 1840 and 1857 ceased to exist after the
Chinese Government dealt with opium as a commercial commodity by its admission into the country upon the payment of a
duty. Opium was henceforth detached from all political considerations and became a matter of fiscal arrangement.[47] The
opium trade was, consequently, no longer "destructive of all
relations of amity between England and China."[48] Gladstone
rather minimized the evil effects of opium[49] and stressed the
importance of the revenue to the Indian Government.[50] On
the moral side of the problem, the supporters of the Administration's policy asserted that it was taking too exalted a view
of international duty to force England to be more solicitous of
the health and the morals of the Chinese than they themselves
were. England derived a large revenue from the opium traffic,
and the condition of India at the time would not justify the

[44] H. B. Morse and H. F. MacNair, *Far Eastern International Relations*
(Boston, 1931), Chapters X, XIII.
[45] *Hansard* (1870), 201, p. 480 *et seq.*
[46] *Ibid.*, 479 *et seq.*; (1875), 225, p. 571 *et seq.*
[47] *Ibid.* (1870), 201, p. 516.   [48] *Ibid.* (1843), 68, p. 405.
[49] *Ibid.* (1870), 201, p. 517 *et seq.*   [50] *Ibid.*, p. 520 *et seq.*

British in taking any great financial risks for the sake of an idea.[51]

Sir Wilfrid Lawson in 1870 introduced a resolution which condemned the system of raising a large portion of the Indian revenue from opium. In anticipation of the defendants' emphasis on the importance of the trade for India, he stressed the uncertainty of the opium revenue and gave three reasons to support his statement. In the first place, some political situation might cause China to prohibit the importation of opium. Again, a foreign country might take up the trade and destroy the monopoly of Great Britain. Lastly, the Chinese were beginning to grow the poppy extensively. Lawson also attacked the trade from the moral point of view and declared the often repeated argument that the opium trade was no worse than the liquor trade was not true.[52]

The statesmen participating in the opium debates in Parliament particularly Lord Ashley, later the Earl of Shaftesbury, and Sir Wilfrid Lawson of the opposition were fairly familiar with contemporary works on China. Sir Wilfrid quoted the missionaries, Huc, Medhurst, and Wylie, and Lay and Montgomery Martin, representatives of the British Government in China, in his discussion of the evils of the opium traffic. Lord Ashley in his famous speech of 1843 took his material from the writings and conversations of Dunn, the proprietor of the Chinese collection on exhibition in London at that time, Gutzlaff, the missionary, Medhurst, the distinguished representative of the London Missionary Society, Squire, an agent of the Church Missionary Society, Malcolm, an American missionary in China, and Lindsay, a merchant in the East. The speeches of Gladstone and other spokesmen for the Administration indicate no general interest in Chinese affairs except in so far as they directly affected British policy in the East.

Public opinion in America at the time was decidedly against the opium traffic because of the reports of Protestant missionaries who from 1843 to 1860 outnumbered the English two to

[51] *Ibid.* (1875), 225, p. 602.
[52] *Ibid.* (1870), 201, p. 479 *et seq.*; (1875), 225, p. 589.

one. Some of the American merchants in China participated in the opium trade, but a large number opposed it and supported the missionaries in their denunciation of the traffic.[53]

French and German authors, who stressed the moral issues less than the Americans did, were interested in British diplomacy in the Orient and the opium question in general. They considered the first Anglo-Chinese War an inglorious and unjust war against the Chinese for the sake of the Indian opium revenue,[54] and the treaty of Nanking unfair to the Chinese. A French writer, in the *Revue des Deux Mondes*, gave a somewhat objective account of the opium problem with more emphasis on the Chinese point of view than is usually found in the English accounts of the controversy. Rather sympathetic toward the Chinese, this author thought that they were justified in their efforts to suppress the traffic.[55] Their documents, which he quoted copiously, proved the English assertions of the toleration of the opium trade by the Chinese Government to be without foundation. Some local officials probably connived with smugglers to get some of the profits from the traffic. But such agents no more compromised the Chinese Government than the French smugglers on the coast of France compromised their own Government by dealing in contraband goods.[56]

Callery and Yvan, whose book was well known in France and was translated into English,[57] admitted that the French on the whole sympathized with the Chinese, but they tried to justify English policy.[58] The British, they conceded, had carried on a contraband trade on the coast of China precisely similar to the smuggling trade along the French coast. The French, however, had not dared to seize and threaten with death all foreign merchants within their clutches on the pretext

[53] Morse and MacNair, *op. cit.*, 205.
[54] M. J. L. Hervey-Saint-Denys, *La Chine devant l'Europe* (Paris, 1859), p. 74.
[55] "Question anglo-chinoise," *RDM* (1842), 29, p. 670 *et seq.*
[56] *Ibid.*, 662.
[57] "Contemporary Literature of France," *Westm. R.* (1853), 60, p. 631.
[58] Joseph Marie Callery and Melchior Yvan, *The Insurrection in China* (New York, 1853), p. 16; Charles Macfarlane, *The Chinese Revolution* (London, 1853), p. 24.

that their vessels in French harbors were loaded with contra-band goods.[59]

The Germans were interested in the diplomatic aspects of the struggle between China and England rather than in the opium question as it affected the Chinese. Neumann in his history of the Anglo-Chinese Wars, however, discussed the origin and the use of opium, the gradual increase in the sale of the drug to China, the enormous profits arising from the traffic, the laws against its introduction into China, and the evasions of these laws by smugglers.[60] In his detailed account of the "Opium War," Neumann, like many other writers, was unsym-pathetic with the British and took the stand that England forced the war upon China.[61]

The French and German general works, like the English and the American accounts, devoted some space to opium and its related problems.[62] Almost every Western writer on Chinese social conditions described the technique of opium smoking and its moral and its physical effects. The Chinese, therefore, came to be regarded as a nation of opium smokers. Because a large quantity of the drug came from British India, public opinion in England, America, and other countries held the British Govern-ment largely responsible for such conditions in China and almost universally condemned the opium traffic.

[59] Callery and Yvan, *op. cit.*, 16.
[60] K. F. Neumann, *Ostasiatische Geschichte* (Leipzig, 1861), p. 7 *et seq.*; *Geschichte des englisch-chinesischen Krieges* (2nd ed., Leipzig, 1855), p. 22 *et seq.*; A. Wulfert, "Der Opiumkrieg," *Illustrirtes Familienbuch* (1858), 8, pp. 344-48.
[61] Neumann, *Ostasiatische Geschichte*, p. 18 *et seq.*; *Geschichte des englisch-chinesischen Krieges*, p. 45 *et seq.*
[62] Reinhold Werner, *Die preussische Expedition nach China . . . in den Jahren 1860, 1861 und 1862* (2nd ed., Leipzig, 1873), p. 235; R. Lechler, *Acht Vorträge über China* (Basel, 1861), p. 159 *et seq.*

CHAPTER VII

COMMERCIAL AND POLITICAL
INTERESTS

GREAT Britain had carried on trade with China since the seventeenth century, and it naturally included a whole range of commodities. The opium trade became an important element toward the end of the eighteenth century.[1] During the latter part of the seventeenth century French trade began, but it was very insignificant.[2] American merchants of the Atlantic seaboard commenced a lucrative trade with the East immediately after the Revolution.[3] But after 1840 the West chiefly the British and the Americans showed a quickening of interest in the trade with the Orient.[4] An example of England's emphasis on trading possibilities in China is Martin's *China; Political, Commercial...* (1847). In this official report on the position of Great Britain in China, the author made many suggestions on policy which would give political and commercial advantages to England.

Little was written on the trade relations between the East and West from 1840 to 1876, but these years constitute one of the most picturesque and glamorous eras in the annals of the Eastern trade. As a result of the growing demand for a more speedy delivery of Chinese commodities, tea especially, the "Clipper Ship"[5] period of America began about 1843 and

[1] R. M. Martin, *China; Political, Commercial, and Social; in an Official Report to Her Majesty's Government* (London, 1847), II, 145.

[2] *Ibid.*, I, 397.

[3] Tyler Dennett, *Americans in Eastern Asia* (New York, 1922), p. 4.

[4] T. T. Cooper, *Travels of a Pioneer of Commerce in Pigtail and Petticoats* (London, 1871), p. 2.

[5] The "clipper" was a full rigged ship developed by American builders about 1840. Designed for speed, it was characterized by fine lines, an overhanging bow, tall, raking masts, and a large sail area. For thirty years or more after the Napoleonic Wars, little progress was made in the development of British shipping. The high profits and big risks of the neutral trade of Americans during the Wars, however, stimulated the construction of fast

ended approximately with the opening of the Suez Canal in 1869. During those years merchants and sea captains vied with each other in building fast ships of which the *Houqua, Samuel Russell, Sea Witch*, and *Oriental* were the pioneers of a great fleet.[6] The clippers made racing passages between China and America some seven years before the first British clipper appeared in the East.[7] An early ship of this class was the *John Bunyan* which made a trip from Shanghai to England in ninety-nine days, but its record was overshadowed by the famous American clipper, the *Oriental*,[8] whose time was ninety-seven days. The *Stornoway* and the *Chrysolite* are usually mentioned as the first of the British clippers.[9]

Great activity in shipbuilding during these years implies an active and growing trade to make use of these fast carriers. The leading Chinese exports to the United States and Great Britain were tea, silk, raw and manufactured, such as sarsenets, satins, and other silk materials, crêpe shawls, scarves, grass cloths, screens, lacquered ware, mats, vermilion, aniseed, cassia, sweetmeats, and rhubarb. To the United States, in particular, large quantities of matting and firecrackers were shipped.[10] The

---

sailing vessels with the result that in 1843 the first extreme clipper ship was turned out by a New York navy yard. The demand for speed was further strengthened by the California gold rush (1849-56). The policy of American ship builders had an almost immediate effect on ship design in Great Britain. At first the American style of ship was used only in the coasting trade, but when the discovery of gold in Australia caused a rush of emigrants to Melbourne (1851-56) the British bought American clippers and began to construct vessels along American lines. See "Clipper Ships," *Encyclopaedia Britannica* (14th ed.) 20, pp. 509, 544.

[6] Arthur H. Clark, *The Clipper Ship Era* (New York, 1910), Preface.

[7] Basil Lubbock, *The China Clippers* (5th ed., Glasgow, Scotland), p. 37.

[8] *Ibid.*, 109.   [9] *Ibid.*, 110.

[10] Articles of trade are mentioned in the George H. Allen, Letters (Essex Institute); Augustine Heard and Company, *Prices Current;* Letters to Benjamin Newton, New York, July 21, 1851 and July 2, 1852 (Baker Library, Harvard). Yale University has other Heard papers from Hong Kong. See "Commerce of China," *Hunt* (1840), 3, p. 465 *et seq.;* "Commerce of the United States," *ibid.* (1844), 11, p. 54 *et seq.;* "Consular or Commercial Cities," *ibid.* (1849), 21, p. 262 *et seq.;* 422 *et seq.;* "Commercial Character of the Chinese," *De Bow* (1847), 3, p. 440.

chief French import from China was raw silk to feed the silk looms of Lyon. Not so much tea was sent to France as to England and America.[11] After 1840 the West imported fewer of those unusual products of fine workmanship, such as porcelain and lacquer ware and more and more of such staples as tea and silk.[12]

The Occident, England and the United States chiefly, sent to China various kinds of coarse cotton goods, woollen fabrics, lead, spars, iron, coal, and lumber.[13] Prior to 1815 the United States was importing cotton goods from China. This commodity, therefore, was a relatively new export to China in 1840. This shift of cotton from an import to an export, resulting from the mechanization of the textile industry in England and the United States, is of major importance because the Occident no longer regarded China as a source for certain products which could not be readily obtained elsewhere. The West stressed the value of China as a potential and limitless market for Western commodities especially for cotton materials.[14] British merchants and manufacturers continually pointed out the advantages which would accrue to their respective firms and factories if the use of cotton could be introduced among the Chinese. The Board of Trade, however, in an elaborate résumé of commercial affairs in China (1869) seemed to think it very doubtful whether the coarser cottons, the only manufactures exported in large quantities to China, could ever do more than supplement the native production in supplying the great cities accessible to foreign trade.[15] China during the latter years of the East India Company's rule offered a strictly limited outlet for Indian raw cotton, opium, and a few minor tropical products which included drugs and spices.[16]

[11] *Chambre de commerce de Lyon. Commerce de la France avec la Chine* (Lyon, 1860), p. 12.
[12] "Trade with China," *Quar. R.* (1872), 132, p. 380.
[13] See note 10.
[14] "American Trade with China," *De Bow* (1846), 2, p. 395.
[15] "Trade with China," *op. cit.*, 381; Dennett, *op. cit.*, 18 *et seq.*; 73 *et seq.*
[16] A. J. Sargent, *Anglo-Chinese Commerce and Diplomacy* (Oxford, 1907), p. 57.

During the years from 1840 to 1876 such mercantile houses in China as the American firm of Augustine Heard and Company tried to avail themselves of every commercial advantage. An illustration is the expedition under the direction of John Heard, a member of the firm of Augustine Heard and Company, which was made up the Yangtze in the steamer, *Fire Dart*, in 1861. At Shanghai, Heard collected such a cargo as would test the market possibilities thoroughly. Besides the interest in obtaining a sale for various kinds of merchandise, Heard wished to buy land for permanent establishments in the river ports. Those who arrived in these cities earliest would have the first choice. He hoped to buy enough land so that he could sell his surplus at a profit which would pay for his own.

The last stage of the journey was to Hankow where Heard left the remainder of the merchandise in charge of C. D. Williams, an agent for Augustine Heard and Company. With a return cargo containing only one new commodity, "vegetable wax," they went back to Shanghai. Everyone was curious for details about the recently opened river ports. Heard and his associates were convinced that business would be slow in its development in the interior. The merchants in the seaport towns, however, were sceptical, and wished to find out the actual conditions for themselves. Heard immediately sensed an opportunity for making money by using the *Fire Dart* for the carrying trade on the Yangtze. He filled the steamer with freight not his own but other shippers' commodities at twenty dollars per ton and carried passengers at one hundred taels per head. The business paid well and was continued throughout the year.

For once the T'ai P'ing Rebellion proved useful to a merchant. Because of the depredations of the rebels, there was a general exodus to Shanghai from the river ports and adjacent territory. These Chinese were charged twenty taels each for sitting or standing room. It is interesting to note that when the *Fire Dart's* accounts were made up at the end of the year Heard and Company, from their three-fourths' interest in the steamer, had made a clear profit of $175,000 in addition to the twenty-five per cent allowed for the depreciation of the ship's value.[17]

The story of the *Fire Dart* shows the way in which these companies made huge profits, and it also indicates the alertness with which merchants watched for opportunities for the expansion of their interests. The large houses did not confine their activities to great enterprises but engaged in all kinds of small undertakings which would yield substantial returns on their investments. The expedition up the Yangtze was the first of its kind made into the interior of China. This journey paved the way for the expansion of Western merchants' activities into the very heart of the Chinese Empire.

With the establishment of the great commercial houses, such as the British house of Jardine, Matheson and Company[18] which dates from 1782[19] and the American firms of Russell and Company founded in 1825[20] and Augustine Heard and Company established in 1842,[21] the import and export business was gradually and systematically organized on a larger scale. *Prices current* giving full information on the price and supply of commodities were sent at fairly regular intervals to the leading American or British firms trading in the East.[22] These merchants then corresponded directly with the Western firms in China which took care of their cargoes upon their arrival, and also looked after the merchandise to be shipped out. After this change in business methods, the letters of sea captains were more or less restricted to matters affecting their respective ships and any comments on trade were limited more or less to such statements as "Russell and Company will keep you informed on the tea business."[23] The reports, *prices current*, and short

---

[17] John Heard, *Diary*, pp. 127-139; Letter to parents, May 16, 1861.

[18] Archives at Cambridge University, England.

[19] G. T. Yorke, Jardine Matheson Company Archives (Description of papers, typescript).

[20] Dennett, *op. cit.*, 34.

[21] Augustine Heard and Company Papers (Baker Library).

[22] See Augustine Heard and Company and Olyphant and Company, *Prices Current* (Essex Institute).

[23] William Cole, Letter to William Appleton and Company, July 20, 1857 (Baker Library).

business letters, sent out from time to time by the larger firms, did not give the minute details on the China trade which made up a large part of the informal letters of sea captains to the owners of the ships under their commands or even of the earlier letters of the merchants to each other.

After 1870 little is written about the business acumen of ship captains as traders in the Orient or their marvellous feats in bringing their graceful sailing vessels which were filled with costly and carefully selected Eastern products to England or to the Atlantic ports of America. A new era dawned with the advent of the steamer. It could transport bulky commodities for the large mercantile houses more economically, more speedily, and more safely than sailing vessels could.

The Western nations long before 1870 realized that their growing commercial interests required easy communication. The French, particularly the members of the Chamber of Commerce of Lyon who were chiefly interested in the trade because the mills of their city required raw silk, stressed the need of a steamship line between France and the Orient.[24]   As early as 1848 T. Butler King, a member of the committee on Naval Affairs, introduced into the American House of Representatives a report which recommended the establishment of steam navigation from the Pacific coast to China. In the course of his speech he expressed the opinion that England in the future would be dependent upon the United States for the raw material for her cotton trade with China. It was demonstrated that Americans could successfully compete with England in the sale of cheap cotton goods, and it merely remained for the American manufacturer to study more carefully the problem of adapting his fabrics to the wants and tastes of the Chinese. In spite of the increasing production of cotton in India, King believed that the Americans could monopolize the cotton market in China if the transportation problem between America and the Orient were solved.[25]   The question of steam communication claimed the

[24] *Chambre de commerce de Lyon, op. cit.,* 7; "Die Eisenbahnverbindung zwischen China und Europa," *Westermann Mh.* (1874), 36, pp. 445-47.

[25] Dennett, *op. cit.,* 183; *House Reports, 30th Congress, 1st sess.* (1847-48), Doc., 596, pp. 9-10.

attention of Congress intermittently from 1848 until 1865 when
Congress finally subsidized the project for steam navigation
across the Pacific.[26] Because of the increased commercial connections between Great Britain and China after 1842, merchants
and others stressed the value of telegraphic communication with
the Chinese Empire.[27]

About 1860 the British became deeply interested in reopen-
ing between India, Burma, and Western China, by way of
Bhamo, trade routes which had been in disuse since 1854 as a
result of the T'ai P'ing Rebellion.[28] They realized the importance of connecting India and Burma with Western China.
The British hoped to divert their trade with Shanghai and
other cities of the Chinese coast to Rangoon or some other port
which they controlled on the Bay of Bengal and thereby spare
their tea ships the long and arduous journey through the China
seas. The British merchantmen in time of war could easily be
protected on their courses from Rangoon and neighboring ports
out to the open sea. By shortening the distance from England
to China by one third, freight charges and other expenses would
be greatly reduced.[29]

In 1868 the Indian Government sent an exploring party
of fifty men under Major Sladen to Yun-nan, but the expedition
was unsuccessful presumably because the King of Burma wished
to retain a monopoly on the trade with China.[30] In 1874 Lord
Salisbury, whose favorite scheme was to open up a commercial
route between India and China, encouraged another mission
from Rangoon under Colonel Horace Browne. Augustus Mar-

[26] Ma Wên-hwan, *American Policy toward China As Revealed in the
Debates of Congress* (Shanghai, 1935), p. 39; "Commercial Chronicle and
Review," *Hunt* (1849), 20, p. 533.
[27] "Telegraphic Communications with China," *Chamb. J.* (1862), 38,
p. 287; "Commercial Progress in China," *Dub. Univ. M.* (1872), 80,
p. 536.
[28] *Annual Register* (1875), pp. 94-101; Capt. A. Bowers, *Bhamo Expedition. Report of the Practicability of Opening the Trade Route between
Burma and Western China* (Rangoon, 1869), p. 8.
[29] "The Road into Western China," *Sat. R.* (1868), 25, p. 482.
[30] *Annual Register, op. cit.,* p. 96; E. B. Sladen, *Official Narrative of
the Expedition to Explore the Trade Routes to China via Bhamo* (Calcutta,
1870).

gary of the Chinese consular service, who was sent from Shanghai, reached Browne's party at Bhamo without serious difficulties, but the former was killed while reconnoitering near by. The development of this line of communication was of tremendous importance to the English mercantile community and to the British Indian possessions.[31]

Besides the expeditions sponsored by the Indian or British Governments, others were undertaken. Clement Williams while on duty at the Burmese capital decided to look into a trade route project by way of the Irawaddy River as far as it was navigable and thence across the narrowest part of the watershed to Yun-nan or some other point on the Chinese frontier. Finally toward the end of 1862 after he had overcome the jealousies and obstructions of the Burmese officials, he received a royal commission to make the expedition up the Irawaddy. On the basis of his investigations, he advocated the opening of a trade route from India to Western China *via* Burma.[32]

After a conversation with Williams who had just returned from his trip up the Irawaddy to Bhamo, Cooper proposed to make an overland journey from India to China in 1862. He was unable to carry out his plans, however, for a trip from Rangoon to China. In 1867 James Hogg, a merchant in Shanghai, induced him to make an overland journey from China to Calcutta. Hogg's personal knowledge of Blakiston's efforts to reach India *via* the Yangtze and Tibet in 1860 led him to advise Blakiston's suggested route leading from the farthest navigable point on the Yangtze *via* Likiang in the northern part of Yun-nan to Sadiya on the Brahmaputra in Northern Asia and thence to Calcutta. Cooper set out on his journey in 1867, but he was forced to retreat before he reached Sadiya. He came to the conclusion, however, that the rugged mountains in the two hundred miles of territory between Tatsienlu and Batang would prevent the development of lucrative trade along this route between India and China.[33]

The traders and missionaries who went to China in large

---

[31] *Annual Register* (1875), p. 97; Clement Williams, *Through Burmah to Western China* (Edinburgh, 1868), Preface, p. ix.

[32] *Ibid.*, Preface.   [33] Cooper, *op. cit.*, 5 *et seq.*, 408 *et seq.*

numbers after 1840 clamored for a further opening up of China so that they might carry on their work without restrictions.[34] Certainly by 1870 many Westerners felt a definite responsibility for China. They believed it their duty as strong and superior powers with a virile and Christian civilization to "civilize" China. Various groups had been working toward this end. Prior to 1870 the missionaries by their usual methods of preaching and distributing tracts tried to introduce Western culture and Christianity, but their system was losing prestige during the seventies because they had made such slow progress. The man of business wanted the country opened to trade, manufactures introduced, and the mineral resources developed. The idea of using China as a place for the investment of foreign capital seems to have emerged in the decade of the sixties. Expeditions such as Baron von Richthofen's were made to determine the extent and nature of mineral deposits.[35] The French mission to China sought special concessions as early as 1843 so that their engineers could develop the mines.[36]

During these years the British were also studying the problem of railroad building in China. The organization of a company in England to send out a competent engineer and the means to build a good railroad from Canton to Hunan was considered a good project in which to invest money. The proposed railroad would be extremely advantageous to trade because it would not only take care of the enormous traffic at that time, but would eventually lead to the development of a much larger amount of business in coal and articles of commerce which were then unprofitable because of excessive costs of carriage.

Everywhere in China capital was scarce. An influx of foreign money into the East with proper securities and under able administration would lead to adequate transportation facilities and the development of natural resources on a larger scale. China would soon be modernized and industrialized.[37]

[34] Dennett, op. cit., 181.

[35] J. R. Browne, "Under the Dragon's Footstool," *Overland* (1871), 6, p. 234.   [36] Martin, op. cit., I, 401.

[37] W. Dickson, "Trip through Hunan, from Canton to Hankow," *JNCBRAS* (1864), I, no. 1, p. 170; "Eisenbahnen in China," *Westermann Mh.* (1865), 17, p. 668.

Ruskin's commentary on the business man's notion of civilizing China is noteworthy. He wrote in 1874:

We have Philistines out here, and a Philistine is a perfect Goliath. When he imagines that anything is wrong, he says—let it be a Coolie or an Emperor—"Give him a thrashing." The men of this class here propose their usual remedy: "Let us have a war, and give the Chinese a good licking, and then we shall have the audience question granted, and everything else will follow." This includes opening up the country for trade, and civilizing the people, which according to their theories can be best done by "thrashing them." The missionaries are working to civilize the people here in another way—that is, by the usual plan of tracts and preaching; but their system is not much in favour for they make such small progress among the 360,000,000, the conversion of which is their problem. The man of business wants the country opened up to trade, wants manufactures introduced, the mineral wealth to be used, and generally speaking the resources of the country to be developed, "and that sort of thing, you know—that's the real way to civilize them". . . . I am here giving the tone of the ideas I hear expressed around me. It was only the other day that I heard some of these various points talked over. We were sailing on the river in a steam launch, which was making the air impure with its smoke, snorting in a high-pressure way, and whistling as steam launches are wont to do. The scene was appropriate to the conversation, for we were among a forest of great junks—most quaint and picturesque they looked— so old-fashioned they seemed that Noah's Ark, had it been there, would have had a much more modern look about it. My friend to whom the launch belonged, and who is in the machinery line himself, gave his opinion. He began by giving a significant movement of his head in the direction of the uncouth-looking junks, and then pointing to his own craft with its engine, said "he did not believe much in war, and the missionaries were not of much account. This is the thing to do it," he added, pointing to the launch; "let us get at them, with this sort of article, and steam at sixty pounds on the square inch; that would soon do it: that's the thing to civilize them—sixty pounds on the square inch."[38]

By 1870 the business man's method of civilizing China through the introduction of Western machinery and other mate-

—————
[38] John Ruskin, *Works* (Library ed., London, 1903-12), XXVIII, 105.

rial improvements was taking precedence over the missionary way with its emphasis on spiritual matters.

Western merchants and statesmen, however, disclaimed any political interests in the Orient. It is not surprising that Occidental countries with constantly increasing commercial and missionary interests soon developed political ambitions in the East. Even as early as the Anglo-Chinese War (1839-1842) when Europeans, the English chiefly, advocated the opening of China to trade, mention was made of acquiring areas of Chinese territory as bases to aid the growth of commerce. Much was written at the time to convince the Government of Great Britain that Hong Kong was an unhealthy and unprofitable place[39] while Chusan was both productive and advantageously situated to serve Britain's political and commercial interests as a colony.[40] Located off the coast of Central China, Chusan held a key position in relation to England's northern and southern trade and might have formed an admirable site for the establishment of a force to hold the Chinese to their treaty obligations. The island because of its strategic location could also have formed an emporium of trade which might have soon rivalled any other in Asia.[41]

Others favored the choice of Hong Kong for a colony. Situated at the mouth of the Canton River and in the immediate neighborhood of an immense trading center, it was an excellent point from which the manufactures of other countries could be distributed to the treaty ports.[42] The importance of Hong Kong in the event of another war would be tremendous. If British merchants were expelled from the mainland ports, they could transfer their property to Hong Kong which could be defended by British ships.[43] The reception of the treaty of Nanking in Manchester and other manufacturing towns was

[39] H. C. Sirr, *China and the Chinese* (London, 1849), I, 1 et seq.
[40] *Ibid.*, I, Preface, p. ix, p. 241; Martin, *op. cit.*, II, 396.
[41] J. E. Bingham, *Narrative of the Expedition to China* (London, 1842), II, 3 et seq.; George Smith, *Narrative of an Exploratory Visit to Each of the Consular Cities of China* (New York, 1847), p. 233.
[42] G. F. Davidson, *Trade and Travel in the Far East* (London, 1846), p. 237 et seq.　[43] *Ibid.*, 247.

cited to show the satisfaction of the merchants with the choice of Hong Kong.[44]

If the first Anglo-Chinese War had been settled by a commercial treaty, the China question might have remained economic for some years, but England took Hong Kong which was to serve as a base of operations in the Far East. The occupation of this island caused other powers to desire territorial bases as well as commercial agreements.[45] In 1840 the American Government was first confronted with the task of forming a policy in regard to China. The American merchants of Canton because of their perilous situation during the Anglo-Chinese War sent a Memorial to Congress. They asked for a naval force to protect American lives and property and for a commissioner to arrange a commercial treaty.[46]

The treaty of Wanghia which was negotiated by Caleb Cushing in 1844 marked the entrance of the United States into Far Eastern politics. Prior to this treaty America had been interested only in undisturbed commercial relations, but after 1845 its commerce became immensely important, and Americans foresaw that their trans-Pacific commerce would reach vast proportions in the future. The Americans were ever on the alert to see that no other power made a move which would interfere with American interests or gained privileges to which the United States was not a party.[47]

After the first Anglo-Chinese War the French were likewise eager for commercial and diplomatic advantages. The celebrated French mission which was headed by Langrené went to China in 1843.[48] The mission was also accompanied by shrewd, intelligent representatives of the more important industries. They took with them choice specimens from the factories of Paris and other French cities and hoped to induce the Chinese to import more commodities from France.[49] As a result of Langrené's negotiations, the French obtained a treaty

[44] *Ibid.*, 280.   [45] Dennett, *op. cit.*, 181.
[46] *Ibid.*, 122 *et seq.*; 175 *et seq.*; *House Journal, 26th Congress, 1st sess.* (1840), p. 189.   [47] Dennett, *op. cit.*, 179 *et seq.*
[48] *Chambre de commerce de Lyon, op. cit.*, 7.
[49] *Ibid.*

which gave them political and commercial privileges in China similar to those obtained by England in 1842.[50] During the years following that date, the Germans lived in China on a footing of equality with the nationals of countries which had made treaties with China. Not until after the war of 1860 did Germany ask for a treaty when Graf Eulenberg, acting for Prussia and other members of the German Zoll und Handels-Verein, was commissioned to negotiate a treaty with China. As the German merchants carried on their trade and German ships visited the shores of China with the same freedom that other Western traders enjoyed after 1842, the Chinese Government was surprised at their request for a treaty but eventually granted to the Germans commercial and extraterritorial rights comparable to those of other nations in the Chinese Empire.[51]

The right of extraterritoriality[52] was allowed to a limited extent by the respective treaties which China signed with Western countries immediately following the first Anglo-Chinese War. The English obtained in practice extraterritoriality after 1784. In that year three Chinese were injured by a salute fired from a British vessel, the *Lady Hughes*. When one of them died the following day, the Chinese demanded the surrender of the guilty person who had temporarily disappeared. After the death of the second Chinese, the authorities again demanded the surrender of the gunner. This demand was refused. The Chinese to force the issue imprisoned the supercargo of the *Lady Hughes*, surrounded the factories with soldiers, and stopped all trade. The other nations, represented at Canton, made common cause with the British. The supercargo then wrote to the captain of the *Lady Hughes* to request him to send the gunner to the Chinese for examination. The accused was

[50] Martin, *op. cit.*, I, 400; R. Lindau, "Le commerce étranger en Chine," *RDM* (1861), 35, p. 770.

[51] H. B. Morse, *The International Relations of the Chinese Empire* (London, 1910-18), II, 50 *et seq.*

[52] The material on the subject of extraterritoriality is taken from *Senate Documents, 28th Congress, 2nd sess.* (1844-45), Docs. 58, 67; Dennett, *op. cit.*, 86 *et seq.*, 145 *et seq.*; H. B. Morse and H. F. MacNair, *Far Eastern International Relations* (Boston, 1931), p. 131 *et seq.*, 210; "Treaty with the United States," *C. Repos.* (1845), 14, pp. 410-23.

surrendered upon the assurance that he would be returned safely within sixty days. The gunner was strangled, however, by the Chinese authorities. This case determined the attitude of the British toward the extraterritoriality question. After the *Lady Hughes* affair the English submitted no homicide cases to the Chinese.[53]

In the latter part of the eighteenth and in the early nineteenth century, the Americans pursued a policy of submission to the Chinese authorities. The American position on the matter was clearly expressed at the time of the Terranova case in 1821. Francis Terranova, a sailor from the American ship, *Emily*, anchored at Whampoa, was accused of causing the death of a boat woman. Terranova who was demanded by the Chinese was ultimately surrendered to them. After a trial he was strangled and his body returned to the *Emily*.

The American merchants' attitude toward the case is expressed in the following excerpt from a statement which they drew up and presented to Houqua for the Chinese authorities: ". . . We are bound to submit to your laws while we are in your country, be they ever so unjust. We will not resist them. . . ." Dennett says that "it is hardly to be doubted that the decisions of the Americans in submitting to Chinese jurisdiction in the Terranova case represented fairly accurately the state of American public opinion on the rights of Americans in China."

The Americans continued to accept Chinese jurisdiction until about 1844. That year while Caleb Cushing was in China to negotiate a commercial treaty, some Americans were attacked by a Chinese mob. During the affray a Chinese, Hsü A-man, was accidentally killed. Upon acting viceroy Ching's demand for the surrender of the murderer, the matter was referred to Cushing and Kiying, the High Commissioner for Foreign Affairs. The former, refusing to deliver the man to the Chinese authorities, ordered the case to be tried before a jury of Amer-

---

[53] George Keeton, *The Development of Extraterritoriality in China* (London, 1928), I, 40 *et seq.*; C. H. Peake, "Recent Studies on Chinese Law," *PSQ*, March, 1937, p. 118 *et seq.*

icans and according to American law. The verdict of acquittal on the ground of self-defense was accepted by Kiying. Cushing made this case a precedent in the matter of jurisdiction over Americans accused by Chinese. He maintained:

The United States ought not to concede to any foreign State, under any circumstances, jurisdiction over the life and liberty of any citizen of the United States, unless that foreign State be of our own family of nations; in a word, a Christian State.

The States of Christendom are bound together by treaties, which confer mutual rights and prescribe reciprocal obligations. They acknowledge the authority of certain maxims and usages received among them by common consent, and called the law of nations, but which, not being acknowledged and observed by any of the Mohammedan or Pagan States, which occupy the greater part of the globe, is *in fact* only the international law of Christendom. . . .[54]

As China did not recognize international law even though it was a highly civilized country, Cushing demanded extraterritorial privileges for citizens of the United States in China and succeeded in obtaining such privileges by the treaty of Wanghia in 1844. Although the English some years earlier took the stand that none of their nationals should be surrendered to Chinese criminal jurisdiction, the treaty of Nanking contained no provision for extraterritoriality. Both the Chinese and the English, however, understood that the system was to be introduced. Article XIII of the General Resolutions, issued in 1843, contained a provision for the application of English law by English consuls for the punishment of English criminals in China. The French by the treaty of Whampoa (1844) also obtained jurisdiction over Frenchmen in China in criminal cases. They declared, however, the repression of crimes by French citizens in the treaty ports to be the underlying motive.

The demand for extraterritorial rights after 1840 was due in part to the application of the death penalty in homicide cases and the Chinese principle of responsibility which made the captain of a vessel responsible for the offence of a subordinate. In the nineteenth century because there was much emphasis on

[54] *Senate Documents, 28th Congress, 2nd sess.* (1844-45), Doc. 58, p. 12.

penal and prison reform in Europe, Westerners were horrified by the severity of Chinese punishments, the unsanitary condition of prisons, and the cruel treatment of prisoners. The West for many years after 1840 regarded Chinese law as primitive and backward in contrast to European codes and did not wish to submit cases to Chinese jurisdiction.[55]

The various treaties, signed by Great Britain, France, Russia, and the United States in 1858, by Prussia and the North German Confederation in 1861, and by other powers in later years, contain the stipulation of extraterritoriality. Since those years the consuls have effectively exercised jurisdiction over their nationals, and Western powers have tenaciously adhered to the principles of extraterritoriality.[56]

Even though the countries of the West during this period demanded extraterritorial privileges, they desired no Chinese territory according to their representatives.[57] Prior to 1876 only casual references were made to the partition of China by European powers. As early as 1844 Martin had in mind a possible dismemberment when he wrote:

The position which England has assumed, the treaty which she has forced on China (which has thus been opened to all Europe and America), and the shock which the late war has given to the Tartar Government, and which may probably end in the dismemberment, if not destruction, of the Tartar empire of China, all indicate the great responsibility we have incurred.

England can not remain passive in China—there, as elsewhere, she must advance or recede; the latter is impossible; and the former, if uncontrolled, will plunge her into the greatest difficulties. The abandonment of Chusan, in January 1845, and the retention of Hong Kong as the sole settlement of Great Britain in China, will, ere long, by the force of peculiar circumstances, lead to our territorial

---

[55] Peake, op. cit.; John Heard, Diary, p. 50.

[56] H. B. Morse, The Trade and Administration of China (3rd ed., London, 1920), p. 200.

[57] Cushing said in 1844 that the United States wanted only personal and not territorial jurisdiction. Senate Documents, 28th Congress, 2nd sess. (1844-45), Doc. 67; "Treaty with the United States," C. Repos. (1845), 14, p. 413.

occupancy on the mainland of China; a measure greatly to be deprecated and condemned.[58]

At the time of the Chinese Rebellion, Humphrey Marshall, American commissioner to China, voiced a similar opinion. In 1853 he said:

. . . the highest interests of the United States are involved in sustaining China—maintaining order here, and gradually engrafting on this worn-out stock, the healthy principles which give life and health to governments, rather than to see China become the theatre of widespread anarchy, and ultimately the prey of European ambition.[59]

In 1857 Lord Napier, then British minister at Washington, in the course of a series of conferences with the United States which preceded the revision of the treaties with China, gave the following official statement of British policy with reference to the integrity of China:

The dissolution of the Chinese Empire and the separation of its provinces could not fail to be accompanied by the interception of communications, the diminution of wealth, the destruction of industry, by all the calamities which check the powers of production and consumption. Such a result would be most prejudicial to Great Britain both in reference to our exportation to China, and to our importation of tea, which is at once a source of revenue and a necessary of life.[60]

Both America and England, the two countries most interested in China from the practical business and commercial standpoint, insisted that they desired only adequate trading facilities and protection for their markets. But many Westerners, chiefly the French, during the T'ai P'ing Rebellion thought that the Chinese Empire, then in a state of virtual collapse, was in danger because certain Western nations especially England might help themselves to Chinese territory.[61]

[58] Martin, op. cit., II, 395-96.   [59] Dennett, op. cit., 215.
[60] Ibid., 223 et seq.; "The China Question," Liv. Age (1857), 54, p. 319.
[61] J. P. E. Jurien de la Gravière, "Le Céleste empire depuis la guerre de l'opium," RDM (1851), 11, p. 843; "Shang-Hai et les Chinois du nord," ibid. (1852), 13, p. 1146.

During the difficult years following 1860 the disputes between the foreign powers and China were amicably arranged
by the ministers agreeing to act in concert and giving to each
of the treaty powers an equal share in all advantages obtained
in the Eastern Empire.[62]   This "co-operative policy" was
strongly supported by Anson Burlingame who headed the first
Chinese mission to the Western powers in 1868.[63]   He believed
that "if the treaty powers could agree among themselves to the
neutrality of China, and together secure order in the treaty
ports, and give their moral support to the party in China in
favor of order, the interest of humanity would be subserved. . . ."
He tried, therefore, to bring America and the powers of Europe
in harmony with the policy of co-operation which he thought
would prevent a partition of the Empire.[64]

The mission, sailing from Shanghai, February 25, 1868, for
San Francisco, received a warm and enthusiastic reception there
and in other American cities.   Burlingame made many eloquent
speeches on his tour through the United States.   At the San
Francisco banquet he declared that his mission meant that China
was launched on the path of peace and progress and appealed
to the memory of "Ricci, Verbiest, Morrison, Milne, Bridgman, Culbertson and an army of others who have lived and
died in that far land, hoping that the day would soon arrive
when this great people would extend its arms towards the shining banners of western civilization."   He said that "that hour
has struck, the day has come."[65]   He sounded the same note
in his speech at a banquet given June 28 in New York:

China, seeing another civilization approaching on every side, has
her eyes open. . . . She finds that by not being in a position to

---

[62] "The Chinese Embassy to the Foreign Powers," *Harper* (1868), 37,
p. 598.

[63] For an account of the Burlingame mission see H. B. Morse, *The Inter-
national Relations of the Chinese Empire* (London, 1910-18), II, Chap. IX;
Dennett, *op. cit.*, Chap. XX; F. W. Williams, *Anson Burlingame and the
First Chinese Mission to Foreign Powers* (New York, 1912); Henri Cordier,
Histoire des relations de la Chine avec les puissances occidentales, 1860-1900
(Paris, 1901), I, Chap. XX.

[64] Dennett, *op. cit.*, 373.   [65] Morse, *op. cit.*, II, 194 *et seq.*

compete with other nations for so long a time she has lost ground. She finds that she must come into relations with this civilization that is pressing up around her, and feeling that, she does not wait but comes out to you and extends to you her hand. She tells you she is ready to take upon her ancient civilization the graft of your civilization. . . She invites your merchants, she invites your missionaries. She tells the latter to plant the shining cross on every hill and in every valley. . . .[66]

After Burlingame had popularized his ideas, negotiations were opened in Washington between him and William H. Seward, the Secretary of State, for a treaty which was signed July 28, 1868. The first two articles of the treaty declared that China should have full sovereign rights over its territory. In article VIII, which was considered extremely important at the time, the United States renounced "any intention or right to intervene in the domestic administration of China in regard to the construction of railroads, telegraphs, or other material internal improvements."[67]

In Boston where Burlingame previously lived for several years a banquet was given in honor of the Chinese embassy at the Saint James Hotel, August 21, 1868. Many prominent persons including Emerson and Caleb Cushing were present and made speeches in which they stressed the friendship of America and China and paid tribute to certain superior features of Chinese civilization. Emerson, for example, praised the teachings of Confucius.[68]

Burlingame, after pointing out the similarities of Chinese and American institutions and those things which each country could learn from the other with profit, made a few remarks on the treaty which the United States and China had just concluded. It had its origin, he said, "in the desire to give the control of China to herself in opposition to that aggressive spirit which would take it from her to give it to the caprice of interest

[66] Dennett, op. cit., 384 et seq.   [67] Ibid., 381.

[68] Reception and Entertainment of the Chinese Embassy by the City of Boston (Boston, 1868), p. 52 et seq.; F. I. Carpenter, Emerson and Asia (Cambridge, Massachusetts, 1930), Chap. IX; Arthur Christy, The Orient in American Transcendentalism (New York, 1932).

and to the rude energy of force. It had its origin in the belief that institutions which had withstood all the mutations of time, have something in them worthy of consideration, in the belief that institutions cherished unanimously by one-third of the human race may possibly be the best institutions for the people of China and that at least they are entitled to hold on to them until they shall be changed by fair agreement."[69]

The eloquence of Burlingame's speeches which emphasized the friendship of China for the West and its readiness to welcome missionaries and merchants aroused much enthusiasm, but such assertions of magnanimity were unwarranted by facts and created false impressions of actual conditions in China. Missionaries and other residents in the East were alarmed at Burlingame's extravagant assertions of Chinese progress. They thought that the disillusionment which Westerners would experience upon their arrival in the Orient might seriously impede any movement toward co-operation between China and the Western powers.[70]

The mission did not receive the flattering welcome in England that it had in America. The Queen finally granted an audience to the envoys after they had declared that only the Chinese Emperor's minority prevented him from receiving foreign envoys. On December 4, 1868, Lord Clarendon, Secretary of the Foreign Office in the first Gladstone ministry, received Burlingame for the first time and a little later made the following statements on British policy:

1. The Chinese Government is fully entitled to count upon the forbearance of the foreign nations, and the British Government has neither a desire nor intention to apply unfriendly pressure to China to induce her government to advance more rapidly in her intercourse with foreign nations than is consistent with safety and with due and reasonable regard for the feelings of her subjects.

2. On the other hand, China must observe the treaties and protect British subjects within her empire.

[69] *Reception and Entertainment of the Chinese Embassy, op. cit.,* 24.
[70] See Johannes von Gumpach, *The Burlingame Mission* (Shanghai, 1872), Preface.

3. The British Government announces its preference rather for an appeal to the central government than to local authorities for the redress of wrongs done to British subjects. It is for the interest of China that her central government be not only fully recognized but also established within the empire.

4. The British agents in China have been instructed to act in the spirit and with the objects as explained above.[71]

Burlingame accomplished his aims in England through regular diplomatic channels and did not try to arouse the British public by enthusiastic speeches about Chinese friendship for the Occident. From London the mission went to Paris, but it failed to obtain either a treaty or statement of policy. The French were rather sceptical of any change in the Chinese Government's attitude and policy toward the West. The Tientsin massacre of 1870 during which a mob destroyed an orphanage and the church near by and murdered the French consul and several other French nationals seems to be a justification for such scepticism.[72]

The mission proceeded from Paris to Stockholm, Copenhagen, the Hague, and Berlin where it received a declaration similar to but less definite than Lord Clarendon's. The envoys then went to St. Petersburg, but upon Burlingame's death there, Chih Kang became head of the mission, and after a visit to Brussels and to Rome, the envoys returned to China in October, 1870. The mission did not meet with the same success on the Continent as in England and America although it was well received socially.

Contemporaries believed that if Burlingame and his associates could have obtained the same declarations from Russia, France, and England as were found in the Burlingame treaty of 1868, an effective check could have been made to the policy of absorption in so far as Asia was concerned.[73] The changes which the mission induced Western governments to make in

[71] Dennett, op. cit., 387.

[72] H. Blerzy, "Les Affaires de Chine," RDM (1871), 94, p. 53.

[73] R. J. Hinton, "A Talk with Mr. Burlingame about China," Galaxy (1868), 6, p. 614.

their policies were advantageous for China, and at the time the apparent success of the mission in the United States and England encouraged the Chinese Government to oppose further foreign aggression. Its resistance together with Burlingame's efforts to arrive at a policy of co-operation, and the domestic problems of France, Germany, and Russia undoubtedly did stay the dissolution of China.

CHAPTER VIII

CHINESE SOCIETY

AFTER the Anglo-Chinese War of 1840, Westerners had opportunities to learn about social life in China. From 1840 to 1876 they were conscious of their misconceptions of and their inability to understand the Chinese people. Because few foreigners had attempted to interpret their character and those acquainted with the Chinese and their literature were too partisan to give a balanced and unbiased analysis of their character and their customs, no absolutely reliable body of critical opinion on these subjects was available in European languages.[1]

CHARACTER

Westerners held divergent views about the Chinese. Some said they were the most infamous people in the world; others thought the "Celestials" were a most excellent people. Many writers, taking a middle course, pointed out both their good and their bad traits. The reason for these varied opinions was due chiefly to the different circumstances under which the foreigners observed the Orientals with whom they were associated.[2]

The most praiseworthy characteristics of the Chinese were mildness, docility, and adaptability.[3] Conforming to their surroundings, they quickly learned a trade. Many Occidentals admired their submissiveness to authority.[4] Sir John Davis

---

[1] "Introductory Essay," *C. & J. Repos.* (1863), 1, p. 9; T. T. Meadows, *The Chinese and Their Rebellions* (London, 1856), p. 376.

[2] "Traits of Chinese Character," *C. Repos.* (1842), 11, p. 480.

[3] J. F. Davis, *China: A General Description* (London, 1857), I, 299; "The Hindu-Chinese," *Liv. Age* (1875), 126, p. 448; Arthur Fisher, *Personal Narrative of Three Years' Service in China* (London, 1863), p. 81; John L. Nevius, *China and the Chinese* (New York, 1869), p. 278; H. C. Sirr, *China and the Chinese* (London, 1849), I, 213; T. T. Meadows, *Desultory Notes on the Government and People of China* (London, 1847), p. 203; Alexander Williamson, *Journeys in North China* (London, 1870), I, 3; "Fortune and Huc," *Quar. R.* (1857), 102, p. 156.

[4] "China," *No. Brit. R.* (1847), 7, p. 390; G. T. Staunton, *Miscellaneous Notices Relating to China* (London, 1822-50), p. 127.

attributed this trait to early discipline and training.[5] The Chinese seemed to endure with the greatest composure injuries and insults which would enrage a Westerner. The Orientals considered self-control a necessary part of civilization and a hasty temper indecent.[6] They were also noted for their stoicism and fortitude.[7] Because of their strange notions of death, they preferred to lose a child rather than see it suffer.[8] This attitude toward death, puzzling to Europeans, Huc attributed to their soft and lymphatic temperament and to their entire want of religious sentiments.[9]

Whether or not the Chinese were a courageous people was a debatable question. Notwithstanding their reputation for cowardice which was probably a trait of the masses,[10] English army officers commended the bravery of the Chinese soldiers upon the capture of Amoy by the British in 1841. One officer cut his throat; another walked into the sea and drowned himself.[11] Patterson said that it was both true and false to credit the Chinese with great bravery. While they endured adversity or pain without a murmur, they were deficient in active courage.[12]

An excellent trait of the Orientals was their friendliness.

[5] Davis, op. cit., I, 304.   [6] Meadows, op. cit., 202.

[7] E. B. de Fonblanque, Niphon and Pe-che-li; or, Two Years in Japan and Northern China (London, 1862), p. 206; Arthur Cunynghame, An Aide-de-camp's Recollections of Service in China (London, 1844), I, 189 et seq.; Charles Macfarlane, The Chinese Revolution (London, 1853), p. 64; William Lockhart, The Medical Missionary in China (2nd ed., London, 1861), p. 164; Sirr, op. cit., II, 422; John Scarth, Twelve Years in China (Edinburgh, 1860), p. 101; J. E. Bingham, Narrative of the Expedition to China (London, 1842), II, 21; W. L. G. Smith, Observations on China and the Chinese (New York, 1863), p. 192.

[8] "Manners and Customs in China," Liv. Age (1874), 122, p. 98.

[9] E. R. Huc, The Chinese Empire (New ed., London, 1859), p. 295.

[10] Scarth, op. cit., 107; Bingham, op. cit., II, 391.

[11] J. R. Peters, Miscellaneous Remarks upon the Government, History, Religions, Literature, Agriculture, Arts, Trades, Manners, and Customs of the Chinese: As Suggested by an Examination of the Articles Comprising the Chinese Museum (Philadelphia, 1847), p. 104 et seq.

[12] R. H. Patterson, Essays in History and Art (Edinburgh, 1862), p. 301; T. T. Meadows, Desultory Notes, p. 199.

They were extremely open, frank, and good-natured. They were also civil, obliging, and hospitable.[13] Travellers made long journeys with little fear of danger from the country people who were only too glad to welcome them in their homes.[14] They were generous to a fault. Their desire to appear well often led them into expenditures entirely out of proportion to their means.[15] The Chinese were not devoid of gratitude; several expressed their great indebtedness to the foreign surgeons who restored them to health.[16]

The characteristic, particularly amazing to Westerners, was their almost excessive politeness. The persistent, graceful, and successful efforts of a retiring visitor to pass through perhaps two or three courts without turning his back on his host and his continuous expressions of gratitude and respect had a peculiar elegance and dignity.[17] The Chinese were refined also in their speech. The correspondence of literary men contained delicate compliments and expressions of respect for the person addressed.[18]

The rules of their traditional habits of politeness date back three thousand years. All the Chinese, having been brought up in the same school, were masters of the arts of urbanity, courtesy, compliments, and genuflexions. This politeness, acquired in their earliest childhood, seemed very natural.[19] Even though Europeans conceded the "Celestials" to be the most

[13] "Trade with China," *Liv. Age* (1872), 113, p. 589; W. T. Power, *Recollections of Three Years' Residence in China* (London, 1853), p. 138; F. E. Forbes, *Five Years in China* (London, 1848), p. 3.

[14] Thomas W. Blakiston, *Five Months on the Yang-tsze* (London, 1862), p. 215 *et seq.*

[15] J. L. Nevius, *op. cit.*, 240; John Thomson, *The Straits of Malacca, Indo-China, and China* (New York, 1875), p. 219; George Mogridge, *The Celestial Empire* (London, 1844), p. 37.

[16] Charles Alexander Gordon, *China from a Medical Point of View in 1860 and 1861* (London, 1863), p. 430.

[17] Huc, *op. cit.*, pp. 17, 72 *et seq.*; Alexandre Bonacossi, *La Chine et les Chinois* (Paris, 1847), p. 282; Cunynghame, *op. cit.*, II, 59 *et seq.*; J. L. Nevius, *op. cit.*, 239; Sirr, *op. cit.*, I, 152.

[18] Nevius, *op. cit.*, 240.

[19] "The Paper Wall of China," *All the Year* (1860), 3, p. 322.

polite people on the face of the earth, they often questioned the sincerity of their etiquette. Williams wrote that their politeness seldom had its motive in goodwill, and when the veneer was off the coarseness of the material was obvious. But the same author thought that this exterior polish did prevent quarrels because both parties were careful not to overstep the bonds of etiquette.[20]

Many Westerners were favorably impressed by Chinese industry. As a people, they were neat, orderly, and skillful. Rarely were they excelled in handicrafts. They made excellent house servants, and when taught by French cooks it was difficult to find better cooks.[21]

The Chinese were quick, shrewd, and practical. As business men, they were remarkably energetic, efficient, and adroit.[22] Merchants were said to be extremely systematic in their operations. They seemed to have an innate spirit of association which made it possible for them to carry on their enterprises without the distrust and jealousy common to foreign traders.[23] The honesty of the Chinese merchant was proverbial among both Americans and British. It was customary in Shanghai and Foochow to intrust large sums of money or great amounts of opium to native traders to purchase tea and silk in the interior, but foreigners rarely suffered any losses through their Chinese agents' dishonesty.[24]

An Asiatic trait which many Occidentals admired was tolerance. Because of their innate urbanity, they were more tolerant of opposition and less addicted to excessive idolatry

---

[20] S. W. Williams, *The Middle Kingdom* (New York, 1848), II, 98.

[21] C. W. Brooks, "The Chinese Labor Problem," *Overland* (1869), 3, p. 413; "John Chinaman in Australia," *Liv. Age* (1858), 57, p. 861.

[22] R. S. Maclay, *Life among the Chinese* (New York, 1861), p. 122; Laurence Oliphant, *Narrative of the Earl of Elgin's Mission to China* (New York, 1860), p. 29; Davis, *op. cit.*, I, 416; James D. Johnston, *China and Japan* (Philadelphia, 1861), p. 85.

[23] William Cole, Letter to William Appleton and Company, October 7, 1856 (Baker Library); Williams, *op. cit.*, II, 397.

[24] John Heard, *Diary*, p. 34; Scarth, *op. cit.*, 110; R. B. Forbes, *Remarks on the China Trade* (Boston, 1844), p. 19.

than almost any other people.[25] Throughout the history of China, religious persecution was almost unknown.[26] From the Western point of view, there was a less favorable aspect of Chinese character. They were noted for lying. Many good principles, wrote Meadows, were taught by the sages who urged sincerity and honesty. But still a rigid adherence to truth received little emphasis. A lie itself was not considered wrong; it might be meritorious. Even Confucius believed a falsehood told by a child to help a parent was commendable.[27] Although some persons undoubtely spoke the truth and fulfilled their promises, the Chinese, in general, were supposed to be notorious liars.[28] The disregard for truth, it was said, had done more to lower their character in the eyes of Christendom than any other fault.[29]

The Orientals were also supposed to be sensuous and licentious,[30] although a general regard for outward decency existed among them. A very common habit among the masses was the use of obscene language. This practice seems to have taken the place of profanity in Western countries.[31]

Occidentals cited incident after incident to illustrate the cruelty of the Chinese people who seemed oblivious to all suffering.[32] Parents looked on with pride while their children dismembered insects. A cook could not kill a fowl without first torturing it. No spectacle so much delighted a mob as the flogging, mutilation, or execution of a compatriot.[33] An ex-

[25] Samuel Kidd, *China* (London, 1841), p. 186.
[26] G. T. Lay, *The Chinese As They Are* (Albany, 1843), p. 69; William Gillespie, *The Land of Sinim* (Edinburgh, 1854), p. 152; R. J. L. M'Ghee, *How We Got to Pekin* (London, 1862), p. 46.
[27] Meadows, *Desultory Notes*, p. 213, *passim*; Huc, *op. cit.*, 178.
[28] Blakiston, *op. cit.*, 5; Maclay, *op. cit.*, 125; Meadows, *op. cit.*, 214.
[29] John Thomson, *The Straits of Malacca, Indo-China, and China* (New York, 1875), p. 467; Williams, *op. cit.*, II, 96.
[30] Power, *op. cit.*, 202; George Smith, *A Narrative of an Exploratory Visit to Each of the Consular Cities of China* (New York, 1847), p. 259; Maclay, *op. cit.*, 136.
[31] J. L. Nevius, *op. cit.*, 274; Justus Doolittle, *Social Life of the Chinese* (New York, 1865), II, 273; Sirr, *op. cit.*, I, 35.
[32] Gordon, *op. cit.*, 219 *et seq.*
[33] De Fonblanque, *op. cit.*, 239 *et seq.*; Bingham, *op. cit.*, II, 71.

ample of Chinese indifference is related by Bernard. A fishing boat was upset, but none of the other boats near by would pull toward the two drowning men. They were saved, however, by a boat from a steamer.[34] Some of the incidents which were cited to prove the inhumanity of the Chinese are not very convincing. They indicate that Westerners had a preconceived notion of their cruelty and had some difficulty in finding striking examples.

As the Chinese had a reputation for treachery and unscrupulousness, it was necessary for foreigners to keep a sharp lookout even upon the actions of the very highest officials and those with whom they were on most friendly terms.[35] Thieves were extremely adroit[36] and very numerous.[37] Helen Nevius in her *Life in China,* after mentioning a trifling incident about the theft of a few household articles, remarked that a narrative of experiences in China would be considered uninteresting and incomplete without tales of a few robberies. In deference to the Chinese, this writer said that the incident mentioned was the only loss of any value by theft which she had experienced during her sojourn in the Orient.[38]

Bands of pirates infested the rivers and, pretending to be customs officials, boarded and plundered every trading boat within their reach. Transportation by land was equally dangerous. Carriers were so often waylaid that the magistrates issued orders which prohibited the search of natives on journeys.[39] As early as 1846 the increase in robberies, both on land and on sea, became a serious problem.[40] The European travellers doubtless exaggerated the prevalence of plundering,[41]

---

[34] W. D. Bernard, *Narrative of the Voyages and Services of the Nemesis* (London, 1844), II, 487; Meadows, *op. cit.,* 208.
[35] Cunynghame, *op. cit.,* II, 50.
[36] G. W. Cooke, *China* (London, 1858), p. 103; Maclay, *op. cit.,* 134; Thomson, *op. cit.,* 65.   [37] Williams, *op. cit.,* II, 97.
[38] Helen Nevius, *Life in China* (New York, 1869), p. 99 *et seq.*
[39] James Holman, *Travels in China* (2nd ed., London, 1840), p. 226 *et seq.;* J. F. Davis, *China During the War and Since the Peace* (London, 1852), II, 206; W. L. G. Smith, *op. cit.,* 177.
[40] Davis, *op. cit.,* II, 206.
[41] Robert Fortune, *Two Visits to the Tea Countries of China* (London, 1853), II, 100.

but the practice was so frequently mentioned by writers that theft was regarded as a national trait. Westerners, aware of these good and bad points of the Chinese, stamped them as a matter of fact people, great utilitarians ready to sacrifice everything for present profit or pleasure, decidedly low in their appreciation of beauty, and lacking in religious sentiments.[42]

The many superstitions of the Chinese seem paradoxical.[43] One author pointed out that the philosophic indifference of the learned groups had not checked the growth of superstition among the lower classes. Their credulity was supposed to be unlimited, the objects of their fears numberless, and the ceremonies by which they hoped to ward off the wrath of evil spirits or obtain the favor of good ones amazed foreigners.[44] Sickness, accidents, and all misfortunes were due to malicious spirits. To escape from bad luck, the superstitious consulted priests who tried to exorcize the demons by compelling the clients to make pilgrimages, to do penance, to make gifts to the priests and temples and offerings to the gods.[45]

Charms to drive away evil spirits were used. A common practice consisted in burning paper on which characters were written and blowing away the ashes. By this performance the disease was supposed to be carried off. Other charms consisted of mysterious words on papers which were hung up in certain ways. Ofter a charmer would repeat the words again and again.[46] A common charm was the "hundred families' lock." To procure it a father called upon a hundred friends for coins to which he added enough to buy an ornament in the form of a lock. He fastened it around the child's neck to lock it to life and to make one hundred persons concerned in his reaching old age.[47]

Because the people of China constantly feared evil, the for-

[42] James Henderson, "The Medicine and Medical Practices of the Chinese," *JNCBRAS* (1864), no. 1, p. 29.
[43] Power, *op. cit.*, 159 *et seq.*; *Hegel's Philosophy of the State and of History*, G. S. Morris, ed. (Chicago, 1887), p. 144.
[44] "China and the Chinese," *Westm. R.* (1857), 67, p. 550.
[45] Power, *op. cit.*, 159 *et seq.*   [46] Mogridge, *op. cit.*, 240 *et seq.*
[47] J. F. Davis, *China* (London, 1857), II, 96.

tune teller did a thriving business.[48] His table or a geomancer's shop was at the corner of every street. A common method of divination was to hold up a bamboo root cut in halves, resembling in size and color a common potato, and let the pieces drop as the petition was made.[49] Many other methods of fortune telling and divination were sketched in the various books on social customs. The "Celestial Empire," the paradise of shams, was by nature the most fertile soil for all sorts of humbugs, remarked Eitel, a missionary. He thought that probably all those spiritualistic tricks, which since the beginning of the nineteenth century had engaged by their novelty the attention of the whole civilized world, came from China.[50]

The Chinese were impressed by the marvellous, and, never having been taught the scientific explanations of ordinary phenomena, attributed them to supernatural agencies. Thunder was the voice, and lightning was the messenger of the thunder god. Clouds made the dragon of the air, and rain was the water ejected from his mouth. The sea roared when the dragon of the deep was enraged. If the earth dragon moved, an earthquake might follow.[51] The Chinese were especially addicted to practices which arose from fear caused by earthquakes, eclipses, comets, meteors, inundations, famines, locusts, and other phenomena of nature, all of which were regarded as indications of Heaven's displeasure.[52]

One of the strangest superstitions was *Feng Shui*. It was called *Feng* because it was like wind which could not be comprehended and *Shui* because it was like water which could not be grasped.[53] The term, *Feng Shui* might be construed by the word, luck. In a country like China, where nearly all long journeys were made by water, "a good wind and water," or in

[48] Doolittle, *op. cit.*, II, 331; Kidd, *op. cit.*, 313 *et seq.*
[49] Williams, *op. cit.*, II, 276 *et seq.*
[50] E. J. Eitel, "Somnambulism in China," *N. & Q. on C. & J.* (1868), 2, p. 19.
[51] A. W. Loomis, "Occult Sciences in the Chinese Quarter," *Overland* (1869), 3, p. 160.   [52] Kidd, *op. cit.*, 300.
[53] E. J. Eitel, *Feng Shui; or, the Rudiments of Natural Science in China* (Hong Kong, 1873), p. 2 *et seq.*

other words, good luck on a journey by degrees came to signify good luck, generally.

The origin of *Feng Shui* was traced to an ancient idea according to which the whole universe was a living organism. The trinity of heaven, earth, and man shared a common life; each member of the triad was influenced by and acted upon the other two. *Feng Shui* was a species of geomancy or a belief in the good or ill-luck attached to definite locations. Before a house was built or a burial place chosen, a professor of the occult science was consulted. For an adequate fee he examined the proposed site. The outlines and general character of the earth's surface were supposed to determine the destinies of its inhabitants. Rising grounds, groups of trees, pools of water, and winding roads, properly situated and combined, contributed towards health, peace, happiness, and wealth.

Feng Shui was a kind of terrestrial astrology, but Westerners thought it superior to astrology. The former had a great advantage over the latter because its phenomena were in reach of the spade, and there was much room for man to aid nature.

This superstition attracted foreigners' attention because it had made much trouble for them. When they proposed to erect a few telegraph poles, to build a railroad, or a tramway to provide for the transportation to and from the coal mines of the interior, the Chinese officials opposed such projects because of *Feng Shui*.[54]

PERSONAL APPEARANCE

Westerners not only pointed out all the odd customs and superstitions of the Chinese but also emphasized the peculiarities of their personal appearance which was at first irresistibly ludicrous to Occidentals. Their cracked whining voices, the peculiar twanging, guttural sound of the language, their effeminate dress, their exaggerated politeness, and their long queues, fans, beads, and embroidery amused foreigners.[55] People in Europe, Davis remarked, had been confused in their notions of

[54] *Ibid.;* "Feng Shui," *Cornh.* (1874), 29, p. 337 *et seq.;* Davis, *op. cit.,* II, 99.

[55] Power, *op. cit.,* 103 *et seq.;* Cunynghame, *op. cit.,* I, 85 *et seq.*

Chinese physiognomy by the figures, usually mere caricatures, on the pieces of Canton porcelain. A Chinese, he wrote, might as well form his ideas of Europeans from *Punch's* illustrations.[56]

On the whole, Western comments after 1840 were rather favorable.[57] After giving details as to facial features, Sirr said that although the Chinese could not be called a handsome race, their expressions were intelligent and pleasing. He remarked, however, that although women's complexions and features corresponded closely to men's, their countenances were devoid of expression.[58] The Chinese women were said to possess little beauty. The broad upper face, low nose, and linear eyes were considered very homely features. In size the women were small in comparison to European women. The Chinese as a race, however, were well built but not as muscular as the European or as agile as the Hindu.[59]

Western travellers and residents were interested in Chinese dress. It presented striking contrasts to Western costume. The Board of Rites at Peking was the sole dictator of fashions. It not only prescribed the forms of worship on all occasions, but the costumes which were worn for the ceremonies conformed to minute regulations. The dresses of all ranks about the Imperial Palace had to meet specific requirements as to cut, color, and material.[60]

The full costume of the Chinese was commodious, graceful, and elegant. Unlike European dress the Chinese costume had remained in its general style the same for centuries. Garments of fur or silk were handed down from parent to child, and the antique cuts of their clothes attracted no attention.[61] Westerners marvelled at the beautiful materials used in Chinese

---

[56] Davis, *op. cit.*, I, 310 *et seq.*

[57] Williams, *op. cit.*, I, 36 *et seq.*; Sirr, *op. cit.*, I, 314; W. B. Langdon, *Descriptive Catalogue of the Chinese Collection* (London, 1844), p. 35; Mogridge, *op. cit.*, 28 *et seq.*; Lay, *op. cit.*, 51; Oliphant, *op. cit.*, 140.

[58] Sirr, *op. cit.*, I, 314.

[59] Williams, *op. cit.*, I, 36 *et seq.*; Lay, *op. cit.*, 51.

[60] Davis, *op. cit.*, I, 391.

[61] Williams, *op. cit.*, II, 29; Davis, *op. cit.*, I, 390; Henrietta Shuck, *Scenes in China* (Philadelphia, 1853), p. 169.

clothing.[62] They also commented upon the discretion and judgment of the Orientals in their mode of dress. For example because of the frequent changes in temperature, they either put on or took off an extra jacket as the weather demanded.[63] They like all Eastern peoples attached great value to jewelry. Rings, made by native jewellers, were equal to those of France or England in workmanship.[64]

A universal accessory of both men and women was the fan. Nothing was more novel than a fan in the hand or belt of a soldier, scholar, or priest. Officers, Occidentals observed, went to battle waving fans. On the authority of eye-witnesses of the attack on the Bogue forts in 1841 the native soldiers on the battlements cooled themselves with fans in the midst of the fighting.[65]

An odd Chinese custom was allowing the nails of the left hand to grow very long. The reason for such a curious fashion among both men and women, Westerners said, was to indicate a life of ease and of luxury.[66] Most writers commented on the curious practice, but Milne said it was an exception rather than a rule.[67]

FOOD

Because of the popularity of Chinese restaurants, in America and Europe, it is interesting to note that as early as 1840 Occidentals were appreciative of Chinese culinary art. Huc commented upon the remarkable Chinese gift for good cooking. Williams did not think so highly of Chinese dishes as Huc. The former's pithy comment was that their cooking consisted chiefly of stews of various kinds in which garlic and grease were more abundant than salt and pepper.[68] Huc said many writers found it amusing to make the Western public believe that the Chinese prepared food with castor oil and some of their favorite dishes were shark's fins, fish gizzards, goose feet, pea-

---

[62] Mogridge, op. cit., 31; Davis, op. cit., I, 389; Sirr, op. cit., I, 311.
[63] Sirr, op. cit., I, 309.   [64] Ibid., I, 317.
[65] W. C. Milne, Life in China (London, 1859), p. 15.
[66] Ibid., 14.
[67] Cunynghame, op. cit., II, 17.   [68] Williams, op. cit., II, 50.

cocks' combs, and other "delicacies." Because such dishes were seen nowhere else except at Canton and Occidentals upon their arrival in the East were always eager for an invitation to a Chinese dinner, it was probable that the Canton merchants served such dishes for Westerners who had never dined at a Chinese table.[69]

The following description of a Chinese dinner, written by one Captain Laplace of the French navy and quoted in full by at least two Western authors,[70] gives a more or less accurate account of the method of serving a Chinese dinner and a sketch of the food:

> The first course was laid out in a great number of saucers of painted porcelain, and consisted of various relishes in a cold state, as salted earth-worms, prepared and dried, but so cut up that I fortunately did not know what they were until I had swallowed them; salted or smoked fish and ham, both of them cut into extremely small slices; besides which, there was what they called Japan leather, a sort of darkish skin, hard and tough, with a strong and far from agreeable taste, and which seemed to have been macerated for some time in water. All these et-caeteras, including among the number a liquor which I recognized to be soy, made from a Japan bean, and long since adopted by the wine-drinkers of Europe to revive their faded appetites or tastes, were used as seasoning to a great number of stews which were contained in bowls, and succeeded each other uninterruptedly. All the dishes, without exception, swam in soup. On one side figured pigeons' eggs, cooked in gravy, together with ducks and fowls cut very small, and immersed in a dark-coloured sauce; on the other, little balls made of sharks' fins, eggs prepared by heat, of which both the smell and taste seemed to us equally repulsive, immense grubs, a peculiar kind of sea-fish, crabs, and pounded shrimps.

> Seated at the right of our excellent Amphitryon, I was the object of his whole attention, but, nevertheless, found myself considerably at a loss how to use the two little ivory sticks, tipped with silver,

---

[69] Huc, *op. cit.*, 126 *et seq.*; Fortune, *op. cit.*, I, 113; De Fonblanque, *op. cit.*, 252 *et seq.*; R. H. Cobbold, *Pictures of the Chinese* (London, 1860), p. 200 *et seq.*; Davis, *op. cit.*, I, 371.

[70] *Ibid.*, I, 363 *et seq.*; Langdon, *op. cit.*, 52 *et seq.*; "Chinese Ladies, Dinners and Love-letters," *Nat. M.* (1853), 3, pp. 242-45.

which, together with a knife that had a long, narrow, and thin blade, formed the whole of my eating apparatus. I had great difficulty in seizing my prey in the midst of those several bowls filled with gravy: in vain I tried to hold, in imitation of my host, this substitute for a fork between the thumb and two first fingers of the right hand; for the cursed chopsticks slipped aside every moment, leaving behind them the unhappy little morsel which I coveted. It is true that the master of the house came to the relief of my inexperience (by which he was much entertained) with his two instruments, the extremities of which, a few moments before, had touched a mouth whence age, and the use of snuff and tobacco, had cruelly chased its good looks. I could very well have dispensed with such an auxiliary, for my stomach had already much ado to support the various ragôuts, each one more surprising than another, which I had been obliged, *nolens volens,* to taste of. However, I contrived to eat with tolerable propriety a soup prepared with the famous birds'-nests, in which the Chinese are such epicures. The substance thus served up is reduced into very thin filaments, transparent as isinglass, and resembling vermicelli, with little or no taste. . . .

To the younger guests, naturally lively, such a crowd of novelties presented an inexhaustible fund of pleasantry, and, though unintelligible to the worthy Hong merchant and his brother, the jokes seemed to delight them. . . . The wine in the meanwhile circulated freely, and the toasts followed each other in rapid succession. The liquor, which to my taste was by no means agreeable, is always taken hot, and in this state it approaches pretty nearly to Madeira in colour, as well as a little in taste; but it is not easy to get tipsy with it, for, in spite of the necessity of frequently attending to the invitations of my host, this wine did not in the least affect my head. We drank it in little gilt cups, having the shape of an antique vase, with two handles of perfect workmanship, and kept constantly filled by attendants holding large silver vessels like coffee-pots. The Chinese mode of pledging is singular enough, but has at the same time some little resemblance to the English. The person who wishes to do this courtesy to one or more guests gives them notice by an attendant; then, taking the full cup with both hands, he lifts it to the level of his mouth, and, after making a comical sign with his head, he drinks off the contents: he waits until the other party has done the same and finally repeats the first nod of the head, holding the cup downwards before him, to show it is quite empty.

After all these good things, served one upon the other, and of which it gave me pleasure to see the last, succeeded the second course, which was preceded by a little ceremony, of which the object seemed to me to be a trial of the guests' appetites. Upon the edges of four bowls, arranged in a square, three others were placed filled with stews, and surmounted by an eighth, which thus formed the summit of a pyramid; and the custom is to touch none of these although invited by the host. On the refusal of the party, the whole disappeared, and the table was covered with articles in pastry and sugar, and in the midst of which was a salad composed of the tender shoots of the bamboo, and some watery preparations, that exhaled a most disagreeable odour.

Up to this point the relishes, of which I first spoke, had been the sole accompaniments of all the successive ragôuts; they still served to season the bowls of plain rice which the attendants now, for the first time, placed before each of the guests. I regarded with an air of considerable embarrassment the two little sticks, with which, notwithstanding the experience acquired since the commencement of the repast, it seemed very doubtful whether I would be able to eat my rice grain by grain, according to the belief of Europeans regarding the Chinese custom. I therefore waited until my host should begin, to follow his example, foreseeing that, on this new occasion, some fresh discovery would serve to relieve us from the truly ludicrous embarrassment which we all displayed: in a word, our two Chinese, cleverly joining the ends of their chopsticks, plunged them into the bowls of rice, held up to the mouth, which was opened to its full extent, and thus easily shovelled in the rice, not by grains, but by handfuls. . . . The attendants cleared away everything. Presently the table was strewed with flowers, which vied with each other in brilliancy; pretty baskets filled with the same, were mixed with plates which contained a vast variety of delicious sweetmeats as well as cakes, of which the forms were as ingenious as they were varied. This display of the productions of nature and of art was equally agreeable to the eyes and the tastes of the guests: by the side of the yellow plantain was seen the *litchi*, of which the strong, rough, and bright crimson skin defends a stone enveloped in a whitish pulp, which, for its fine aromatic taste, is superior to most of the tropical fruits. . . . With these fruits of the warm climates were mingled those of the temperate zone, brought at some expense from the northern provinces; as walnuts, chestnuts (small and inferior to those of France), apples, grapes, and Peking pears, which last, though their lively colour and pleasant smell attracted the attention, proved to be tasteless. . . .

. . . At length, we adjourned to the next room to take tea,— the indispensable commencement and close of all visits and ceremonies among the Chinese. According to custom, the servants presented it in porcelain cups, each of which was covered with a saucerlike top. . . . The boiling water had been poured over a few of the leaves collected at the bottom of the cup; and the infusion, to which no sugar is ever added in China, exhaled a delicious fragrant odour, of which the best teas carried to Europe can scarcely give an idea.[71]

This description, written with a certain amount of vivacity and levity, capitalizes Chinese idiosyncrasies in the choice of food. It illustrates the tendency of Europeans to stress the bizarre and the unusual rather than the ordinary fare. This letter, quoted by Davis, was widely read and was in part responsible for Occidentals' strange ideas about Chinese food. In reality such unsavory articles formed almost no part of their dinners or their ceremonial feasts. Because travellers often, as the above quotation shows, spoke of birds' nest soup, dogs' hams, rats, snakes, and worms, Westerners believed these articles formed a large proportion of the Chinese diet.[72]

As the struggle for existence in China was at times very hard, every sort of organic matter was used for food.[73] But on the testimony of the most reputable authors, the wide and almost universal notion that rats, cats, and dogs were articles of general consumption was an example of a local custom being taken for a national practice.[74]

In general the foreigners who lived in China approved of the food, and whatever criticisms they made were the results of individual tastes. Although the Chinese dishes were too rich

[71] Davis, op. cit., I, 363 et seq.

[72] Williams, op. cit., II, 42; Cobbold, op. cit., 203.

[73] "Facts about the Chinese," Chamb. J. (1844), I, p. 356; "How China is Peopled," Ecl. M. (1857), 41, p. 477 et seq.; Martha N. Williams, A Year in China (New York, 1864), p. 196; Cooke, op. cit., 366.

[74] J. L. Nevius, op. cit., 245; Milne, op. cit., 27; T. T. Cooper, Travels of a Pioneer of Commerce in Pigtail and Petticoats (London, 1871), p. 431.

in oils and such seasoning as garlic, for the average Englishman or American to relish, many Westerners especially the French liked many of their preparations.[75]

The common beverages were tea and a fermented liquor made from rice. The taste of the latter was sometimes pleasing, Huc wrote, but Westerners usually did not care for this drink. The same writer also mentioned a brandy which was made from millet. Its unpleasant taste was counteracted by putting green fruits or aromatic herbs into the brew. The Chinese drank their beverages steaming hot. Even though Huc stressed the prevalence of drunkenness, it was not a common practice. Most authors, who were impressed by the absence of intoxication, wrote that the temperance of the Chinese was their most redeeming characteristic.[76]

HOMES

Books on the social life of the Chinese usually described their houses especially those of the wealthy. Chinese mansions were estimated by the space which the buildings covered and by the size and number of the compartments. Courts, galleries, and trellis work often extended far and wide. The walks of figured tiles were neat and attractive. The ponds which contained golden carp, and the intricate flower arrangements added much to the beauty of the gardens. The triple gateway entrance used in elaborate houses was rather imposing. The outer wall of brick which had no windows looked dull and heavy. The enclosed courts, the colonnades, the granite platforms, and the elaborately decorated roofs, however, gave the building a picturesque appearance.[77]

The worst feature of Chinese houses was their lighting facilities. As glass was little used and imperfect, almost the only method of letting in light and excluding cold at the same time was the use of lattice work windows, lined inside with

[75] F. E. Forbes, *Five Years in China* (London, 1848), p. 97; Maclay, *op. cit.*, 278.

[76] S. W. Williams, *op. cit.*, II, 46; Huc, *op. cit.*, 484 *et seq.*; Davis, *op. cit.*, I, 370.

[77] Mogridge, *op. cit.*, 284; Davis, *op. cit.*, I, 403 *et seq.*

very thin transparent paper. Sometimes a single pane of glass was placed in the center of the window. In other instances the whole was covered with the lining of oyster shells which afforded a rather poor light.[78] The interiors of Chinese houses were beautifully arranged and were most unique as to furniture and decoration.[79] Some of their wardrobes and bedsteads were elegantly ornamented with carved work which was inlaid with various kinds of wood.[80] The general style of the handsome, massive, and substantial furniture was in some respects similar to the furniture of the Elizabethan period.

The Chinese often arranged chairs in rows against the walls with small tables between each two or three chairs for tea or samshoo cups. On the couches they placed small tables about a foot high usually of ebony or lacquer ware. The former were richly carved, and the latter were profusely decorated. These small tables were used for tea or cards. Tables of different forms and sizes were scattered throughout the rooms. They were of marble, granite, ebony, or lacquer ware and were highly ornate with gilding or mother-of-pearl. Curios, antiques, and knick-knacks lay carelessly on the tables.[81]

The walls of the rooms were usually adorned with scrolls of silk or paper hanging from the ceiling to the floor. On these scrolls were written or painted maxims of the philosophers. The Chinese considered these scrolls far more decorative than the finest paintings.[82]

The most striking feature of Chinese homes were the lanterns suspended by silk cords from the ceilings. Lanterns were showy specimens of the national taste and ingenuity. They were made in every form and size from the small ones carried

[78] Bernard, op. cit., II, 248; Doolittle, op. cit., I, 42.

[79] Cunynghame, op. cit., II, 121; D. F. Rennie, The British Arms in North China and Japan (London, 1864), p. 172; De Fonblanque, op. cit., 208 et seq.

[80] Frank Leslie's Historical Register of the United States Centennial Exposition, 1876, Frank H. Norton, ed. (New York, 1877), p. 245; New York Tribune . . . Guide to the Exhibition (New York, 1876), p. 2; Bernard, op. cit., II, 248.   [81] Sirr, op. cit., I, 322.

[82] William Speer, The Oldest and the Newest Empire: China and the United States (Hartford, Connecticut, 1870), p. 90.

by pedestrians to the large ones, eight or ten feet high and three feet in diameter, which were found in the halls of the rich. The most costly were made of transparent silk, decorated with landscapes, birds, flowers, and fantastic ornaments of dazzling brightness. The framework was richly carved and the tassels by which they were suspended were often of gold thread. To own fine lanterns was an ambition of the Chinese, and they spent large sums to gratify their fancy.[83]

TRAVEL

Just as the houses of the wealthy, although rather large and lavishly decorated, were not equal in luxury and comfort to the homes of well-to-do Westerners, the inns in China were not as elegant as the better hotels of Europe. Western travellers, whose modes of living were not too luxurious, might find a room in one of the better Chinese inns rather pleasant. Adjoining such an inn was ordinarily a spacious courtyard which contained feeding troughs for the travellers' horses or mules. The interior of these inns was usually very rude. Every room had a *k'ang* or sleeping place through which ran a flue connected with a small container of fuel. Only in the inns of the larger towns could a traveller have a private room.[84]

The network of rivers and canals in China made water carriage the most common and convenient mode of transportation. This was especially true in the South. The river craft of the Chinese was unique. The small draft of water and the great burden and stiffness of the vessels, the perfect ease with which they slipped through the most dangerous passages, and their unusual accommodations amazed Westerners. Travellers, wishing a voyage of luxury and pleasure, Huc advised to get a mandarin junk, in which they might glide leisurely on rivers and canals through many parts of China.

In the North the means of transportation were less tedious but more tiresome. Travellers either rode horses, asses, or mules or made trips in palanquins or coaches which had neither

---

[83] *Ibid.*, 91; S. W. Williams, *op. cit.*, II, 82.

[84] Huc, *op. cit.*, 522; "The Great Wall of China," *Once a Week* (1862), 6, p. 668.

springs nor seats. The Orientals had used coaches before the Europeans had, but the Chinese coaches were inferior to the Western coaches.[85]

AMUSEMENTS

Occidentals were also curious about the recreations and forms of amusement which the Chinese people enjoyed.[86] The Chinese game of chess, which afforded fewer opportunities for brilliant and powerful combinations, Europeans regarded as inferior to the Western game.[87]

Foreigners marvelled at the ability of jugglers whose dexterity, sleight of hand, and conjuring were almost incredible.[88] Chinese skill in gymnastic feats impressed foreigners. While tossing innumerable balls through hoops in quick succession, they could keep twelve in constant play for a quarter of an hour.[89]

The most popular outdoor game was kite flying. The Orientals showed their superiority in the heights to which they made their kites go and in the construction of their kites which had strings stretched across holes. When the wind whistled through the strings, they sounded like Aeolian harps. Kite flying was the national amusement of China.[90]

Combats between crickets were contested with great spirit. Two well chosen fighters were put into a basin and irritated with a straw until they rushed upon each other with the "utmost fury." Quails' fights were common sport. Westerners looked upon such fights with amusement usually. A missionary author remarked that even though they were not sublime

[85] Huc, *op. cit.*, 521 *et seq.*; Davis, *op. cit.*, I, 407 *et seq.*; "Commercial Progress in China," *Dub. Univ. M.* (1872), 80, p. 531.

[86] W. L. G. Smith, *op. cit.*, p. 94.

[87] "Chinese Chess," *C. & J. Repos.* (1865), 3, p. 582; Davis, *op. cit.*, I, 378.

[88] Sirr, *op. cit.*, I, 177; Thomas Allom, *The Chinese Empire Illustrated: Being a Series of Views from Original Sketches . . . with Historical and Descriptive Letterpress by the Rev. G. N. Wright* (London, 1858-59), I, 153; W. L. G. Smith, *op. cit.*, 93 *et seq.*

[89] Sirr, *op. cit.*, I, 194; Langdon, *op. cit.*, 38; Lay, *op. cit.*, 107.

[90] Langdon, *op. cit.*, 42; Davis, *op. cit.*, I, 379; Mogridge, *op. cit.*, 235.

sports, they were less inhumane than the prize fights and the bull-baits of Christian countries.[91]

The Chinese, who had no regular day of rest, made much of holidays and festivals. Although they were a plodding and industrious people, they needed a period of relaxation.[92] Their holidays, which gave them a respite, commemorated traditional customs, the great changes in nature, the interment of the dead, and the seasons devoted to the worship of certain gods.[93] New Year's day was an important day. Public offices were closed twenty days before the New Year to give time for suitable preparations and twenty days after that date for proper observation of the prescribed ceremonial.[94]

The Feast of Lanterns was a general illumination which occurred throughout every province, city, town, and village in China. Large and small lanterns of every description were made of glass, horn, mica, pearl, shell, paper, cotton, and silk. An odd, fish-shaped lantern spouting forth sparks of firework was described by the one author. Another lantern represented a hideous dragon with glaring eyes and hissing snakes and streams of fire coming out of its mouth. Lanterns were lighted with oil and cotton wicks and were noted for their great number and lavish decorations rather than for intensity of light. Yet the brilliance and splendor of the Feast of Lanterns was unrivalled.[95]

A peculiar institution was the birthday celebration. Every tenth birthday after fifty called for a great amount of pomp and expense particularly in wealthy families and those connected with the Government. Westerners, although they were amazed at the bizarre customs connected with Chinese festivals, enjoyed the pageantry and beauty. Missionaries, however, re-

[91] Williams, *op. cit.*, II, 90, 91; Mogridge, *op. cit.*, 234.
[92] "Chinese Festivals," *All the Year* (1875), 30, p. 256; Doolittle, *op. cit.*, II, Chapters I, II, III.
[93] Kidd, *op. cit.*, 301; Davis, *op. cit.*, I, 345.
[94] Kidd, *op. cit.*, 301 *et seq.*
[95] Mogridge, *op. cit.*, 281; Davis, *op. cit.*, I, 347 *et seq.*

coiled at the pagan practices, such as offerings to the gods during the festivals.[96]

"CONTRARIETY" OF CHINESE CUSTOMS

The ceremonies connected with births, marriages, and funerals, were very odd to foreigners. As late as 1874 a Western writer admitted that the Occidentals knew little about Chinese marriage customs.[97] The ceremonies of betrothal and marriage were supposed to be very absurd while those inflicted upon an infant during the first three days of his life were the most ridiculous of all.[98]

Funeral customs, which differed widely from those of Western countries, were described with great detail.[99] The curious mortuary procession was as follows:

The former [mortuary processions], like all Chinese marches, are a heterogeneous gathering of incongruous objects. Ragged, semi-clad coolies staggering along without order or precision, bearing the most singular burdens; the dead person with the white fowl fluttering ahead, trays with baked meats, perhaps a whole pig, and ducks, heaps of paper money in baskets, clothes, shoes, both real and made of paper, trays of cakes, umbrellas, fans, &c. The friends, carried in chairs, wrapped in white cloths, only their eyes and nose appearing, looked like so many corpses going to their own funerals; and it would be too tedious to enumerate the objects which do go to a Chinese interment. The general effect is comic rather than solemn, lively rather than sad, disorderly rather than methodical.[100]

Everything the Chinese did was exactly opposite to the parallel custom of the West. A writer in the *Chinese Repository* wrote that "if we examine some of the minuter shades of his [a Chinese's] character we shall at once perceive that he was cast in a different mold from 'us barbarians'; and albeit the outlines of the two are alike, their finish is quite diverse." Some of these differences are grouped in the following sketch:

[96] Doolittle, *op. cit.*, II, 217 *et seq.*
[97] "Married Life in China," *All the Year* (1873), 31, p. 42.
[98] "Celestial Ceremonies," *Chamb. J.* (1866), 43, p. 668.
[99] "Funeral Rites in China," *All the Year* (1873), 30, p. 162.
[100] "Manners and Customs in China," *Liv. Age* (1874), 122, p. 99.

On inquiring of the boatman in which direction our port lay, I was answered west-north; and the wind, he said, was east-south. "We do not say so, in Europe," thought I, but imagine my surprise when in explaining the utility of the compass, he added that the needle pointed south. On landing, the first object that attracted my attention was a military mandarin, who wore an embroidered petticoat, with a string of beads around his neck, and a fan in his hand. His insignia of rank was a button on the apex of his sugar-loaf cap, instead of a star on his breast, or epaulettes on his shoulders; and it was with some dismay, I observed him mount on the right side of his horse. Several scabbards hung from his belt, which of course I thought must contain a dress-sword or dirks, but on venturing near through the crowd of attendants, I was surprised to see a pair of chopsticks and a knife-handle sticking out of one, and soon his fan was folded up and put into the other, whereupon I concluded he was going to a dinner instead of a review. The natives around me had their hair all shaven on the front of their head, and let it grow as long as it would behind; many of them did not shave their faces, but their mustaches were made to grow perpendicularly down over their mouths, and lest some straggling hairs should diverge cheek-ways, the owners were busily employed pulling them down. "We arrange our toilettes differently in Europe," thought I, but could not help acknowledging the happy device of chopsticks, which enabled these gentlemen to put their food into the mouth endwise, underneath the natural fringe.

On my way to the house where I was to put up, I saw a group of old people, some of whom were graybeards; a few were chirruping and chuckling to singing birds, which they carried perched on a stick or in cages; others were catching flies to feed the birds; and the remainder of the party seemed to be delightedly employed in flying fantastic paper kites, while a group of boys were gravely looking on, and regarding these innocent occupations of their seniors with the most serious and gratified attention. As I had come to the country to reside for some time, I made inquiries respecting a teacher, and the next morning found me provided with one who happily understood English. On entering the room, he stood at the door, and instead of coming forward and shaking my hand, he politely bowed, and shook his own before his breast. I looked upon this custom as a decided improvement upon our mode, especially in doubtful cases; and requested him to be seated. I knew I was about to study a language without an alphabet, but was somewhat astonished to find him begin at what I had all my life previously considered the end of the book. He read the date of the publication, "The fifth year, tenth month and first day." "We arrange our dates differently," I observed, and begged him to read, which he did from the top to the bottom, then proceeding from right to the left. "You have an odd book here," remarked I, taking it out of his hands; and looking farther, saw that the running title was on the edge of the leaves instead of the top; that the paging was near the bottom; that the marginal notes were on the top of the page. . . .

Giving the book back to him, I begged him to speak of ceremony. He commenced by saying, "When you receive a distinguished guest, do not fail to place him on your left hand, for that is the seat of honor; and be cautious not to uncover the head, as it would be an unbecoming act of familiarity." This was a severe blow to any established notions, but requested him to continue. He reopened the volume and read with becoming gravity, "The most learned men are decidedly of the opinion, that the seat of the understanding is in the belly." "Better say it is in the feet and done with it," exclaimed I, for this so shocked all my principles of correct philosophy, that I immediately shut up the book, and dismissed my moonshe to come another day.

On going abroad, I met so many things contrary to all my preconceived ideas of propriety, that I really assented to a friend's observation "that the Chinese were our antipodes in many things besides geography." "Indeed," said I, "it is so; I shall almost expect shortly to see a man walking on his head; look, there's a woman in trousers, and a party of gentlemen in petticoats; she is smoking a segar, and they are fanning themselves"; but I was taught not to trust to appearances too much, when on passing them, I saw the latter wore tight under-garments. We soon after met the comprador of the house dressed in a complete suit of white, and I stopped and asked him what merry-making he was invited to; with a look of the deepest concern, he said, he was just returning from burying his father. Soon we passed a house, where we heard sobbing and crying, and desiring to alleviate grief, I inquired who was ill. The man, suppressing a smile, said, "it is a young girl just about leaving her father's house to be married and she is lamenting with a party of her fellows." I thought, after these unlucky essays, I would ask no more questions; but carefully use my eyes instead.

Looking into a shop, I saw a stout strapping fellow sewing lace on a bonnet; and going to the landing-place, behold, there all the ferry-boats were rowed by women; and from a passage boat just arrived, I saw the females get out of the cabin which was in the bow. "What are we coming to next?" said I, and just by I saw a carpenter take his foot-rule out of his stocking, to measure some timber, which his apprentice was cutting with a saw that had the blade set nearly at right angles with the frame. Before his door sat a man busily engaged in whitening the soles of a pair of shoes with white lead. We next passed a fashionable lady who was just stepping out of her chair, hobbling, I should rather say; for unlike our·ladies with their compressed waists, her feet were not above three inches long; and her gown, instead of having gores sewed into the bottom, was so contracted by embroidered plaits as apparently to restrain her walking. "Come let us return home," said I, "for I am quite whirled about in this strange land."[101]

SOCIAL VICES

Much space in books and magazine articles was devoted to social vices. The one which attracted most attention in the West, because of the importance of the opium question, was the use of opium. Writers described in great detail the method of smoking. Opium dens with all their horrors were depicted.[102] An author, publishing his work in 1849, sketched the evil effects of the drug, mentally, physically, and economically. The victim was unable to perform any task which required concentration. He did not have the strength to engage in normal labor and neglected his business. The wide use of opium, therefore, was making the entire nation poorer and poorer.[103] Notwithstanding the opinion, which almost universally prevailed in

---

[101] "Illustrations of Men and Things in China," *C. Repos.* (1841), 10, p. 106 *et seq.;* "Chinese Domestic Life," *Liv. Age* (1874), 121, p. 442; "National Contrasts," *House. W.* (1858), 18, p. 473.

[102] Bingham, *op. cit.,* I, 126 *et seq.;* Cooke, *op. cit.,* 178; Doolittle, *op. cit.,* II, 349 *et seq.;* Reinhold Werner, *Die preussische Expedition nach China* (2nd ed., Leipzig, 1873), p. 235; "How the World Smokes," *All the Year* (1860), 3, p. 247; "Chinese Players," *House. W.* (1854), 8, p. 282.

[103] Doolittle, *op. cit.,* II, 353 *et seq.;* Langdon, *op. cit.,* 79; Huc, *op. cit.,* 19; George Smith, *A Narrative of an Exploratory Visit to Each of the Consular Cities of China* (New York, 1847), p. 380 *et seq.;* Maclay, *op. cit.,* 137; "Opium Smoking," *C. Recorder* (1868), 1, p. 93.

Europe, that the drug was injurious except when used as a medicine, some writers stressed the harmless and pleasing qualities of the drug.[104] A European, holding a middle position on the baneful effects of opium, wrote that there were doubtless evils arising from the excessive use of opium but he had known many Chinese who had used it for years without obvious injury. Opium, he said, was taken more as a sedative than as a narcotic, and its general effects were similar to those of wine, whisky, or brandy.[105]

Different opinions are found on the extent of opium smoking. It was so universal, observed one Westerner, that the proclamations against the use of opium had no effect on the practice.[106] Among the lower ranks it was unusual to see an individual suffering from the effects of the drug, and the victims were almost entirely among the wealthier groups, another traveller noted.[107] The number of addicts was exaggerated, Robert Fortune maintained. Although a large quantity of the drug was yearly imported into China from India, the vast extent of the Chinese Empire and its population of three hundred million people should have been considered in comparison with the annual consumption of opium.[108]

Another Chinese vice widely practised was gambling.[109] Betting was also common.[110] Although gambling did prevail among the lower classes, society attached so much infamy to the practice that the government officials and the more respectable people refrained from this pastime, Davis and Langdon commented. All classes from the lowest to the highest, wrote Sirr,

[104] "The Opium Trade with China," *For. Quar. R.* (1840), 24, p. 117; Charles Alexander Gordon, *China from a Medical Point of View* (London, 1863), p. 131.

[105] Scarth, *op. cit.*, 296 *et seq.*

[106] James Holman, *Travels in China* (2nd ed., London, 1840), p. 254; Sirr, *op. cit.*, I, 221.

[107] Power, *op. cit.*, 203; Rennie, *op. cit.*, 202.

[108] Fortune, *op. cit.*, I, 176.

[109] George Smith, *op. cit.*, 364; Bingham, *op. cit.*, II, 69 *et seq.*; Williams, *op. cit.*, II, 89 *et seq.*; Doolittle, *op. cit.*, II, 283 *et seq.*; Fortune, *op. cit.*, I, 66; J. L. Nevius, *op. cit.*, 274; Davis, *op. cit.*, I, 377 *et seq.*; Huc, *op. cit.*, 482.

[110] Speer, *op. cit.*, 101.

were gamblers, and the laws prohibiting the practice were dead letters.[111]

Infanticide received much attention from Western writers.[112] The edicts published by the Government against the practice were sufficient proof of its occurrence, but infanticide was not universal. It had not reached the proportions which were attributed to it. The Chinese were too fond of their children in most cases to commit such a crime.[113] Many Occidentals, thinking the whole Chinese nation brutal and barbarous, assumed that the practice of infanticide was tolerated by the Government and public opinion. This was not the case, Huc wrote. An infant's murder was a crime in China, and the magistrates continually protested against this abuse of paternal authority.[114]

A few writers referred to the frequency of suicides.[115] Petty disputes, the discontent, caused by poverty, sullen resentment at reproof, and dread of punishment for the violation of a law made Chinese hang or throw themselves into the bottom of a well. In the West if a man wished to wreak veangeance on an enemy, he tried to murder him. In China he killed himself, because the law threw the responsibility of a suicide on those who theoretically caused the act. By committing suicide, a person might make serious trouble for his enemy who would immediately fall into the hands of justice to be tortured or ruined if not deprived of his life. The family of the suicide usually obtained considerable damages. In killing his enemy on the contrary the individual exposed his own relatives and

[111] Langdon, *op. cit.*, 41; Davis, *op. cit.*, I, 377; Sirr, *op. cit.*, II, 420; Holman, *op. cit*, 219; J. L. Nevius, *op. cit.*, 274; Huc, *op. cit.*, 322.

[112] Milne, *op. cit.*, 32; Doolittle, *op. cit.*, II, 203-9; J. L. Nevius, *op. cit.*, 252.

[113] Charles Lavollée, *La Chine contemporaine* (Paris, 1860), p. 90; Sinibaldo de Mas, *La Chine et les puissances chrétiennes* (Paris, 1861), I, 37; Bernard, *op. cit.*, II, 257; Werner, *op. cit.*, 232 *et seq.*; T. T. Meadows, *Desultory Notes on the Government and People of China* (London, 1847), p. 210; "How China Is Peopled," *Ecl. M.* (1857), 41, p. 478; J. F. Davis, *Sketches of China* (London, 1841), I, 173; Davis, *China* (London, 1857), I, 305.

[114] Huc, *op. cit.*, 496 *et seq.*; Lay, *op. cit.*, 60.

[115] Holman, *op. cit.*, 222; Huc, *op. cit.*, 181.

friends to injury, disgrace, and poverty and deprived himself of funeral honors. Public opinion did not disapprove of suicides but glorified them.

Footbinding caused much comment. Although its origin about the end of the T'ang dynasty was obscure, several explanations of its beginnings were given.[116] According to one theory the practice arose from the desire to imitate the club feet of a popular empress. It gradually became a custom because the Chinese admired small feet. Men were said to have imposed the practice upon their wives to prevent them "gadding."[117] It might in part be ascribed to the same principle which dictated the fashion of long nails. Both customs conveyed the idea of exemption from labor and therefore of gentility. The Chinese admired the women's appearance of helplessness and compared their gait to the waving of the willow in the breeze.[118] Authors described fully the process of binding.[119] In almost all parts of the Empire girls had to submit to this nearly universal prac- tice. In the sections of the country which Nevius visited, all women conformed to the custom except those of a certain class from Canton and Tartar women. This author pointed out that country women and those of a low social status compressed their feet about half the natural size, and women of the higher classes had feet about three inches long.[120] Authors also discussed the results of footbinding. Lockhart, a medical missionary, reported several cases of diseased ankle bones which were treated in the hospital at Shanghai. But in comparison to the vast number of girls who suffered this distortion, such cases were few. How far foot binding was injurious to the health could not be de- termined. From the observation of both women and children,

---

[116] A. Ecker, "Die künstlichen Missstaltungen der Körperform," *Wester- mann Mh.* (1862), 12, p. 632 *et seq.*

[117] De Fonblanque, *op. cit.*, 191; Williams, *op. cit.*, II, 38.

[118] Davis, *op. cit.*, I, 312 *et seq.*

[119] "'Small Feet of Chinese Ladies," *N. & Q.* (1869), 3, p. 301; Cooke, *op. cit.*, 218; Charles Taylor, *Five Years in China* (New York, 1860), p. 110.

[120] J. L. Nevius, *op. cit.*, 242; Fortune, *op. cit.*, I, 192; Milne, *op. cit.*, 8 *et seq.*; "Ladies Feet in China," *All the Year* (1873), 30, p. 571.

the practice did not cause as much misery as might have been expected.[121]

A practice of Chinese society, particularly condemned by Westerners, was polygamy. In China the "wife" was the woman united by the usual marriage ceremonies to her husband. She was the head of all women in the household. The other women who were of a subordinate and inferior status were called concubines by Westerners. The Chinese maintained that additional women were not taken into the household without the wife's consent and that these domestic arrangements did not disturb family peace.[122] The laws permitted polygamy, although they did not sanction such a system, Davis stated. A Chinese could have but one wife who was distinguished by that title. He could have as many inferior wives as he chose.[123]

Because no statistics were available, the extent of polygamy was difficult to estimate. Among the laboring classes it was rare to find a man with more than one wife, but tradesmen, officials, landholders, and others in easy circumstances frequently took one or more wives in addition to the first. More than one wife would probably be found in two-fifths of such homes, wrote Williams.[124]

The position of the wife taken by the prescribed formalities and the status of women purchased as concubines were carefully defined in law. The degradation of the former or the elevation of the latter was prohibited. Other laws forbade the marriage of persons with the same surname or of close relationship. These restrictions, Williams remarked, not only gave a certain dignity to marriage, but the emphasis on early marriages, which were arranged by parents, contributed greatly toward morality. A

---

[121] William Lockhart, *The Medical Missionary in China* (2nd ed., London, 1861), p. 334; W. T. Power, *Recollections of Three Years' Residence in China* (London, 1853), p. 298; T. T. Cooper, *Travels of a Pioneer of Commerce in Pigtail and Petticoats* (London, 1871), p. 48; Gordon, *op. cit.*, 10; Bingham, *op. cit.*, II, 18; Doolittle, *op. cit.*, II, 197 *et seq.*; Milne, *op. cit.*, 13.

[122] W. L. G. Smith, *op. cit.*, 85 *et seq.*; George Smith, *op. cit.*, 148.

[123] Davis, *op. cit.*, I, 323 *et seq.*

[124] Williams, *op. cit.*, II, 60; Milne, *op. cit.*, 157; Lay, *op. cit.*, 57; Sirr, *op. cit.*, II, 47.

result of the method of Chinese marriage arrangements was the divorce which was granted not merely for determinate causes but by mutual consent. It was natural enough, commented Huc, that persons who were married without their own consent should at least have permission to separate if they could not agree. The husband, however, could repudiate his wife for the following legal reasons: sterility, immorality, disobedience to her husband's parents, talkativeness, theft, jealous temper, and habitual ill-health.[125]

POSITION OF WOMEN

Although Oriental women spent their lives in seclusion, nineteenth-century writers thought that former accounts, stressing absolute seclusion of women, exaggerated the situation.[126] A Chinese, however, never introduced the women of his family to casual acquaintances.[127] "Ladies of quality" were rarely seen but spent their time playing musical instruments, embroidering, playing chess, smoking, and drinking tea.[128] That women's education except in unusual instances was limited and restricted but not entirely neglected, was the opinion of most Occidentals.[129] Davis said that women were "not often deeply versed in letters, but celebrated instances are sometimes quoted of those who have been skilled in composing verses."[130] Despite the general disadvantages of women, Davis thinks their position retained a certain amount of dignity because of widows' authority over their sons and the respect which sons owed to their mothers.[131] Williams thought that De Guignes' statement "that though their lot is less happy than that of their sisters in Europe, their ignorance of a better state renders their present

[125] Huc, op. cit., 445; Williams, op. cit., II, 61 et seq.; Davis, op. cit., I, 326 et seq.; Doolittle, op. cit., I, 106 et seq.

[126] "China," No. Brit. R. (1847), 7, p. 416 et seq.; Lay, op. cit., 57.

[127] Blakiston, op. cit., 109.

[128] Langdon, op. cit., 36; "Traits of Chinese Character," C. Repos. (1842), 11, p. 84.

[129] Lay, op. cit., 59; Henrietta Shuck, Scenes in China (Philadelphia, 1853), p. 163; George Smith, op. cit., 107; "The Paper Wall of China," All the Year (1860), 3, p. 321; "Traits of Chinese Character," op. cit.

[130] Davis, op. cit., I, 322.   [131] Ibid.

or prospective one supportable," was applicable to the condition of Chinese women in the middle of the nineteenth century.[132]

GENERAL CHARACTER OF CHINESE SOCIETY

The most dominant influence in Chinese society was the principle of filial piety. It was the starting point of Chinese virtue and social duty, the basis of family ties, government, and the fundamental law of the country.[133] According to the rules of filial piety, children must revere their parents, give them unlimited obedience, and provide them with all needs. Marriage did not release a son from obligation but rather extended it to his wife.[134] The most distinguished philosophers taught this doctrine of filial piety by precept and example from the remotest ages.[135] Every crime, every act against the property or life of any person was treated as filial disobedience. Acts of virtue, devotion, compassion toward the unfortunate, commercial honor, and bravery in battle were attributed to filial piety.[136] Westerners greatly admired the obedience of the Chinese to their parents. They considered filial piety the redeeming feature of their national character.[137]

Occidentals did not have a great respect for Chinese morality.[138] While it abounded in the noblest maxims which were founded on eternal truths, it was an incomplete system of ethics. It praised the observance of private and public duties but left the universal rights of man—that is, social justice, untouched. It proclaimed the reciprocal obligations between man and man but had no valid sanction to give them. It protested against abuse of power yet could not prevent it. According to Chinese ethics, every human being was responsible for his own acts, but

---

[132] Williams, *op. cit.*, II, 62 *et seq.*
[133] "The Paper Wall of China," *op. cit.*, 323.
[134] Holman, *op. cit.*, 214 *et seq.*
[135] Meadows, *Desultory Notes*, p. 206.
[136] Huc, *op. cit.*, 54.
[137] William Gillespie, *The Land of Sinim* (Edinburgh, 1854), p. 15 *et seq.*; Meadows, *op. cit.*, 205 *et seq.*; Kidd, *op. cit.*, 190 *et seq.*; "Celestial Intelligence," *Chamb. J.* (1850), 14, p. 170; "Manners and Customs of China," *Liv. Age* (1874), 122, p. 97.
[138] De Fonblanque, *op. cit.*, 236; Williams, *op. cit.*, II, 96; Holman, *op. cit.*, 213 *et seq.*

the son became the compulsory partner of his father's crime. Filial piety was exalted in China, but the wife, mother, and daughter were supposedly in a state of degradation. Such is the darker side of Chinese morality.[139] Other writers, viewing the subject in a more favorable light, thought that the positive features of Chinese moral teachings contributed toward high ethical standards.[140]

A feature of society, which caused much comment, was the prevalence of extreme poverty; beggars were everywhere.[141] Cooke did not think they were as numerous in the large Chinese cities as in Naples, and Davis believed there were no more in Canton than in the large cities of Europe.[142]

A general impression prevailed that the Chinese were not charitable, but probably as many institutions for orphans and other helpless persons were found in China as in Christian countries. Charity organizations existed in almost every important city.[143] Public opinion, however, expected people in easy circumstances to support their relatives. The state refused to aid those who could work or had families able to take care of them.[144]

Another criticism constantly levelled at the Chinese was their entire lack of sanitation. Personal cleanliness was not a strong point. The style of dress made laundering infrequent, and they used little linen in their households. Skin diseases were, therefore, common.[145] Some Westerners did mention bath houses, which contributed toward cleanliness in the cities.[146] Chinese towns and cities were far behind those of the West in sanitation and hygiene. Writers often described the filthy con-

[139] "The Paper Wall of China," op. cit., 320; Kidd, op. cit., 192 et seq.
[140] Gillespie, op. cit., 122; Lay, op. cit., 52; J. L. Nevius, op. cit., 288.
[141] Charles Taylor, Five Years in China (London, 1842), p. 99 et seq.; Bingham, op. cit., II, 281; Robert Fortune, Two Visits to the Tea Countries of China (London, 1853), II, 254 et seq.; Doolittle, op. cit., II, 259 et seq.
[142] Cooke, op. cit., 361; Davis, op. cit., I, 457.
[143] Milne, op. cit., 39 et seq.; J. L. Nevius, op. cit., 213 et seq.
[144] Davis, op. cit., I, 458.
[145] Charles Gutzlaff, Journal (London, 1840), p. 269; Bingham, op. cit., I, 272; Williams, op. cit., II, 34.
[146] "The Medical Missionary in China," Liv. Age (1869), 69, p. 254; Fortune, op. cit., I, 197; Milne, op. cit., 191.

dition of the streets. Yet in spite of such conditions, the Chinese were very healthy. Their freedom from epidemics was a matter of wonder to European travellers.[147]

The most remarkable and unique characteristic of the social order in China was the absence of well-defined classes. Some observers saw no trace of a noble class. Others pointed out two kinds of nobility, the one hereditary and the other official. The first group consisted of all who were related to the ruling family. They lived within the confines of the Imperial Palace and had little influence on the country as a whole. The real nobility of the "Celestial Empire," however, consisted of the mandarins, a numerous, brilliant aristocracy. The most influential groups in China next to the learned class included the bankers and the merchants. Just below them in the social scale were the manufacturers. The actual tillers of the soil, farmers and farm laborers, had the lowest position.[148]

As no definite line was drawn between these different groups, no caste system existed. Only the sons of barbers, players, and persons of a few other proscribed occupations, were excluded by birth from an equal competition for all the dignities of the state.[149]

PUBLIC EXAMINATIONS

The chief basis of rank in Chinese society was "cultivated talent."[150] A literary person, though poor, was much more respected and had a greater practical influence than the wealthy but comparatively illiterate merchant or landed proprietor.[151] Westerners were profoundly impressed by the stress put upon education and learning. Emerson praised the high esteem of

---

[147] Ibid., 317; W. L. G. Smith, op. cit., 100; Williams, op. cit., II, 12; Gillespie, op. cit., 239 et seq.

[148] Alexandre Bonacossi, La Chine et les Chinois (Paris, 1847), 102 et seq.; M. J. L. Hervey-Saint-Denys, La Chine devant l'Europe (Paris, 1859), p. 35; Meadows, The Chinese and Their Rebellions, p. 399. Slavery existed in China, but little was written on the subject. See James Holman, Travels in China (2nd ed., London, 1840), p. 269; J. F. Davis, China (London, 1857), I, 288; William Gillespie, The Land of Sinim (Edinburgh, 1854), p. 121; Justus Doolittle, Social Life of the Chinese (New York, 1865), II, 213.

[149] Meadows, op. cit., 398.   [150] Davis, op. cit., I, 261.

[151] Meadows, Desultory Notes, p. 137.

the Chinese for education. By requiring candidates for public
office to pass comprehensive literary examinations, they made
education an indispensable passport to the higher levels of
society.[152]

As the highest officials of the Empire were theoretically the
best scholars regardless of social rank a uniform system of instruction was given in Chinese schools for all classes. It was
based upon the reading and the explanation of a small number
of texts which were supposed to contain all the essential documents of morals, philosophy, and legislation. Only a few persons could hope to achieve after long and serious study complete
mastery of these difficult books. After they had passed a series
of examinations, the successful candidates gained the coveted
literary degrees. Only a small number received the very highest
degree. The aim of this system was to group around the throne
the greatest intellectuals of the Empire. Even though the
Chinese carried their system too far according to European
ideas, their method of choosing civil servants, even with all of
its defects, was of special interest to Western countries which in
the middle of the nineteenth century were devising means to
test the merits of applicants for government positions.[153]

The Chinese method of filling public offices had many advantages from the Western point of view. It caused education
and liberal culture to be esteemed and was responsible for a
better class of officials. The system also tended to limit the
Emperor's authority. Without competitive examinations the
more important offices might have been filled by hereditary
nobles, and the minor posts might have been farmed out to
Imperial favorites.[154] The choice of officials by examinations
prevented legislation in favor of special classes. Government
employees came from all ranks of society.[155]

[152]*Reception and Entertainment of the Chinese Embassy by the City of
Boston* (Boston, 1868), p. 52 *et seq.*
[153] Édouard Biot, *Essai sur l'histoire de l'instruction publique en Chine*
(Paris, 1847), p. 1 *et seq.*
[154] W. A. P. Martin, "Competitive Examinations in China," *No. Amer. R.*
(1870), 111, p. 75; J. L. Nevius, *op. cit.*, 61 *et seq.*
[155] R. H. Graves, "Chinese Triennial Examinations," *Overland* (1872),
8, p. 265.

Since the earliest contacts between the East and the West, the French had spoken favorably of the Chinese civil service. The Jesuits and, later, Voltaire greatly admired China's Government. If there ever was a country, said Voltaire, in which life, honor, and property had been protected by law, it was the Chinese Empire. Brunetière, in the *Revue des Deux Mondes*, wrote that the French plan of a civil service, whose personnel was recruited by competitive examinations, undoubtedly owed its origin to the Chinese system which was popularized in France by the philosophers especially Voltaire.[156]

This system, according to Meadows, its most ardent admirer, was *the* institution of China and was responsible for the unification of the different provinces into a homogeneous whole. It had produced a "fundamental belief" throughout the body politic. It was through this system of examinations that Confucian morality and philosophy became the creed of all Chinese aspirants for public office.[157]

During the controversy over civil service reform in England from about 1830 to 1853 when the patronage system was overthrown and the merit system was introduced,[158] much was heard about the example of China. Meadows, in his *Desultory Notes on the Government and People of China*, the main object of which was to urge the adoption of public service competitive examinations, gave a complete description of the Chinese system and also outlined an elaborate plan for its introduction into England. This system, if applied to the different branches of the executive, Meadows argued, would greatly improve the administration of that department of government.[159]

[156] F. Brunetière, "L'Orient dans la littérature française," *RDM* (1906), 35, p. 699 *et seq.*; W. L. Schwartz, *The Imaginative Interpretation of the Far East in Modern French Literature, 1800-1925* (Paris, 1927), p. 2. (The French plan of civil service was put into operation before 1840).

[157] "Administrative Reform à la Chinoise," *Sat. R.* (1856), 2, p. 357.

[158] Herbert Welsh, *A Sketch of the History of Civil Service Reform in England and in the United States* (Philadelphia, 1889), p. 6.

[159] Meadows, *The Chinese and Their Rebellions*, pp. xxii, xlvi, 607. Meadows would not introduce the examination method into the legislative and judicial branches of the Government because England owed its "freedom and greatness" to Parliament, the Bench, and the Bar. Meadows, *op. cit.*, xxv.

Although Trevelyan and Northcote, who were appointed by the Crown to look into the condition of the British civil service, made only casual references to Chinese examinations in their *Report,* the opponents of their plan for reform through the introduction of competitive examinations denounced the system as foreign and Chinese.[160] It was also pointed out that such examinations might be all right in theory, but in practice this method of choosing candidates would not work. In China officials were notoriously corrupt, and money would buy almost any office. Western countries, others argued, should borrow the idea of the competitive examinations from China and develop it to suit their individual needs rather than discard the whole method because China had not been able to put its theories into practice.[161]

In the United States the question of civil service reform was first put before Congress, December 20, 1865, when Jenckes of Rhode Island introduced his first reform bill into the House of Representatives. Although the majority of Congress greeted his plan with scorn and the first act for civil service reform was not passed until 1883, public opinion favored the movement. As in England, many advocates of the spoils system protested against the use of examinations to determine candidates' fitness for office because they considered such a plan Chinese, foreign, and un-American. The Civil Service Commission in its report, however, declared that "with no intention of recommending either the religion or the imperialism of China, we could not see why the fact that the most enlightened and enduring government of the Eastern world had required an examination as to the merits of candidates for office, should any more deprive the American people of that advantage, if it might be an advantage, than the facts that Confucius had taught

[160] *Papers Relating to the Re-organization of the Civil Service* (London, 1855), pp. 47, 159; *Civil Service Reform, Observations on the Report of Sir C. E. Trevelyan and Sir S. H. Northcote on the "Organization of the Permanent Civil Service," with Quotations from the Leading Journals, the Debate in the House of Lords . . . by a Civil Subaltern* (London), p. 42 et seq.

[161] R. H. Graves, "Chinese Triennial Examinations," *Overland* (1872), 8, p. 265.

political morality, and the people of China had read books, used the compass, gunpowder, and the multiplication table, during centuries when this continent was a wilderness, should deprive our people of those conveniences."[162]

Whether or not the Chinese system of civil service influenced civil service reform in the West especially in England[163] and America in the nineteenth century is a matter of opinion and further research. It is sufficient to note, however, that with the timely publication of Meadows' *Desultory Notes on the Government and People of China* which explained the Chinese system of competitive examinations and a few articles in periodicals on the same subject, the British and American public became familiar to some extent with the Chinese method of selecting government officials while civil service reform was an important issue.

"CHINESE SOCIALISM"

In the middle of the nineteenth century when there was much agitation for all kinds of reform, social as well as political, an article was published on Chinese socialism in *Chamber's Journal* and reprinted in *Living Age*.[164] This paper was probably inspired by Huc's comment which was quoted at the beginning of the article. He wrote: "It is a curious fact that the greater part of those social theories which have lately thrown the public mind of France into a ferment, and which are represented as the sublime results of the progress of human reason, are but exploded Chinese Utopias, which agitated the Celestial Empire centuries ago."[165]

In the eleventh century, Wang An-shih, one of the most prominent statesmen of his time and also a literary scholar of considerable fame, undertook to distribute equitably the resources of the Empire so as to give every one the greatest possible amount of material happiness. To prevent oppression

[162] *House Executive Documents, 43rd Congress, 1st sess.* (1873-74), Doc. 221, p. 24.
[163] Competitive Civil Service Examinations were introduced into India in 1854.
[164] "Chinese Socialism," *Chamb. J.* (1855), 24, pp. 93-95; *Liv. Age* (1855), 46, pp. 691-94.   [165] Huc, *op. cit.*, 307.

by any social group, the state was to assume control over agriculture, industry, and commerce so that the working classes would not be crushed by the wealthy. During the reign of Jen Tsung, Wang An-shih was allowed to carry out his plans. Upon the death of this Emperor, the reactionary forces which were led by Ssu-ma Kuang came into power and tried to wipe out all traces of the reforms. They were again put into practice only to be abandoned shortly.[166]

Wang An-shih's theories were said to be similar to the principles of the French and English Socialists, although the Europeans were not influenced by or even familiar with the Chinese reformer's ideas. It is only in the twentieth century that Chinese historians have recognized Wang An-shih's abilities as a statesman and Western scholars have studied his theories.[167]

[166] H. Kopsch, "Wang An-shih, the 'Innovator,'" *CR* (1874-75), 2, pp. 29-33, 74-80.
[167] T. K. Chuan, "Wang An-shih and His Critics," *The China Critic* (1935), 10, p. 15 *et seq.*; H. R. Williamson, *Wang An-shih, A Chinese Statesman and Educationalist of the Sung Dynasty* (London, 1935-37), I, Preface, p. viii.

CHAPTER IX

LANGUAGE AND LITERATURE

KNOWLEDGE of the language and literature of China was limited to a comparatively small number of missionaries, a few consular officials who during their residence in the East had studied Chinese, and certain scholars who had delved into the vast field of Chinese literature in the Oriental collections of the West, especially in Paris.

While the date, 1840, tends to mark a turning point in the general Western attitude toward China, no abrupt change took place in the progress of literary researches. The work which Abel Rémusat began in the decade of the twenties, French scholars continued throughout the nineteenth century, and English and German Sinologists began to make more extensive researches in language and literature. But scientific study of Chinese on a large scale obviously had not advanced very far by 1840.[1] The philologists as such were slow to become interested in Chinese. Max Müller was the only important philologist who recognized the significance of the Chinese language to students.[2]

Many circumstances made the study of Chinese imperative for Europeans during this period. First for cultural reasons this long neglected branch of learning should have been studied in the interest of comparative philology and literature. Without an adequate knowledge of this language, it was impossible for Europeans to conduct researches in Chinese history and literature. To understand Chinese civilization, it was absolutely necessary for Westerners to be familiar with these subjects. Not only could Westerners appreciate Chinese theories of economics

---

[1] T. T. Meadows, *Desultory Notes on the Government and People of China* (London, 1847), p. 25; Samuel Kidd, *China, or, Illustrations of the Symbols, Philosophy, Antiquities, Customs, Superstitions, Laws, Government, Education and Literature of the Chinese* (London, 1841), p. 1.

[2] Joseph Edkins, "Chinese Philology," *CR* (1872), 1, p. 184.

and ethics through the medium of the Chinese language, but they could also communicate a knowledge of Western literature, science, law, and religion to the Chinese. The distinguished missionary scholars devoted their time and energy to learning the language primarily to present to the Chinese the doctrines of Christianity. Westerners were rapidly extending their trade relations with China, and a command of Chinese might greatly expedite all commercial intercourse. It might also lessen misunderstandings between the East and the West.[3]

Chinese was considered extremely difficult to learn. Even linguists asserted as late as 1862 that it required almost a lifetime to master this language.[4] Callery said that twenty years of study convinced him that a European could never become as proficient in Chinese as a native.[5] A few writers, however, minimized its difficulties. One writer said that Chinese was an easy language to speak and understand and required a shorter period of study than French, German, or other European languages.[6] Abel Rémusat predicted that in time Chinese would become as easy a language to learn as other Oriental and, perhaps, certain European languages.[7] Williams said that the acquisition of sufficient Chinese to speak intelligently, to write, and to read with some facility was not so herculean a task as foreigners had supposed it to be, but this limited knowledge could not be gained without diligent study.[8]

Because Chinese was so different from European languages, its peculiarities brought forth many comments from Western authors. In Williams's opinion, Chinese was undoubtedly the

[3] Kidd, *op. cit.*, 15; James Holman, *Travels in China* (2nd ed., London, 1840), p. 295 *et seq.*; Robert K. Douglas, *The Language and Literature of China* (London, 1875), p. 58.
[4] "The Chinese Language and Literature," *Nat. Quar. R.* (1862), 5, p. 3; "Der chinesische Roman," *Europa* (1864), p. 1127.
[5] J. M. Callery, *Li-Ki, ou mémorial des rites* (Turin, 1853), Introduction, p. xx.
[6] Alfred Lister, "On the Supposed Difficulty of Chinese," *CR* (1873-74), 2, p. 104; E. R. Huc, *The Chinese Empire* (New ed., London, 1859), p. 207.
[7] Abel Rémusat, *Élémens de la grammaire chinoise* (Paris, 1857), Preface, p. v.
[8] S. W. Williams, *The Middle Kingdom* (New York, 1848), I, 498 *et seq.*

most ancient language then spoken, and probably with the single exception of the Hebrew the oldest written language.[9] The characteristics, said Huc, which distinguished Chinese from all other languages were its originality, its great antiquity, its immutability, and its wide use in the most densely populated country of Asia.[10]

Europeans pointed out what they considered glaring defects in Chinese. Its grammar was extremely limited; it had no rules, inflection, or agglutination. The relation of words to each other in a sentence could be determined only by their position.[11] Another weakness of the Chinese language from the Western point of view was its vague expression of time. They supposedly had ample words to express past, present, and future time, but Chinese writers, to achieve terseness of expression, discarded every unessential word particularly those denoting time.[12] The Chinese language was, in the opinion of Staunton, who admired many of its features, not adequate for logical accuracy and inductive reasoning.[13] Wingrove Cooke, the English journalist, branded it the most intricate, cumbrous, and unwieldy vehicle of thought ever developed by any people.[14]

Although Europeans, especially the more or less casual students of the language were emphasizing its defects, scholars who had made a thorough study of Chinese philology and literature were profoundly impressed by the beauty and simplicity of the language. Its richness in synonyms and metaphors and its brevity and terseness of expression appealed to them. These features were largely lost in translation. Because the Chinese had studied the art of poetry longer and more extensively than any other people, delicacy, grace, and refinement naturally became most conspicuous attributes of the language.[15] Contrary to prevailing opinion, a leading French Sinologist argued that

[9] *Ibid.*, I, 460.   [10] Huc, *op. cit.*, 201.

[11] J. F. Davis, *China: A General Description* (New ed., London, 1857), II, 110; Douglas, *op. cit.*, 10 *et seq.*   [12] Williams, *op. cit.*, I, 497.

[13] G. T. Staunton, *Miscellaneous Notices Relating to China* (2nd ed., London, 1822-50), p. 65.

[14] "China and the War," *Quar. R.* (1860), 107, p. 86.

[15] Staunton, *op. cit.*, p. 65.

Chinese was not a confused jargon without rules but a beautiful and noble language important as a political and commercial medium and beginning to be appreciated by Westerners as a great literary language.[16] For twenty centuries it had fulfilled all requirements of thought sufficiently to allow the Chinese authors to discuss intelligibly all literary and scientific topics.[17]

Various branches of Chinese literature, which Europeans divided into three or four categories, were written in rather definite styles. Rémusat observed three, the "style antique" found in the ancient *Classics*, the "style littéraire" in the compositions of the candidates for examinations and in similar treatises, and the "langue des magistrats" or "langue mandarinique," the style in which the instructions and proclamations of the Government were written.[18] Meadows spoke of still another form of the Chinese written language, the "business style." While the ancient style was so concise as to become vague, the business style, although concise and terse, was clear. This style was used in statistical works, the collected statutes of the Empire, and the penal code. The addresses of the high mandarins and the Boards at Peking to the Emperor, the edicts of the latter, and all mercantile legal papers, such as contracts for the purchase of commodities, were drawn up in the business style. Still another form noted by Meadows was the "familiar." It lay between the business and the colloquial and was found in the lighter forms of literature. It is the least concise of all the Chinese written styles. Although Westerners often commented upon the categories of style into which Chinese literature was divided, they did admit that the lines of demarcation between these classifications were not well defined. Historical writings were composed in a style which was a mixture of the ancient and business styles, and many works could scarcely be assigned to any particular form.[19]

[16] Antoine Bazin, "Mémoire sur les principes généraux du Chinois vulgaire," *JA* (1845), 5, p. 346.

[17] Stanislas Julien, *Syntaxe nouvelle de la langue chinoise* (Paris, 1869-70), I, 1 *et seq.*

[18] Rémusat, *op. cit.*, 35 *et seq.*; W. A. P. Martin, "Remarks on the Style of Chinese Prose," *New Eng.* (1872), 31, p. 234 *et seq.*

[19] Meadows, *op. cit.*, 14 *et seq.*

Westerners who had studied Chinese literature appreciated its conciseness, which was the most significant general characteristic of their literary style. Next in importance was the Chinese love for the law of symmetry. It was the expression of correlated ideas in corresponding or parallel phrases. Every sentence was balanced with the utmost precision. The most obvious defect in the Chinese mode of composition was a servile imitation which not only circumscribed the thoughts and ideas of literary men but made their writings appear stilted and affected. Notwithstanding their tendency to imitation, Chinese authors, an American writer contended, were as individualistic as those of other countries. If they had a certain amount of original genius, they gave their writing the stamp of their own individuality. If they were not creative, they reproduced in their own composition those traits of early authors who most impressed and influenced them.[20]

From 1840 to 1876 several translations of examples of imaginative literature were made by European scholars who were distinctly interested in the novels, drama, and poetry of the Chinese.[21] Authors of general works usually devoted a chapter or more to the subject, but their material was taken largely from the works of the comparatively few translators and students of this field of literature.[22] Articles containing the critical views of Sinologists,[23] a short Chinese tale,[24] an abstract

[20] W. A. P. Martin, *op. cit.*, 238 *et seq.*

[21] Sir John Bowring, *Hwa Tsien Ki, the Flowery Scroll* (London, 1868); J. F. Davis, *Chinese Novels* (New ed., London, 1843); Stanislas Julien, *Yu Kiao Li; ou, les deux cousines* (2nd ed., Paris, 1864); *P'ing-Chan-Ling-Yen ou les deux jeunes filles lettrées* (Paris, 1860); *Les Avadânas contes et apologiques indiens . . . suivis de fables, de poésies et de nouvelles chinoises* (Paris, 1859), II, 125-251, III, 272 pp.; *Nouvelles chinoises* (Paris, 1860); Guillard d'Arcy, *Hao-Khieou-Tchouan, ou la femme accomplie* (Paris, 1842); Théodore Pavie, *San Koue-Tchy, ou histoire des trois royaumes* (Paris, 1845); Antoine Bazin, *Le Pi-Pa-Ki ou l'histoire du luth* (Paris, 1841); M. J. L. Hervey-Saint-Denys, *Poésies de l'époque des Thang* (Paris, 1862).

[22] Williams, *op. cit.*, I, Chap. XII; Paul E. D. Forgues, *La Chine ouverte; aventures d'un fan-kouei dans le pays de Tsin* (Paris, 1845), p. 287 *et seq.*

[23] "Chinese Literature," *For. Quar. R.* (1841), 26, pp. 127-44.

[24] "Wang Keaou Lwan, A Chinese Tale of Bygone Years," *Chamb. J.* (1847), 7, pp. 179-83; "The Lost Child," *Liv. Age* (1860), 64, pp. 43-47.

or criticism of a Chinese novel,[25] or excerpts from various Chinese dramas[26] were published occasionally in periodicals. But the public in America, England, Germany, and even France, where Chinese *belles lettres* received much attention from the more serious students of Oriental literature, was not deeply interested in the polite literature of the East.[27]

The main reason for Western interest in Chinese fiction and drama was the richness of a large number of tales, romances, and novels, both social and historical, in the most minute details on social customs and manners.[28] As early as 1756, Thomas Percy discovered among the papers of Wilkinson, a neighbor, an English translation of the Chinese novel, *Hau Kiou Choaan*, with the exception of the last quarter which was in Portuguese. This translation was made by James Wilkinson, an English merchant at Canton. Percy edited and published the English translation which he had completed in 1761, and French, German, and Dutch translations of his version were soon published. Since 1761 when the first important example of Chinese imaginative literature was printed in a European language, Westerners have been interested in Chinese novels as mirrors of life and manners rather than as specimens of creative art.[29] Davis agreed with Julien who said, "It seems to me that before treating questions of high erudition . . . it would be better to translate works . . . which will enable us to understand the history, religious customs, usages, and literature of the Chinese."[30] West-

[25] "A Chinese Love Story," *Fraser* (1874), 10, pp. 484-503, 585-610; J. T. Doyen, "A Leaf from a Chinese Novel," *Overland* (1868), 1, pp. 95-98; Edmund Le Blant, "Les deux jeunes filles lettrées," *Corres.* (1861), 53, pp. 402-9; E. Egger, "Les deux cousines," *Corres.* (1864), 63, pp. 564-72; "Der chinesische Roman," *Europa* (1864), pp. 1127-31; H. Hensler, "Chinesische Novellen," *Unterhaltungen* (1859), pp. 209-14.

[26] "The Literature of the Chinese," *Chamb. J.* (1844), 2, pp. 290-93.

[27] Douglas, *op. cit.*, 117; Julien, *Les Avadânas*, I, Avertissement du traducteur, p. vii; "A Chinese Love Story," *op. cit.*, 484.

[28] "Der chinesische Roman," *Europa* (1864), p. 1127; Davis, *China*, II, 161; *Chinese Miscellanies* (London, 1865), p. 91.

[29] Ch'en Shou-yi, "Thomas Percy and His Chinese Studies," *CSPSR* (1936), 20, p. 202 *et seq.*; W. F. Mayers, "Chinese Works of Fiction," *N. & Q. on C. & J.* (1867), 1, p. 154.

[30] Davis, *Chinese Miscellanies*, p. 72 *et seq.*

erners could gain more information on Chinese private life and manners by reading one novel than by spending a lifetime among the Orientals, wrote Stent.[31]

NOVELS

Novels concerned with social life met with considerable favor among European critics. "It is in picturing the details of social life," observed Abel Rémusat, "that the authors of Chinese romance excel, approaching very nearly in this respect to Richardson and Fielding, but above all, to Smollett and Miss Burney. Like these novelists, the Chinese produce a high degree of illusion by the truth of their portraiture of the passions and of character. Their personages possess all possible reality. One seems to make their acquaintance by reading of their actions, by hearing them talk, and by following the minute particulars into which their conversations enter."[32]

The Fortunate Union[33] is a good example of an accurate portrayal of Chinese life and manners. The interest and bustle of the scene, the spirit of the dialogue, the strong delineation of the characters, and the moral which is conveyed throughout created a favorable impression of Chinese taste. The story begins with an act of generous devotion on the part of the hero. The gratitude of the person whom he has aided enables him to triumph over his enemies. The profligate, the malicious, and the base, after they have exhausted all their resources, meet with their just rewards. The righteous through prudence and courage ultimately win out. In the hero's and the heroine's conversations are clearly set forth the principles of Confucian philosophy with its profound admiration for virtue and its emphasis on self-sufficiency.[34]

Another novel, *Les deux cousines,* noted for its grace and

---

[31] G. C. Stent, "Chinese Lyrics," *JNCBRAS* (1871-72), 7, p. 94.

[32] "The Literature of the Chinese," *Chamb. J.* (1844), 2, p. 292; Davis, *China,* II, 163.

[33] Translated by Sir John Francis Davis into English and by Guillard d'Arcy into French under the title of *La Femme accomplie.*

[34] Davis, *op. cit.,* II, 163 *et seq.; Chinese Miscellanies,* p. 105; "The Literature of the Chinese," *op. cit.*

purity of style,[35] is a picture of middle-class manners. The author, a "man of humor, intellect and cultivation" treats of small and everyday events. War and politics form no part of the book; it contains no sensational occurrences. Successes and failures in the examinations, upon which public promotion is based, play an important part. The description of the innocent enjoyment of wine and poetry, flowers and beautiful scenery, and the suavity and elegant manners of the characters creates a pleasant atmosphere throughout the book.[36] On the whole this novel was considered the best Chinese novel by Europeans.[37]

A novel not so well known outside of France as the two mentioned above was the *Les deux jeunes filles lettrées* which was translated into French by Julien in 1860. One critic highly commended the novel because of its intrinsic natural charm and its faithful picture of good Chinese society in which letters were highly cultivated. The composition and style of this particular novel were much admired. Its arrangement was said to campare favorably with any European novel.[38]

The Dream of the Red Chamber is considered one of the greatest pieces of Chinese fiction, but it is at a great disadvantage because of its bulk.[39] The length, the large number of characters, the complicated and tedious introductory chapters, and the prolix[40] and minute style were said to make the novel very monotonous to the general reader. It does, however, give an excellent idea of the life of the upper classes. This novel, Lister wrote, was a work of art of which any nation might be proud.[41]

Historical romances form an important class of fiction. The most renowned novel of this group is the *San Kuo Chih Yen-ye*, which is a popular version of the *History of the Three King-*

[35] "Nouvelles littéraires, les deux cousines," *J. Savants* (1863), p. 675.
[36] "A Chinese Love Story," *op. cit.*, 484 *et seq.*
[37] Alfred Lister, "An Hour with a Chinese Romance," *CR* (1872-73), 1, p. 287.
[38] Jules Barthélemy-Saint-Hilaire, "Les deux jeunes filles lettrées," *J. Savants* (1861), p. 147.   [39] Lister, *op. cit.*
[40] J. T. Doyen, "A Leaf from a Chinese Novel," *Overland* (1868), 1, p. 95.
[41] Lister, *op. cit.*; Mayers, *op. cit.*, 166 *et seq.*

doms.[42]   The earliest of its class, it served as a model for subsequent authors.   Chinese critics praised its absolute perfection of style.[43]   Because of the popularity of this novel in China, it appealed to Western readers.   Both English and French writers made numerous comments on the work.   No complete translation of it was made, however, by 1875.[44]

In every historical novel are found certain types of characters, the wily and favored counsellor, the plain-spoken but unappreciated minister of state, the sovereign either founding a dynasty by martial virtues or losing a throne through effeminacy and weakness, the priest with flowing robes concealing a repertory of magic arts, and finally the champion or hero who brandishes sword, lance, and club, all of enormous size and weight.[45]

A characteristic of Chinese fiction which impressed European critics was what one critic called the "tame extravagance" of both life and style.   All was ceremonious; everything was strictly confined within customary channels.   The modes and impulses of human life might be compared to canals rather than to rivers.   They were artificial, methodical, and joined in formal networks.   Human life, therefore, was supposed to be carefully regulated in every respect.   With all phases of human activity being made to conform to specific rules, the treatment of emotions and sentiments was according to a definite pattern. Another explanation offered for the so-called tameness of effect is that in the depiction of emotions there is a lack of perspective. The trivial compliments of life were said by Westerners to be so emphatic that Chinese writers had left no adequate means of expression when stronger feelings were described.[46]   The chief defects in Chinese romances and novels consisted in their

[42] *Ibid.,* 102 *et seq.*   [43] *Ibid.*

[44] Stanislas Julien, *Nouvelles historiques* (1834).   This work contained one chapter from the *History of the Three Kingdoms.* Théodore Pavie in 1845 published one volume of a translation supposed to include five or six volumes.   See Mayers, *op. cit.,* 1, p. 103.   A more recent translation is C. H. Brewitt-Taylor's, *San Kuo or Romance of the Three Kingdoms* (Shanghai, 1925).

[45] Mayers, *op. cit.,* I, 87.

[46] "Hwa Tsien Ki," *Liv. Age* (1868), 99, p. 635 *et seq.*

long descriptions of trifling incidents and various places and their numerous characters. Because of their minute details, Chinese novels were irksome and tedious for Western readers.[47]

DRAMA

The drama also comprises an important part of Chinese literature; the Chinese were especially fond of the theatre.[48] The most celebrated plays belong to a collection dating from the thirteenth century and entitled the "Hundred Plays of the Youen Dynasty." Some of these plays were translated into European languages by Julien, Davis, and Bazin.[49] As late as 1816 the only example of the Chinese theatre in a European language was *L'Orphelin de la famille de Tchao*, a tragedy composed of verse and prose and incompletely translated by Prémare. In 1816 Sir John Francis Davis translated a comedy entitled *An Heir in his Old Age*, with those sections in verse omitted. Brugière de Sorsum put Davis's version into French shortly afterwards. The play which Prémare translated much earlier, Davis put into English in 1829 under the title of the *Sorrows of Han*, but in this work the translator also omitted the poetic passages.

Julien decided to give Europeans a Chinese drama in its entirety. In 1832 he published a comedy, the *Cercle de Craie*, with both the prose and verse translated. In 1834, his translation of *L'Orphelin de Tchao* appeared. He also translated the first act of a very famous drama, *L'Histoire du pavillon d'occident*. Bazin added to the limited knowledge of Chinese dramatic art in the West by publishing in 1838 a volume, *Théâtre chinois*, which contained four complete plays, and in 1841 his version of a celebrated drama, *P'i-Pa-Chi* or *Story of the Guitar*.[50] These few translations, the critical commentaries accompanying them, and articles, published by these scholars

[47] Williams, *op. cit.*, I, 563.   [48] Huc, *op. cit.*, 169.

[49] Douglas, *op. cit.*, 109; "The Literature of the Chinese," *Chamb. J.* (1844), 2, p. 290 *et seq.*; Williams, *op. cit.*, I, p. 581.

[50] Charles Magnin, "Théâtre chinois," *J. Savants* (1842), p. 257 *et seq.* The article attempts to summarize European knowledge of the Chinese theatre. Material is drawn largely from Bazin's writings.

in learned journals, furnished the basis for European opinion of Chinese drama during the years preceding and following the date of 1840.[51]

General descriptive works, travellers' accounts, and magazine articles often refer to the Chinese theatre but only to the more superficial aspects. Whatever literary criticism they give is usually drawn from the opinions of the French scholars, Bazin, Julien, and Rémusat, and Davis, the English diplomat and Sinologist.[52]

Westerners made various classifications of Chinese drama, but Bazin maintained that the Chinese recognize seven different kinds of dramatic works. Historical dramas form an important category, and other plays draw their themes from the practices of Taoism, a system of philosophy which in the course of time became more like a superstitious religion. Five comedies of character, the *Prodigal Child*, the *Buddhist*, the *Libertin*, the *Miser*, and the *Fanatic* are in the repertory of the dynasty of Youen. The comedies of intrigue in which the courtesans play an important part are more numerous than the comedies of character. Another group of dramas which Bazin classified as domestic concern the ordinary affairs of life and portray the customs of the lower classes. The dialogue of these plays, which is written in the form of ordinary conversation, is a monument to the Chinese spoken language of the fourteenth century. Six mythological dramas were included in the collec-

---

[51] Antoine Bazin, "Le Siècle des Youên," *JA* (1850), 15, pp. 5-48, 101-58, 16, pp. 428-75, (1851), 17, pp. 5-51, 163-211, 309-77, 497-533, 18, pp. 247-89, 517-52, (1852), 19, pp. 435-519; Davis, *Chinese Miscellanies*, p. 91 *et seq.*; G. de Bourboulon, "Le Théâtre . . . en Chine," *Corres.* (1862), 56, pp. 69-99.

[52] Julia Corner, *The History of China and India, Pictorial and Descriptive* (3rd ed., London, 1847), p. 115 *et seq.*; James Holman, *Travels in China* (2nd ed., London, 1840), p. 244; G. T. Lay, *The Chinese As They Are* (Albany, 1843), p. 40 *et seq.*; *The People of China* (Philadelphia, 1844), p. 153; W. T. Power, *Recollections of Three Years' Residence in China* (London, 1853), p. 191; H. C. Sirr, *China and the Chinese* (London, 1849), II, 128; Williams, *op. cit.*, I, 581; "Chinese Players," *House. W.* (1854), 8, pp. 281-83; "China and the Chinese," *Westm. R.* (1857), 67, p. 554 *et seq.*; "Chinese Amusements," *All the Year* (1865), 13, p. 14 *et seq.*

tion of Youen but were pronounced mediocre by Bazin. Chinese mythology, he thought, was not sufficiently poetic to furnish dramatic authors adequate materials. Lastly the *Hundred Plays of Youen* contained sixteen judicial dramas. Many of the principal incidents were found in a collection of judgments of Pao-kong, who was already popular at the beginning of the dynasty of Youen.[53] The *Cercle de craie* or the *Chalk Ring or Circle*, a judicial piece, strikingly resembled the *Judgment of Solomon*.[54] Two women claim to be the mother of a child. The judge before whom the case is brought has a chalk ring drawn on the floor of the court room into which the contested child is placed. The judge declares that the child is to be given to the woman who can pull the child outside the circle. The real mother because of her concern for the child does not exert her whole strength while the other woman succeeds in getting the child out of the ring. The wise and humane judge, who senses the situation, awards the child to its own mother.[55]

The Chinese make no regular distinction between comedy and tragedy. But the line is fairly clear. The former is characterized by the ordinary or ludicrous characters and incidents. The historical or mythological character of the personages and the grandeur and seriousness of the subject distinguish the latter.[56] The great historical dramas are, from Bazin's point of view, the most beautiful monuments of Chinese literature in the century of Youen. They give a picture of national customs which can not be found in annals and memoirs. These dramas supplement the annals by adding color and richness of design to the historians' bold, bare outline. They offer a picture filled with minute detail on Chinese society from the year 607 B.C. until the tenth century A.D.[57]

The *P'i-Pa-Chi* or *Story of the Guitar*, written under the Ming dynasty, was regarded by Westerners as the masterpiece of the Chinese theatre. The exposition of the subject in the

---

[53] Bazin, "Le Siècle des Youên," *JA* (1851), 17, p. 163 *et seq.*

[54] *Ibid.*, p. 173; Davis, *China*, II, 154.

[55] Stanislas Julien, *Hoeï-Lan-Ki ou l'histoire du cercle de craie* (London, 1832).

[56] Davis, *China*, II, 144.   [57] Bazin, *op. cit.*, 17, p. 166 *et seq.*

first scene is simple, clear, and natural; the style of the dialogue has vivacity and movement. The play holds the interest by the recital of facts, variety of incidents, and by the singular beauty of details. The characters are clearly drawn with distinct personalities. Again this drama is peculiarly valuable for those who are interested in Chinese customs. The student can obtain an exact idea of the modifications in Chinese religious opinions and philosophy from the fifteenth century to the middle of the nineteenth century.[58]

Because of much interest in drama, Western contemporary writers expected to see public theatres in China. Magnin wrote that theatrical spectacles were not found in the Orient as in the great cities of the West. But some public buildings in North China, remarked Bazin, were used for music, song, and dance. These buildings were often given over to dramatic productions. In the provinces of the South, the stages, which were erected by subscription, were only temporary.[59] Both Huc and Doolittle, Catholic and Protestant missionaries respectively, who were familiar with Chinese life and customs, commented upon the general prevalence of theatres. Doolittle wrote that no buildings existed solely for theatrical purposes as in Western lands but every temple with few exceptions had a stage.[60] Huc merely remarked that theatres were numerous. The large towns were full of them, and every little village had its theatre which was usually situated opposite its pagoda or formed a part of it.[61] The Chinese theatre was always erected simply and contained few scenic effects. Scenery was not changed during the course of production. Europeans were most agreeably impressed, however, with the elaborate stage costumes of gay silks, elaborately embroidered.[62] Westerners appreciated Chinese acting. The Orientals were said to be actors by nature;

---

[58] Antoine Bazin, *Le Pi-Pa-Ki ou l'histoire du luth* (Paris, 1841), Avertissement, p. xiv *et seq.;* "Nouvelles littéraires," *J. Savants* (1841), p. 637.

[59] Magnin, *op. cit.*, 270; Huc, *op. cit.*, 169; "Chinese Amusements," *All the Year* (1865), 13, p. 14.

[60] Justus Doolittle, *Social Life of the Chinese* (New York, 1865), II, 295.

[61] Huc, *op. cit.*, 169.

[62] Davis, *op. cit.*, II, 143; Williams, *op. cit.*, II, 85.

their inherent cunning made them observing, resourceful, and clever. These qualities enabled them to assume almost any rôle.[63]

Although students of Chinese literature admired the drama which they thought compared favorably with that of the West, Occidentals, generally speaking, pronounced Chinese plays rude and artificial.[64] The Oriental dramatists did not display those fine shades of character or bits of humor which enlivened the Western theatre.[65] A criticism not infrequently levelled at Chinese dramatic productions was their obscenity. On this point, Bazin merely commented: "Unfortunately the Chinese joke is never very fine or spiritual. It is even a little heavy and sometimes deviates from the rules of decency and decorum."[66] Because of these features, the temporary quarters for theatrical productions, and the lack of scenic effects, many Western observers considered the Chinese theatre very backward. The dramatic genius of the Chinese like other features of their civilization was supposed to have remained stationary for centuries.[67]

FOLK-LORE

Europeans were only incidentally concerned with Chinese folk-lore. A series of articles on this subject did appear in the *China Review* during 1874 and 1875.[68] The author, N. B. Dennys, attempted to do for the folk-lore of China what had been done for the same subject in other countries. General works and articles contained many scattered allusions to the myths or superstitious beliefs of China, but no systematic study of the entire subject was made before 1875.[69] Watters gave

[63] Douglas, *op. cit.*, 110.

[64] V. de Mars, "De la Musique chinoise," *RDM* (1860), 29, p. 255; G. de Bourboulon, *op. cit.*, 69 *et seq.*

[65] Power, *op. cit.*, 191 *et seq.*; Holman, *op. cit.*, 134; Lay, *op. cit.*, 43 *et seq.*

[66] Bazin, "Le Siècle des Youên," *JA* (1851), 17, p. 170; "Chinese Amusements," *All the Year* (1865), 13, p. 16; Doolittle, *op. cit.*, II, 297.

[67] Corner, *op. cit.*, 115 *et seq.*

[68] N. B. Dennys, "The Folklore of China," *CR* (1874-75), 3, pp. 269-84, 331-42; (1875-76), 4, pp. 1-9, 67-84, 139-52, 213-27, 278-93, 364-75; (1876-77), 5, pp. 41-55, 83-91. This work also appeared in a separate volume.   [69] *Ibid.*, 3, 271.

some curious information in his article on "Chinese Notions about Pigeons and Doves,"[70] and Stent, in his paper on "Chinese Legends,"[71] introduced the West to some bizarre tales and romances.[72]   Again, Dennys's investigations of Chinese folk-lore is another illustration of the inclusion of various phases of the culture of China in the realm of comparative studies.

Chinese folk-lore in its details was said to be similar to that of Europe with here and there some unexpected differences. Many of the superstitions were equally childish whether found in a Cornish hamlet or in a Chinese village, commented one author.   It is none the less interesting to find that they often existed in almost identical form in places far apart.[73]

PROVERBS

Another conspicuous feature of Chinese literature is its rich collection of proverbs.[74]   The Chinese constantly used them in their writings and conversations.   They adorned their houses by copying them on elegant scrolls, carving them on monuments, or embroidering them on banners.   Western writers have compiled lists of proverbs to show their similarity to maxims of other countries as well as to introduce this branch of literature to the West.[75]   Some of the proverbs were said to be excellent, while others were considered mediocre, but their chief value was their contribution to the knowledge of Chinese life and character.[76]

[70] T. Watters, "Chinese Notions about Pigeons and Doves," *JNCBRAS* (1867), 4, pp. 225-42.

[71] G. C. Stent, "Chinese Legends," *JNCBRAS* (1872), 7, pp. 183-95.

[72] N. B. Dennys, *op. cit.*, 3, p. 271.   [73] *Ibid.*, 274.

[74] "Chinese Proverbs," *All the Year* (1874), 32, p. 498; *Liv. Age* (1874), 123, p. 123.

[75] William Scarborough, *A Collection of Chinese Proverbs* (Shanghai, 1875); J. F. Davis, *Sketches of China* (London, 1841), II, 94-100; *China*, II, 120-26; Williams, *op. cit.*, I, 586-90; "Chinese Proverbs," *op. cit.*, 498-500; "Chinese Proverbs," *Overland* (1873), 10, pp. 82-85.

[76] William Scarborough, *A Collection of Chinese Proverbs* (Revised and enlarged ed., Shanghai, 1927), Preface; Davis, *Sketches of China*, II, 94; *China*, II, 120.

POETRY

General interest in Chinese literature naturally led to the study of poetry. The Chinese, of all people of the world, were said to be fondest of poetry; all educated Chinese wrote verse.[77] The chief treatise of this branch of literature in English was *Poeseos Sinicae Commentarii* by Sir John Francis Davis, a paper read in 1829.[78] A new and enlarged edition of this work was published in 1870.[79] Whatever ideas English speaking peoples entertained on the subject of Chinese poetry were largely derived from this particular work. *Poésies de l'époque des Thang* (1842) by the Marquis d'Hervey-Saint-Denys was well received in France and tended to stimulate interest in Chinese *belles lettres.* A few articles, the materials of which were drawn from the above cited work, were published after 1860.[80] These articles were concerned largely with the poetry of the T'ang dynasty, and were not résumés of the entire field of Chinese poetry as Davis's work was.

Occidentals did not turn their attention toward Chinese poetry until a comparatively late date. La Charme's translation of the *Book of Verse,* made about 1733, remained in manuscript form until 1830 when it was published by Julius Mohl. The gifted and versatile German poet, Friedrich Rückert put La Charme's version of the *Odes* into German in 1833. By paraphrasing the latter's imperfect translation and using the utmost poetical license, he so entirely transformed La Charme's work that scarcely any poem could be recognized as an ode from the *Shih Ching.* Cramer also made a translation of La Charme's version of the *Book of Odes* in 1844 which was much more literal than Rückert's translation. Bunsen, in his work entitled

[77] C. T. Gardner, "Chinese Verse," *CR* (1872-73), 1, pp. 248-49.
[78] J. F. Davis, "On the Poetry of the Chinese," *Transactions of the Royal Asiatic Society* (London, 1830), 2, pp. 393-461.
[79] ———, *Poeseos Sinicae Commentarii. The Poetry of the Chinese* (New ed., London, 1870).
[80] Émile Montégut, "La Poésie d'une vieille civilisation," *RDM* (1863), 44, pp. 414-45; Victor de Laprade, "Les Poètes classiques de la Chine," *Corres.* (1864), 62, pp. 413-34; Jules Barthélemy-Saint-Hilaire, "De la Poésie chinoise," *J. Savants* (1864), pp. 597-613.

Gott in der Geschichte published in 1858, included some of Rückert's and Cramer's translations of the ancient poems.[81] This work was put into English in 1868.[82] In these various forms, only fragments of the *Book of Odes* were known to Westerners, especially to English speaking peoples before James Legge's translation of the *Shih Ching* was published in 1871.[83]

The poetical value of the *Odes* has been discussed frequently by Sinologists. Roman Catholic missionaries extravagantly praised them along with other features of Chinese culture.[84] But after 1840 when many writers were extremely critical of Chinese literature and civilization, Sir John Davis and also Wells Williams maintained that the majority of the *Odes* did not go beyond the most primitive simplicity.[85] Legge wrote that a few poems had a certain pathos in their descriptions, a genuine expression of natural feelings, and a boldness of figures which appealed to the reader.[86] Although a valuable source for details on the social life of the ancient Chinese,[87] the *Shih Ching* from the Western point of view did not contain a great amount of literary merit. It was said to be little more than a collection of the national songs of ancient China.[88]

Much of the remaining poetry Davis classified as moral or didactic, and descriptive. Many poems or metrical essays have as an object the inculcation of the doctrines and precepts of the

---

[81] C. C. J. Bunsen, *Gott in der Geschichte* (Leipzig, 1857), Part II, Book III, p. 44 *et seq.*; E. J. Eitel, "The She-King," *CR* (1872-73), 1, p. 3; G. Pauthier, *Chefs d'œuvre littéraires . . . Chi-King* (Paris, 1872), Introduction, p. 231; James Legge, *The Chinese Classics* (2nd ed., Oxford, 1895), IV, Part I, Preface p. v, p. 116; "Friedrich Rückert und der Orient," *Unterhaltungen* (1854), 2, p. 829; Henri Cordier, *Bibliotheca Sinica* (Paris, 1904-08), col. 1381.

[82] C. C. J. Bunsen, *God in History*, Translated from the German by Susanna Winkworth (London, 1868), I, 245-50.

[83] Legge, *op. cit.*, IV, Part I, 114 *et seq.*

[84] *Ibid.*

[85] Davis, *China*, II, 19; Williams, *op. cit.*, I, 506.

[86] Legge, *op. cit.*, IV, Part I, 115.

[87] Édouard Biot, "Sur les Mœurs des anciens Chinois d'après le Chi-King," *JA* (1843), 2, pp. 307-55, 430-47; M. J. L. Hervey-Saint-Denys, *Poésies de l'époque des Thang* (Paris, 1862), p. xi.

[88] Biot, *op. cit.*, 2, 307; Pauthier, *op cit.*, Introduction, 236 *et seq.*

great national sages and other important persons.[89] Such works form a part of Chinese literature, but the learned classes in China had little respect for the form or contents of this kind of poetry. In their lighter pieces of literature, Chinese writers often introduced moral reflections in verse. A couplet or a longer passage is often found in a romance or novel usually at the end of one section of the story and at the beginning of another.[90] They usually make some reflection upon what has preceded and what is to follow, but at the same time the stanza contains a pointed moral.[91]

A very extensive department of Chinese poetry is descriptive. This division is said to have some very attractive features. Such verse abounds in figurative expressions which are derived from the most pleasing or striking objects and circumstances in nature. " 'Spring dreams and autumnal clouds' mean flitting visions of happiness. Unattainable good is represented by the 'moon's reflection in the wave.' 'Floating clouds obscuring the day' express the temporary shade thrown by detraction on an illustrious character. Difficulty of acting is figured by the 'grass and tangle in one's path.' " Spring is the emblem of joy, and autumn symbolizes sorrow.[92]

While the odd characteristics of the Chinese language and the rigid rules governing the composition of poetry are peculiarly suitable for short lyric poems, the turn and construction of Chinese verse does not lend itself to epic poetry. It would be almost impossible to preserve perfectly balanced couplets throughout an epic poem.[93]

Not only have the Chinese produced no great epic poems, but they in the opinion of one critic have little aptitude for the composition of long poems. The Li Sao is a proof of their inferiority in this respect. It is not a great poem from the Western point of view. No Homer or Vergil is to be found in the literature of the Chinese, but they do have a poet, Li

[89] Davis, *Poeseos Sinicae Commentarii* (New ed., London, 1870), 49 *et seq.*
[90] *Ibid.*, 50.   [91] *Ibid.*
[92] *Ibid.*, 53; W. H. Medhurst, "Chinese Poetry," *CR* (1875-76), 4, p. 52.
[93] Davis, *op. cit.*, 46.

Tai-po, who compares favorably with Horace.[94]   The greatest period in the development of Chinese poetry was that of the T'ang dynasty.   The poetic language which was perfected under this dynasty by the great poets, Tu Fu, Li Tai-po and Wang Wei, was considered by the Chinese as a model which never was surpassed.[95]

Europeans admired Chinese poetry but felt that something was lacking.   The poems translated by Hervey-Saint-Denys, Victor de Laprade wrote, often described and contemplated nature with a certain love and appreciation, but they conveyed nothing of a superior world or Supreme Being.   This writer admitted, however, that the lofty and serious imagination of Tu Fu opens up some escapes outside the world of senses.   But Chinese poets, because they were imbued with no great religious doctrine, lack depth and perspective[96] according to Westerners. Medhurst said that Chinese verse possessed ample thought and imagery, but that a Chinese poem would not bear reading from beginning to end with the sustained interest of a composition in a European language.[97]

Although Occidentals were somewhat critical of Chinese scholarship and literature, many serious students found much to commend.   Good examples of Chinese research were the encyclopaedias which are merely collections of material and rather concordances than true encyclopaedias.   The best known of these compilations is the *Wên Hsien T'ung K'ao* by Ma Tuan-lin.   "One can not cease to admire," said Abel Rémusat, "the depth of research which the author was compelled to make in order to collect his materials, the sagacity he has shown in the arrangement of them, and the clearness and precision with which he has presented this multitude of objects in every light. . . ."   Of the same work, Williams said, "It elevates our opinion of a nation whose literature can boast of a work like this, exhibiting such patient investigation and candid com-

---

[94] M. J. L. Hervey-Saint-Denys, *Le Li-Sao* (Paris, 1870), pp. xxi *et seq.*

[95] ———, *Poésies de l'époque des Thang* (Paris, 1862), p. xlvii; Barthélemy-Saint-Hilaire, "De la Poésie chinoise," *J. Savants* (1864), p. 601.

[96] Victor de Laprade, "Les Poètes classiques," *Corres.* (1864), 62, p. 427.

[97] Medhurst, *op. cit.*, 55.

parison of authorities, such varied research and just discrimination of what is truly important, and so extensive a mass of facts and opinions upon every subject of historical interest."[98]

Certain phases of Chinese literature were studied carefully by the Sinologists Legge, Davis, Julien, Bazin, Hervey-Saint-Denys, and others, but much of the subject was not tapped by scholars. Authors of general works who relied upon the researches of specialists frequently attempted to give a cursory view of the entire field of Chinese literature, which is extremely voluminous with its numerous biographies, historical collections, statistical studies, topographical works, and encyclopaedias.[99]

[98] Douglas, *op. cit.*, 90 *et seq.*; Williams, *op. cit.*, I, 549.
[99] Alexander Wylie, *Notes on Chinese Literature* (Shanghai, 1867); Williams, *op. cit.*, I, 502-90.

CHAPTER X

PHILOSOPHY AND RELIGION

CHINESE thought especially the philosophy of Confucius and Mencius and to some extent Taoism has attracted European scholars since the latter part of the sixteenth century. Then, the Jesuits first reached China. Sinologists studied Buddhism very little before the nineteenth century. The missionaries were the pioneers in the translation of Chinese philosophical and religious works because they thought an acquaintance with the ideas which were enunciated in the *Chinese Classics*, the *Tao-Tê-Ching*, and Buddhist literature would be of great value to Christian misisonaries who were stationed in China. If they understood Chinese philosophy and the Chinese processes of thought, they might be able to present Christianity in a form which would appeal to the literati and also to the masses. Sinologists and philosophers studied Chinese philosophy and religion because they were interested in these subjects and wished to make comparative studies.

CONFUCIUS AND MENCIUS

The aim of this section is not an interpretation of the philosophy of Confucius and Mencius. With only enough explanation of the contents of the *Chinese Classics*[1] to give some continuity to the discussion, the opinions of the Sinologists chiefly of Legge, the most profound student of the *Classics* during the period and also some of the comments found in the more popular works, which reached a far greater number of readers than Legge's scholarly translations and commentaries, are summarized. The Western opinions on religion and philosophy are largely limited to the missionaries; the mercantile groups were not interested, obviously, in purely intellectual subjects. Davis and Meadows, official representatives of the British Govern-

---

[1] For information on the *Chinese Classics* see H. A. Giles, *A History of Chinese Literature* (New York, 1931), pp. 7-42.

ment, were fairly important interpreters of some phases of Chinese philosophy especially those principles which influenced the civil rights of the people and the Government.

Among the authors of general descriptive accounts, the opinions of Davis, Wells Williams, and Huc have been most often quoted because their books were widely read in the original and in translation. Davis presents his material from the point of view of an intelligent and relatively unbiased layman. Williams, a rather scholarly Protestant missionary from the United States, gives an accurate and comparatively unprejudiced discussion of religion. Huc, the French Lazarist, although critical of the Chinese, was a shrewd observer. His books, which were popular in the West, exercised a great influence on Occidental opinion of China. Any views which these writers express on Chinese philosophy do not belong in the same category with those of Legge, although both Davis and Williams were familiar with the language and their comments are undoubtedly based upon extensive reading and probably upon some original research.

Legge's and Pauthier's criticisms are cited because they represent two different viewpoints. Legge, the distinguished missionary scholar, although he censured certain features of Confucian ethics, consistently tried to be a fair and impartial critic. Pauthier, who as a Sinologist was far inferior to Legge, studied the works of the Chinese sages objectively. He considered their great system of philosophy on a par with the schools developed by the Greeks and other ancient teachers. European philosophers of the nineteenth century, Cousin, Ritter, and Hegel, for example, who lacked training in the language, naturally made no profound study of the Classics and only briefly discussed Confucius and Mencius in their works.[2]

[2] Victor Cousin, Introduction à l'histoire de la philosophie (7th ed., Paris, 1872), pp. 27-28; Course of the History of Modern Philosophy, translated by O. W. Wight (New York, 1852), I, pp. 366-67; Heinrich Ritter, The History of Ancient Philosophy, translated from the German by A. J. W. Morrison (Oxford, 1838), I, 56-59; Georg Wilhelm Friedrich Hegel, Lectures on the Philosophy of History, translated from the German by E. S. Haldane (London, 1892), I, 119-25.

The *Classics* consist of the *Five Canonical Works* and the *Four Books*. The former, the most ancient monuments of Chinese literature, contain the fundamental principles of the earliest creeds and customs. The *I Ching* or *Book of Changes*, a book of divination, is possibly the oldest pre-Confucian work. The text consists of sixty-four short essays in enigmatic and symbolical language on important subjects, mostly of a moral, social, and political nature. Western scholars have made various interpretations of the work. Piper, a German, who made a rather intensive study of the *I Ching* pronounced it, in its essentials, a work on ethics. Others referred to it as a treatise on divination. Authors of general accounts, if they mentioned this classic at all, usually dismissed the subject with the statement that it was scarcely more than nonsense and was treasured by the Chinese because of its great antiquity.[3]

The *Shu Ching* or *Book of History* contains six different kinds of state papers issued by the ancient rulers—namely, Imperial ordinances regarded as unalterable, plans drawn up by statesmen to serve as guides for their sovereign, instructions for the prince, Imperial proclamations, vows taken by the monarch before Shang-Ti on the eve of war, and mandates sent down from the throne to high ministers of state. This work in addition consists of a series of dialogues designed to give a brief history of China from the twenty-fourth to the eighth century B.C.[4] Western missionaries appreciated the merits of the work. The precepts for governing a country scattered throughout its dialogues and its proclamations do their authors credit however little they may have been followed in practice.[5]

On the question of the reliability of the *Shu Ching*, Legge wrote that historical documents which dated from the beginning of the Chou dynasty were more or less authentic. The books of that period were doubtless made public while the events described in them were still fresh in the memory of the people.

[3] "Sacred Books of the Chinese," *Sat. R.* (1883), 55, p. 841 *et seq.*; T. W. Kingsmill, "The Sacred Books of China," *CR* (1883), 11, p. 86.
[4] W. H. Medhurst, *Ancient China, The Shoo King or the Historical Classic* (Shanghai, 1846), Preface.
[5] S. W. Williams, *The Middle Kingdom* (New York, 1848), I, 506 *et seq.*

Legge did not question the credibility of the *Shu Ching* later than the time of Yü whom he believed to have been an historical personage and the founder of the Chinese Empire. Yet nearly all the material on his reign was fantastic and exaggerated. Yao and Shun, he wrote, were real persons who led the earliest Chinese immigrants into the country but should be divested of the grand proportions which they had assumed.[6] Plath, the German Sinologist, on the contrary, concluded that the earlier part of the *Shu Ching* consisted largely of tradition.[7] Legge's theories in regard to Yü's importance, were without foundation, Plath contended.[8]

The *Shih Ching* or *Book of Poetry* was a collection of poems arranged by Confucius. More than three thousand songs were said to have existed originally, but Confucius supposedly discarded mere repetitions and selected those valuable for teaching the principles of propriety and righteousness. On the contrary, evidence tends to indicate that before the birth of Confucius, the *Book of Poetry* existed in more or less the same form as after his death. Although he may have made a few alterations in its contents, his important service to the *Book of Poetry* was his popularization of its poems.[9]

This *Book* consists of four parts. The first, which is the longest and most interesting, is called the "Lessons from the States." The princes of these states, into which China was supposedly divided, collected compositions among their people and presented them to the Emperor. He in turn delivered them to the Board of Music for classification so that he could learn about the manners of the people and the administrations of his vassal rulers. The second and third parts of the *Book of Poetry*, which were composed for state occasions, eulogize great heroes and sages.[10] The fourth and last part, translated

---

[6] James Legge, *The Chinese Classics* (2nd ed., Oxford, 1865-95), III, Part I, 80.

[7] J. H. Plath, "Die Glaubwürdigkeit der ältesten chinesischen Geschichte," *Sitz. d. bay. Ak. d. W.* (1866), 1, p. 526 *et seq.*

[8] *Ibid.*, 573.

[9] Legge, *op. cit.*, IV, Part I, 1 *et seq.*

[10] *Ibid.*, Part II, 245 *et seq.*

by Legge as "Odes of the Temple and the Altar," consists of poems which seem to have been sung in honor of the Emperors when sacrifices were made in the temples. The manner in which this collection of poems came into existence makes it of great value as a mirror of pre-Confucian society.[11]

The *Classic* which probably had the most practical effect upon Chinese life and manners was the *Li Chi* or *Book of Rites*. It contains minute and explicit regulations for all human activities. It was largely responsible for the uniformity and changelessness of Chinese customs. The Chinese moralists formulated definitive rules of propriety by which they hoped to harmonize different opinions, stifle all violence, and maintain a state of tranquillity throughout China. The principles of the *Book of Rites,* therefore, served as a wholesome restraint upon conduct in the Chinese Empire.[12]

Callery, aware of the value of this *Classic* as a source of information upon ancient Chinese customs, pronounced it the most exact and complete monograph which the Chinese nation had given of itself to the rest of the world.[13] Legge, quoting Callery's statement, concurred in this opinion.[14] The philosophical and moral ideas expressed in the *Li Chi* were sound and profound even from the European point of view, but their presentation was often odd and difficult to understand. While portions contained confused ideas, other parts were said to expound a pure and sublime philosophy such as only a great sage could enunciate.[15]

Another historical work besides the *Shu Ching* is the *Ch'un Ch'iu* or the *Spring and Autumn Annals* which contains a chronological record of the chief events in the state of Lu for the period 722-484 B.C. It is generally regarded as the work of

[11] *Ibid.,* IV, Part II, 569; Édouard Biot, "Sur les mœurs des anciens Chinois, d'après le Chi-King," *JA* (1843), 2, p. 308.

[12] Williams, *op. cit.,* I, 509 *et seq.;* J. F. Davis, *China* (London, 1857), II, 22.

[13] J. M. Callery, *Li-Ki ou mémorial des rites* (Turin, 1853), Introduction, p. xiii.

[14] James Legge, *The Li-Ki,* Introduction, p. 12. See Max Müller, *The Sacred Books of the East* (Oxford, 1885), Vol. XXVII.

[15] Callery, *op. cit.,* viii *et seq.*

Confucius whose native state was Lu. Legge, who maintained that a historian must put facts together in such a way as to make an interesting narrative, trace their relations to each other and, perhaps, by portraying the motives of the actors, give important lessons to future generations, felt that the *Ch'un Ch'iu* was a great disappointment as a piece of historical writing. Instead of having an artistic arrangement of events, it contained only brief statements of, or mere notes on happenings in the little state of Lu. The writer gives no details and expresses no opinions. This *Classic*, Legge said, reveals no literary ability or judicial acumen on the part of the author. Legge also questioned the reliability of this work. Confucius, who had no reverence for absolute truth in history, not only ignored and concealed certain events but often distorted facts by giving an imperfect and biased account of actual situations. Because of these defects, the work is supposed to have had an unwholesome influence upon subsequent historical writing which was modeled after the *Ch'un Ch'iu*. It was also largely responsible for the disregard of the Chinese for truth and their inability to face realities.[16]

The contents of the *Ta Hsüeh* or the *Great Learning,* the first of the *Four Books,* are briefly summed up under four heads, the improvement of self, the regulation of a family, the government of a state, and the rule of an empire. The obvious aim of the Chinese philosophers was to point out the duties of a government as well as the obligations of the individual.

In the opinion of Legge, this work undoubtedly had merits because of its enunciation of certain principles which, if observed by a government and in individual behavior, would enhance the happiness and the conduct of humanity. First, the writer had a noble conception of the object of government which is to make its subjects cheerful and virtuous. A sufficient explanation of the methods by which these aims could be attained is not given, but rulers are told to love the people and to rule not for their own benefit but for the welfare of their subjects. Ex-

[16] Legge, *The Chinese Classics,* V, Part I, 38 *et seq.; Hegel's Philosophy of the State and of History,* G. S. Morris, ed. (Chicago, 1887), p. 145.

tremely significant, said Legge, is the statement that rulers have
no divine right except what springs from the performance of
duty. Secondly, the insistence upon personal excellence in those
with authority in the family, the state, and the kingdom is a
good moral and social principle, although it may be overempha-
sized. Thirdly, more important than such excellence is the
statement that goodness must be rooted in the individual and
is the natural outgrowth of internal sincerity. Lastly, the striking enunciation of the Golden Rule, although only in its negative form, is important. Even though commonplace, these
sayings are also eternal truths and deserve careful study, Legge
wrote.[17]

Confucius, the son of a statesman, had devoted himself from
his earliest years almost entirely to moral and political questions
without an investigation of the branches of natural science or
the common superstitions of his country, Legge said. He originated no new doctrines but expounded the teaching of preceding
sages. Legge said of Confucius, "If in anything he thought
himself 'superior and alone,' having attributes which others
could not claim, it was in his possessing a divine commission
as the conservator of ancient truth and rules."[18] Whether or
not Confucius made changes in the ancient creed of China was
a question often asked, but Legge thought that he did not do
so "consciously and designedly."[19]

European Sinologists stressed the agnosticism and the pos-
itivism of Confucius, who concerned himself only with the
human realm and avoided discussions of a deity and allusions
to a future state. He was unreligious rather than irreligious.
By the coldness of his temperament and his intellect, his influence was unfavorable to the development of ardent religious
feeling and tended to prepare the way for the speculations of
later literati which exposed them to the charge of atheism.

---

[17] Legge, *op. cit.*, I, 27 *et seq.* Unless the page numbers or statements
differ with those of the first edition, notes refer to the second edition because
it is more accessible. See G. Pauthier, *Les Livres sacrés de l'orient* (Paris,
1841), p. xiii.
[18] Legge, *op. cit.*, I, 95.
[19] *Ibid.*, I, 98; 1st ed. (Hong Kong, 1861), I, 99.

Confucius himself was not a speculative thinker. Having a practical mind, he investigated only what he could understand and left untouched metaphysical subjects.[20] The testimony of the *Analects* on the subjects he taught is:

His frequent themes of discourse were the Book of Poetry, the Book of History, and the maintenance of the rules of Propriety. He taught letters, ethics, devotion of soul, and truthfulness. Extraordinary things; feats of strength; states of disorder; and spiritual beings, he did not like to talk about.[21]

Confucius, because of his emphasis upon man's obligations to society and because he exalted filial piety above all other social and moral virtues, is primarily responsible for the regimentation of family life and society in China.[22] He prescribed self-cultivation only that the individual might be better fitted to aid the general welfare of humanity. Man was, therefore, only an insignificant member of a vast society.

A serious weakness of Confucius's system, from the missionary point of view, was his position on the doctrine of God. He simply dismissed spiritual matters as beyond the comprehension of mortals. Legge thought Confucius's views on the question of the existence of a Supreme Being fell short of the faith of the older sages. The name "God" was common in the *Shih Ching* and in the *Shu Ching*. Ti or Shang-Ti appeared as a personal Being, ruler in Heaven and on earth, the source of man's moral nature, and the arbiter among nations. Confucius preferred to use the term "Heaven" and not once did he use the personal name for God.[23] Faber, another missionary, wrote that because of Confucius's estrangement from the ancient God, he promoted the worship of spirits without intending to do so.

---

[20] *Ibid.*, I, 97 *et seq.*; 1st ed., I, 98 *et seq.*; Ernst Faber, *A Systematical Digest of the Doctrines of Confucius*, translated by P. G. Mollendorf (2nd ed., 1902), p. 26; Griffith John, "The Ethics of the Chinese," *JNCBRAS* (1860), 2, p. 20; H. G. Creel, "Was Confucius Agnostic?" *TP* (1932), 29, p. 56.

[21] Legge, *op. cit.*, I, 97 *et seq.*; 1st ed., I, 99. See Analects, Book VII, Chapters XVII, XXIV, XX.

[22] *Hegel's Philosophy of the State, op. cit.*, 140 *et seq.*

[23] Legge, *op. cit.*, I, 98 *et seq.*

According to the Christian doctrine, purification and perfection of humanity depends upon God's assistance. Faber maintained that a system of positive ethics was impossible without the intimate relationship to a personal God and without the certainty of immortality. Confucius's silence and ignorance in regard to the future life was, therefore, a serious and fundamental weakness in his whole system of ethics.[24]

The practice of worshipping ancestors which must have originated in a belief in the continued existence of the dead, Confucius recognized as an important institution, but he more or less evaded the whole subject of life after death.[25] When a disciple inquired about death, Confucius's reply was that if a person did not know about life how could he know about death. Still more striking was a conversation with another follower. When Confucius was asked if the dead knew about the services of the living, he made the following reply:

If I were to say that the dead have such knowledge, I am afraid that filial sons and dutiful grandsons would injure their substance in paying the last offices to the departed; and if I were to say that the dead have not such knowledge, I am afraid lest unfilial sons should leave their parents unburied. You need not wish Ts'ze to know whether the dead have knowledge or not. . . . Hereafter you will know it for yourself.[26]

Surely this was not the teaching, fitting for a sage, argued Legge who thought that Confucius should have expressed his real thoughts on such an interesting subject.[27] This scholar maintained that Confucius's position on sacrifices to the dead was closely connected with the most serious charge which could be brought against him—that is, insincerity. Although Confucius stressed truthfulness and honesty as emphatically as Christian moralists, he was not absolutely truthful. Legge cited several examples to prove his point. Confucius could readily excuse himself from seeing an unwelcome visitor on the ground of illness when nothing was the matter with him. Legge pro-

---

[24] Faber, *op. cit.*, 32 *et seq.*
[25] Legge, *op. cit.*, I, 99; 1st ed., 100.
[26] *Ibid.*   [27] *Ibid.*

nounced this example trivial but attached more importance to Confucius's action in deliberately breaking an oath because it was forced upon him. Such examples of untruthfulness in this sage doubtless exercised an unwholesome influence upon the Chinese and caused them to condone deceitfulness and falsehood. The failure to instill sincerity and honesty was the most universal criticism which Westerners made of the whole Confucian system of philosophy.[28]

An appreciation of the moral teachings of Confucius, however, can be traced throughout the writings of most authors on the subject. Joseph Edkins, the English missionary, pronounced Confucius a great moralist who ranked in depth of thought and in influence with Socrates. The two sages were alike in the extent of their influence, their deep moral convictions, and the emphasis they put upon morality. They differed greatly in personal characteristics and in their treatment of the subjects which they taught. Confucius was the stern censor; Socrates was the skillful rationalist and the master of irony. Confucius constantly laid down rules for the government of self, of family, and of state. Socrates sought knowledge and loved virtue for its own sake. Confucius looked into antiquity for his ideas. Socrates depended upon his own resources and was, consequently, more original in many respects.[29] Nevius, another missionary, pronounced Confucianism the purest system of morality which existed independently of Christianity. Confucius, he believed, exerted a greater influence for good than any other uninspired sage of antiquity.[30] Meadows, a layman, stressed the impossibility of drawing a parallel between Confucius and any religious leader. The Chinese sage, Meadows pointed out, never pretended to any superhuman powers but considered himself only a moral philosopher and a statesman. His doctrines had a tremendous influence because they were fundamentally sound and correct.[31]

[28] *Ibid.*, I, 100; 1st ed., 101.
[29] Joseph Edkins, "A Sketch of the Life of Confucius," *JNCBRAS* (1860), 2, p. 1 *et seq.*
[30] J. L. Nevius, *China and the Chinese* (New York, 1869), p. 54.
[31] T. T. Meadows, *Desultory Notes on the Government and People of China* (London, 1847), p. 211.

Confucius's position and influence, Legge attributed to his position as the preserver of the literary monuments of antiquity and the exponent of the maxims of the golden age of China. The devotion of Confucius's disciples also enhanced his popularity and his influence throughout China. The national and the personal were thus blended in him.[32] By 1867 Legge had not formed a very high opinion of Confucius. He wrote:

> . . . I hope I have not done him injustice; but after long study of his character and opinions, I am unable to regard him as a great man. He was not before his age, though he was above the mass of the officers and scholars of his time. He threw no new light on any of the questions which have a world-wide interest. . . . He had no sympathy with progress. His influence has been wonderful, but it will henceforth wane.[33]

Hegel did not admire greatly the philosophy of Confucius who, he wrote, was only a man with a certain amount of practical and worldly wisdom but with no speculative philosophy. He admitted that the conversations of Confucius and his disciples contained commonplace morals in the form of good sound doctrine. But such ideas were as well expressed and sometimes very much better in the literature of other people. For example, Cicero's De Officiis, a book of moral teaching is more comprehensive and superior to all the books of Confucius.[34]

Emerson, the American philosopher, who was interested in China as the center of a great civilization, was never extremely enthusiastic about Chinese philosophy. He frequently quoted

[32] Legge, op. cit., I, 93 et seq.; 1st ed., 94; Théodore Pavie, "Les trois religions de la Chine," RDM (1845), 9, p. 456.

[33] Legge, op. cit. (1st ed., Hong Kong, 1861), I, 113; "Legge's Chinese Classics," Nation (1870), 11, p. 176. The longer Legge studied Confucius, the more tolerant be became of his ideas and the more he came to respect the sage. In 1893, he wrote, ". . . the more I have studied his character and opinions, the more highly I have come to regard him. He was a very great man, and his influence has been on the whole a great benefit to the Chinese, while his teachings suggest important lessons to ourselves who profess to belong to the school of Christ." See Legge, The Chinese Classics (2nd ed., Oxford, 1893), I, 111 and Creel, op. cit., 58 et seq.

[34] G. W. F. Hegel, Lectures on the Philosophy of History (London, 1892), p. 120 et seq.

Confucius, however, to support some of his own ideas.[35] Confucius's most ardent Western admirer was the French Sinologist, Pauthier, who said that if the power of his doctrines were to be judged by the influence they had exercised on humanity, the Chinese point of view that Confucius was the greatest teacher of all times must be accepted. Human reason was never better represented than in the works of Confucius and his school. They contain the most beautiful and noble ideas of any philosophy, wrote Pauthier.[36]

The *Chung Yung* or *Doctrine of the Mean*, presumably composed by K'ung Chi, Confucius's grandson, attempts to illustrate theories about human virtue by describing the behavior of an ideal man who always conducts himself correctly and avoids extremes. Under all conditions he is urged to be calm and moderate. Although much of this book is obscure, it does expound Chinese ideas on the nature of human virtue and adheres to the theory that man's nature is inherently good and becomes corrupt only through evil example. Sections of this work, Legge commended. The very first part was fairly clear, but after a statement of his principles, the author becomes very vague. After several obscure passages, he discourses upon the perfection and nobility of the Chinese sages. Legge thought that this work, because of its exaltation of the philosophers and its definite injunctions to the masses to seek nothing outside of China, contributed toward the development of Chinese pride and sense of superiority.[37] The author of this work introduces few new theories. He enlarges upon certain general principles of Confucius in regard to the nature of man and his proper conduct.

The *Lun Yü* or *Analects of Confucius* in twenty short chapters contains a record of Confucius's words, actions, and his views on many subjects. Not arranged chronologically, its organization is loose and confused, and many passages are almost

[35] F. I. Carpenter, *Emerson and Asia* (Cambridge, Massachusetts, 1930), Chap. IX.
[36] G. Pauthier, *Confucius et Mencius* (Paris, 1841), p. 8.
[37] Legge, *op. cit.*, I, 36 *et seq.*

unintelligible. Among a great number of commonplace statements on morals and politics and curious and trivial details on the character and habits of Confucius, were some profound thoughts which many Westerners admired.[38]

The fourth of the *Books*, the *Works of Mencius*, was probably composed by this sage with the aid of some of his disciples. Mencius's object was to inculcate one of the great principles of Confucius—namely, benevolent government. Mencius travelled as Confucius did with disciples in the different states of China and appeared at the courts of princes with whom he discussed his doctrines and to whom he often gave lessons in politics and government. Like Confucius, Mencius felt responsible for the welfare of all humanity. While communicating his ideas to the princes, he also tried to spread his ideas among the masses. But his main object was to convince the rulers that their power rested upon the good will of the people. Mencius also urged them to obey their sovereigns. With enlightened and benevolent rulers and a subservient population, good government would naturally follow.[39] The value of the *Book* lies in its lessons for the regulation of national policy and individual behavior.

Mencius's views on human nature, Legge said, entitled him to a high rank as a moralist and thinker. Mencius believed that human nature was innately good.[40] He maintained that man had natural principles of benevolence, righteousness, propriety, and knowledge of good and evil.[41] Yet he recognized hatred, improprieties, and unrighteousness as constant features of human life. Mencius admitted that men often committed crimes but did not explain why so much corruption was found in men whose natures were fundamentally virtuous. He did cite, however, the ill effects of unfavorable circumstances and the power of bad example. Legge said that he observed nothing in these teachings of Mencius which were contrary to the teach-

---

[38] *Ibid.*, I, 26 *et seq.* See 1st ed., 12 *et seq.*

[39] G. Pauthier, *Les Livres sacrés de l'orient* (Paris, 1841), p. xvi *et seq.*

[40] Legge, *op. cit.*, II, 56; 1st ed., 58 *et seq.*

[41] *Ibid.*, II, 59 *et seq.*; 1st ed., 62; Book VI, Part I, Chapters VI, VII.

ings of Christianity. Mencius's doctrines on human nature, which failed to embrace the whole duty of man, were defective rather than erroneous. His system supplied a law of conduct worthy of the highest admiration in the opinion of Legge who would naturally regard as inferior any philosophy which said nothing about duty to God. He concluded his criticisms of Mencius's theories on human nature with the suggestion that his limitations resulted from his ignorance of Christianity.[42]

Legge also criticised Mencius's lack of humility. In this respect he was inferior to Confucius, who often admitted his inability to live up to his own ideals. Mencius's faults as a political teacher were substantially the same as Confucius's. He knew as little as Confucius did about foreign countries. A maxim of Mencius, treasured by the rulers and the people, was supposedly responsible for their supercilious attitude toward foreigners and for their own feeling of superiority. "I have heard," said Mencius, "of men using the doctrines of our great land to change barbarians, but I have never yet heard of any being changed by barbarians. I have heard of birds leaving dark valleys to remove to lofty trees, but I have not heard of their descending from lofty trees to enter dark valleys."[43] Some Westerners, believing that China's policy of exclusion was largely due to the teachings of the ancient philosophers, held them partly responsible for the stagnation, decadence, and general backwardness of the Chinese Empire during the nineteenth century.[44]

Abel Rémusat's remarks on the styles and methods of these two philosophers which are quoted by Huc are noteworthy:

The style of Meng-tze less elevated and less concise than that of the prince of letters, Confucius, is more flowery and elegant, and also not deficient in nobleness. The forms of dialogue which he has preserved in his Philosophical Conversations with the great persons of his times, allow of more variety than one can expect to

[42] *Ibid.*, II, 65 *et seq.*

[43] *Ibid.*, II, 76 *et seq.*; 1st ed., 78 *et seq.*

[44] "Legge's Chinese Classics," *Nation* (1870), 11, p. 177; Legge, *op. cit.*, I, 55, II, 76; 1st ed., 78; Justus Doolittle, *Social Life of the Chinese* (New York, 1865), II, 422 *et seq.*

find in the apothegms and maxims of Confucius. The character of their philosophy also differs widely. Confucius is always grave, even austere. He extols the virtuous, of whom he draws an ideal portrait, and only speaks of the vicious with cold indignation. Meng-tze, with the same love of virtue, seems to have more contempt for, than hatred of vice. He attacks it by the force of reason, and does not disdain even to employ the weapon of ridicule. His manner of arguing approaches the irony attributed to Socrates. He does not contend with his adversaries: but endeavours while granting their premises, to draw from them absurd consequences, that he may cover them with confusion. He does not even spare the princes and great men of his time, who often only feigned to consult him in order to have an opportunity of boasting of their conduct, or to obtain from him eulogiums that they supposed themselves to merit. Nothing can be more piquant than the answers he sometimes gives them on such occasions, and nothing more opposed to the too generally entertained opinion of the baseness and servility of Orientals, and especially of the Chinese.

Meng-tze does not resemble Aristippus so much as Diogenes, but without violating decency and decorum. His liveliness does sometimes appear rather of too tart a quality, but he is always inspired by zeal for the public good.[45]

Of Confucius and of Mencius, Legge wrote:

But while we are not to look to Mencius for new truths, the peculiarities of his natural character were more striking than those of his master. There was an element of "the heroical" about him. He was a dialectician, moreover. If he did not like disputing, as he protested that he did not, yet, when forced to it, he showed himself a master of the art. An ingenuity and a subtlety, which we can not but enjoy, often mark his reasonings. We have more sympathy with him than with Confucius. He comes closer to us. He is not so awe-ful, but he is more admirable. The doctrines of the sages take a tinge from his mind in passing through it, and it is with that Mencian character about them that they are now held by the cultivated classes and by readers generally.[46]

[45] E. R. Huc, *The Chinese Empire* (New ed., London, 1859), p. 79 *et seq.*; G. Pauthier, *Confucius et Mencius* (Paris, 1841), Introduction, p. 26 *et seq.*
[46] Legge, *op. cit.*, II, 43 *et seq.*; 1st ed., 45.

Westerners, in general, respected Mencius. Wells Williams regarded him as one of the greatest thinkers of Asia.[47] No Oriental writer, Pauthier thought, could offer more attractions to Europeans especially the French than Mencius, because of the vivacity and vividness of his writings. Regardless of Western scholars' criticisms of the two most famous Chinese philosophers, Europeans agreed that they deserve the attention of all philosophers and all historians because they had enlightened and directed toward civilization a large part of the human race.[48]

TAOISM

Older than Confucius, supposedly, was another great Chinese philosopher, Lao Tzŭ[49] who was one of the most remarkable figures in the history of China.[50] His name is almost as familiar to the Chinese as Confucius's.[51] Very little is known about Lao Tzŭ. During his early life he was a very serious student of early Chinese history and institutions and eventually obtained an office at the court of Chou. But when he saw the kingdom of Chou break up into petty states which were continually at war with each other, the country in ruins, and the people in desolation, he decided to leave. Upon his arrival at the Western pass, the keeper, Yin Hsi said: "If you are going to disappear into retirement, Sir, I hope you will make a book for me." Lao Tzŭ, it was said, wrote a book later called the *Tao-Tê-Ching* which consisted of more than five thousand words. Afterwards he went away and no one knows what became of him. Such is the story of Lao Tzŭ and the *Tao-Tê-Ching* according to Ssu-ma Ch'ien, the great Chinese historian.[52]

[47] Williams, *op. cit.*, I, 521.

[48] G. Pauthier, *Les Livres sacrés de l'orient* (Paris, 1841), p. xvii.

[49] Theodore Pavie, "Les trois religions de la Chine," *RDM* (1845), 9, p. 456 *et seq.*

[50] T. Watters, "Lao-tzŭ," *C. Recorder* (1868), 1, p. 31; G. Pauthier, *Chine description historique géographique et littéraire* (Paris, 1879), p. 120.

[51] H. A. Giles, "The Remains of Lao Tzŭ," *CR* (1886), 14, p. 231.

[52] Watters, *op. cit.*, 58 *et seq.*; John Chalmers, "Tauism," *CR* (1872-73), 1, p. 211; E. H. Parker, *Studies in Chinese Religion* (London, 1910), p. 144 *et seq.*; Victor von Strauss, *Laò-Tsè's Taò Tĕ King* (Leipzig, 1924), p. xliv *et seq.* (1st ed., 1870); Stanislas Julien, *Lao-tseu Tao Te King. Le Livre de la voie et de la vertu* (Paris, 1842), p. xix *et seq.*; Leo Wieger, *A*

Occidentals were slow to begin the study of Taoism. The works which are usually regarded as the earlier classics of this philosophy are the sayings of Lao Tzŭ and the books of Lieh Tzŭ and Chuang Tzŭ. Because the authenticity of the *Book of Lieh Tzŭ* has been seriously challenged,[53] it is only in Chuang Tzŭ's work, a large part of which is considered genuine, that a well developed system has been defined. His philosophy represents the main currents of Taoistic teaching and his book with Kuo Hsiang's *Commentaries* form the most important literature of Taoism. Although Western scholars and writers referred to Lieh Tzŭ[54] occasionally, they emphasized the significance of Chuang Tzŭ, a very celebrated and influential philosopher from whom Taoists derived more opinions than from Lao Tzŭ himself.[55] Sinologists, however, during the years from 1840 to 1875, were undoubtedly more interested in Lao Tzŭ and the *Tao-Tê-Ching*. The first translation of this work was made in Latin by an anonymous Jesuit missionary about 1768. It was preserved in manuscript form in the Library of the Royal Society of England.[56] Prémare, Amiot, and the other Catholic missionaries made studies of the *Tao-Tê-Ching* because they thought the publication of this important book in translation with an interpretation would be of great help to the missionaries in introducing Christianity to the Chinese.[57] Lao Tzŭ was forgotten by most Occidentals until about 1820 when Abel Rémusat produced his memoir on the life and writings of this

History of Religious Beliefs and Philosophical Opinions in China from the Beginning of the Present Time, translated by Edward Charles Werner (Hsien-hsien Press, 1927), p. 145 *et seq.*

[53] Fung Yu-lan, *Chuang Tzŭ* (Shanghai, 1933), p. 2 *et seq.*; H. A. Giles, *Chuang Tzŭ* (London, 1889), Introduction, p. xvi.

[54] "Leih-Tsze," *Cornh.* (1874), 30, pp. 44-64.

[55] Williams, *op. cit.*, II, 245; John Chalmers, "Tauism," *op. cit.*, 213 *et seq.* The first English translation of Chuang Tzŭ's work was made by Frederick Henry Balfour in 1881 and the second was done by Herbert A. Giles in 1889. For a summary of Western translations and studies of the *Tao-Tê-Ching*, see Watters, *op. cit.*, I, 82 *et seq.*; Strauss, *op. cit.*, vii-xiv; Parker, *op. cit.*, 92-95; Wieger, *op. cit.*, 146 *et seq.*

[56] Watters, *op. cit.*, 1, 32; Parker, *op. cit.*, 92.

[57] Julien, *op. cit.*, Introduction, v.

sage, which stimulated Western Sinologists' interest in Taoism.[58] Pauthier in his study which was published in 1831 suggested a similarity between Lao Tzŭ's ideas and the Hindu philosophers' and also compared the former's principles with Schelling's.[59] In 1838 Pauthier published in part a translation of the Tao-Tê-Ching in Latin and French which he had completed as early as 1834.[60] Stanislas Julien in 1842 translated the entire Tao-Tê-Ching into French with copious notes and appendices. The first English translation of this work was John Chalmers's version which was published in 1868. His work was favorably received, by missionaries especially. In the same year Watters wrote a series of papers which Parker said as late as 1910 were "perhaps unequalled so far as accurate inquiry into the life of Lao Tzŭ and the Chinese views of his doctrines are concerned."[61]

Two German translations of the Tao-Tê-Ching were published in 1870 by Reinhold von Plaenckner[62] and Victor von Strauss[63] respectively. Legge wrote that the "former's slender acquaintance with Chinese by no means fitted him for such a task and that von Strauss' knowledge of Chinese, although not equal to Julien's is still very considerable."[64] Von Plaenckner's translation was very unsatisfactory and was criticized severely. Von Strauss's version, however, was carefully and literally done with full notes.[65]

[58] Giles, "The Remains of Lao Tzŭ," op. cit., 232; Julien, op. cit., Introduction, ii; Abel Rémusat, "Mémoire sur la vie et les opinions de Lao-tseu," Mémoires de l'institut royale de France, Académie des inscriptions et belles-lettres (Paris, 1824), VII, 1-55.
[59] Watters, op. cit., I, 32. Chalmers in the introduction to his translation of the Tao-Tê-Ching suggested a possible connection between Chinese and Hindu thought. See John Chalmers, The Speculations on Metaphysics, Polity, and Morality, of "the Old Philosopher" Lau-Tsze (London, 1868), Introduction, p. vii. See also Wieger, op. cit., 146.
[60] Parker, op. cit., 78.   [61] Ibid.
[62] Reinhold von Plaenckner, Lao-tse. Táo-Tĕ-King. Der Weg zur Tugend (Leipzig, 1870).   [63] Strauss, op. cit.
[64] Giles, "The Remains of Lao Tzŭ," op. cit., 233.
[65] Parker, op. cit., 79 et seq. Later translations: Paul Carus, Lao-tze's Tao-Teh-King (Chicago, 1898); Arthur Waley, The Way and Its Power (London, 1934).

The general accounts of China usually described Taoism in a few paragraphs. The Taoists by the third quarter of the nineteenth century were comparatively few in number, and Lao Tzŭ's doctrines were obsolete.[66] The average Western traveller, who had not studied the *Tao-Tê-Ching*, knew nothing of Lao Tzŭ's philosophy and described only the superficial aspects of the cult, such as the priests' style of dress, the temples, and the religious and superstitious practices of the sect. The subject matter of Taoist speculation, however, possessed an intense interest for scholars.

Western Sinologists found the text of the *Tao-Tê-Ching* bewildering because of its uncertainty and confusion. Some native editors, wishing to have only five thousand characters, cut off characters at random without much regard for the author's meaning. Others retained or added characters supposedly to make clear what they thought was the meaning of particular passages. Great variations in the texts, therefore, have produced different interpretations. The extremely terse and concise style of the work makes it very obscure and devoid of much grace or elegance. Watters wrote that the subjects discussed, such as the origin of the universe and man's place and destiny in it as an individual and a member of society are abstract and difficult to understand.[67] Lao Tzŭ's system is purely speculative. He did not give much historical background, nor did he gather and arrange his facts systematically.[68] The main principles of the *Tao-Tê-Ching* are that Tao originates all things, is the everlasting model for all things, and into it all things are finally absorbed.[69] Lao Tzŭ stressed the unification of the various parts of the universe.[70]

Watters said that Lao Tzŭ's philosophy was an ethical or

[66] F. E. Forbes, *Five Years in China* (London, 1848), p. 130 *et seq.;* M. S. Culbertson, *Darkness in the Flowery Land* (New York, 1857), p. 61 *et seq.;* Huc, *op. cit.*, 389; J. F. Davis, *China* (London, 1857), II, 72; W. H. Medhurst, *China; Its State and Prospects* (Boston, 1838), p. 164 *et seq.;* "Leih-tsze," *Cornh.* (1868), 30, p. 60.

[67] Watters, *op. cit.*, 1, 83 *et seq.;* Rémusat, *op. cit.*, 21.

[68] Ritter, *op. cit.*, I, 59.

[69] Watters, *op. cit.*, 1, 107; Strauss, *op. cit.*, xxxii *et seq.*

[70] Chalmers, "Tauism," *op. cit.*, 212.

rather a "political-ethical" system. Lao Tzŭ did not evolve a system of speculative or practical morality but did set forth some clear notions on the subject of ethics. The attributes which characterized the perfect man were described in the *Tao-Tê-Ching*.[71] A very important virtue was freedom from ostentation. The ability to live and work quietly was considered meritorious. Lao Tzŭ did not advocate an active life. All good men should be moderate in everything. To be content was to be rich. Lao Tzŭ also commended humility. An humble man did not claim precedence or merit, but they came to him in the end. Lao Tzŭ gave a very important place to continence.[72] Perfection consisted in being without passion. Then, the harmony of the universe could be contemplated more satisfactorily.[73] About courage, truth, and honesty Lao Tzŭ had little to say. He did emphasize, however, the interdependence of members of society. Watters criticized Lao Tzŭ for his views on learning and wisdom. The Chinese philosopher maintained that learning added to the evils of existence.[74] Although in one chapter of the *Tao-Tê-Ching*, occurs a reference to a life after death, Watters thought that Lao Tzŭ had no conception of immortality. Lao Tzŭ seemed to think that man lost his individuality and that absorption into "universal Nature" was the highest reward for virtue.[75] Rémusat said that, like Pythagoras, the Chinese sage regarded human souls as emanations from an ethereal substance and thought that after death they were united again with it. He also agreed with Plato in refusing to the wicked the faculty of becoming a part of the universal soul after death.[76]

On the subject of the creation of the universe Lao Tzŭ's ideas, Rémusat said, were not ridiculous or preposterous.[77] He referred all existing creatures to an eternal, all-producing unity which he called *Tao*. Lao Tzŭ believed everything had a definite time to exist. All things would eventually decay, and

[71] Watters, *op. cit.*, 1, 108, 209.
[72] *Ibid.*
[73] Huc, *op. cit.*, 385 *et seq.*
[74] Watters, *op. cit.*, 212 *et seq.*
[75] *Ibid.*, 213 *et seq.*
[76] Huc, *op. cit.*, 386 *et seq.*; Rémusat, *op. cit.*, 51; Rémusat, *Mélanges asiatiques* (Paris, 1825), I, 95.
[77] Huc, *op. cit.*, 386 *et seq.*

final dissolution would follow as they returned to Nature. Watters thought that this philosopher's manner of contemplating Nature resembled much more the poetical metaphysician's speculations than the scientist's careful researches.[78] Lao Tzǔ did not, therefore, advocate the study of Nature through detailed investigations. It should be carried on by means of meditation in seclusion. By overcoming affections and emotions, the student reaches serene heights of desireless existence, and in that state he would know all things. Such a method, Westerners thought, would never contribute to the material benefit of humanity. It made an individual sympathetic with his surroundings, and if the philosophers would experiment upon Nature to aid the material progress of mankind, such views as Lao Tzǔ's might not be detrimental to human progress.[79]

On the subject of politics Lao Tzǔ made a number of statements. His own country was in chaos, and he tried to persuade the sovereigns to give their people a good rule. His standard of political excellence may have been ideal and impractical, but Watters found in his principles a genial, human philosophy which the people of the nineteenth century could not absolutely despise. Lao Tzǔ did not consider the sovereign the judge or ruler of the people but their model or instructor. He also regarded the method of government as a very important subject. He compared the administration of a large kingdom to the cooking of a small fish or the handling of a delicate implement. Too much cooking spoiled the fish; too much handling ruined the tool. Too many laws were likewise bad for a state. The first duty of the ruler was to cultivate virtue in himself, in his family, and then in the Empire. He should be serious and grave in his deportment. By levity of conduct he would lose his ministers; by violent measures he would forfeit his throne.

Lao Tzǔ also opposed military oppression. If fighting were absolutely necessary, a decisive blow should be struck at the right time, and then arms should be laid aside.[80] His passage concerning conquerors is rather significant. "The least glorious

---

[78] Watters, *op. cit.*, 131; Chalmers, *op. cit.*, xv.
[79] Watters, *op. cit.*, 131.　　　　[80] *Ibid.*, 154 *et seq.*

peace is preferable to the most brilliant successes of war. The most splendid victory is but the light from a conflagration." "He who adorns himself with laurels loves blood, and deserves to be blotted out from the number of men."[81]

The Chinese philosopher's advice in many respects was unsound. Forcing the people to remain in a state of ignorance and retarding all material advancement, savored of despotism. But even though Lao Tzŭ was condemned for ignoring the individuality of each member of the state, discouraging progress in the mechanical arts, and magnifying the importance of kingship, Watters wrote that barriers to personal liberty as great as these still existed in the nineteenth century.[82]

But Occidental students found much to commend in the philosophy of Taoism. Chalmers called Lao Tzŭ *the philosopher of China*. Conceding that Confucius had a greater name, Chalmers maintained that the former excelled him in depth and independence of thought.[83] Watters also pronounced Lao Tzŭ one of the most remarkable men in the history of China and also in the history of philosophy. He said that the *Tao-Tê-Ching* deserved a high place among philosophical works.[84] The German scholar, Von Plaenckner[85] and Pauthier, the French Sinologist, ardently admired Lao Tzŭ's doctrines. The latter wrote that human wisdom had probably never given expression to more sacred and more profound words than those in the *Tao-Tê-Ching.*[86] Wells Williams, the American missionary, was not enthusiastic about Lao Tzŭ's teachings, although he did not explicitly condemn them. The Chinese philosopher's recommendation of retirement and contemplation as the most effective means of purifying the spiritual element in nature, Williams compared to the spiritual precepts of Zeno. But he thought Confucius, doing all in his power by precept and practice to show the excellence of his ideas, understood his duty

---

[81] Huc, *op. cit.*, 386; Rémusat, *Mélanges asiatiques* (Paris, 1825), I, 94 *et seq.*   [82] Watters, *op. cit.*, 159 *et seq.*

[83] Chalmers, *op. cit.*, Introduction, vii.

[84] Watters, *op. cit.*, 31.   [85] Von Plaenckner, *op. cit.*, vi.

[86] G. Pauthier, *Chine* (Paris, 1879), p. 118 *et seq.*

and his people better than Lao Tzŭ.[87]   Williams probably reached his conclusions after observing the application of Confucian precepts to various social problems by the learned groups in comparison with the corrupt and superstitious practices of the Taoists.

Watters and Chalmers both emphasized the distinction between early Taoism and its later perversions.   All kinds of practices and doctrines distasteful to the orthodox Confucianists were relegated to Taoism.   By the third quarter of the nineteenth century, quack doctors, observers of *Feng Shui*, diviners, exorcists, and writers of charms were either Taoists or closely associated with them in the popular mind.   By 1840 the superstitious practices of the Taoists had become an object of sarcasm and ridicule for the Confucianists, and it is not surprising that Occidentals in general held a rather low opinion of Taoism which they regarded not so much as a philosophy but as a debased and very superstitious form of religion.[88]

BUDDHISM

The third great religion of China, Buddhism, was introduced from India.   This country was, therefore, for the Chinese Buddhists a "Holy Land."   They went to India to venerate the relics of Buddha and also to learn the most accredited theories connected with Buddhist dogma.   They obtained Sanscrit books which they later put into Chinese and also wrote accounts of their pilgrimages with details on the history, geography, and customs of India which could not be found in Sanscrit authors' works.[89]   Abel Rémusat first recognized the value of such accounts, and his translation in 1836 of *Foĕ Kouĕ Ki*, an account of Buddhistic kingdoms by Fa-Hsien, a famous pilgrim, when little was known in Europe of Chinese Buddhist

---

[87] Williams, *op. cit.*, II, 243 *et seq.*

[88] Joseph Edkins, "A Sketch of the Tauist Mythology in Its Modern Form," *JNCBRAS* (1859), no. 3, pp. 309-14; "Leih-tsze," *Cornh.* (1874), 30, p. 60; Charles Hardwick, *Christ and Other Masters* (2nd ed., London, 1863), II, 76 *et seq.*

[89] Stanislas Julien, *Histoire de la vie de Hiouen-Thsang* (Paris, 1843), Preface, p. i; Abel Rémusat, *Foĕ Kouĕ Ki ou relation des royaumes bouddhiques* (Paris, 1836), Introduction, p. v.

literature[90] was regarded by students of India as one of the most valuable aids for their research. Later, Julien translated with copious notes the work of Hsüan-chuang, the most detailed and the richest in facts and information of all the accounts written by Chinese pilgrims to India.[91] Julien's *Histoire de la vie de Hiouen Thsang,* published in 1853, established the importance of Buddhism in China, which from that date became a subject for critical study. Prior to the publication of Julien's work, Westerners generally had a contempt for Chinese Buddhism. It was considered incredible that Chinese literature could supply any information on Indian history.[92]

Until the appearance of Beal's *Travels of Fah-Hian and Sung-Yun* in 1869, European scholars studied the doctrines of Sakyamuni almost entirely in Sanscrit or Pali works.[93] Joseph Edkins, Watters wrote in the same year, was almost the only student who had made profound and extensive researches in the history and development of Chinese Buddhism,[94] and Edkins himself remarked as late as 1879 that very few had ever studied this subject.[95] In 1871 Beal said that, despite the researches in Buddhist history and philosophy of the preceding thirty or forty years, missionaries and scholars generally had made little use of the Buddhist canon found in China. It was well known that many of the larger monasteries in that country possessed complete editions of the Buddhist scriptures.[96] No effort was made in England or in other Western countries to obtain copies of these invaluable works for the national libraries.[97]

[90] Samuel Beal, *Travels of Fah-Hian and Sung-Yun, Buddhist Pilgrims, from China to India* (London, 1869), Preface.
[91] Jules Mohl, "Rapport sur les travaux du conseil," *JA* (1851), 18, p. 180 *et seq.*
[92] "Handbook for the Study of Chinese Buddhism," *Phoenix* (1871), 1, p. 155.
[93] "Life of Buddha," *Sat. R.* (1875), 40, p. 276.
[94] T. Watters, "Buddhism in China," *C. Recorder* (1869), 2, p. 1.
[95] Joseph Edkins, *Chinese Buddhism* (2nd ed., London, 1893), p. xvii.
[96] Samuel Beal, *A Catena of Buddhist Scriptures from the Chinese* (London, 1871), p. 1 *et seq.*; Wilhelm Schott, "Zur Litteratur des chinesischen Buddhismus," *Philo. u. hist. Abh. d. Ak. d. W.* (1873), p. 37 *et seq.*
[97] Beal, *op. cit.,* 1 *et seq.*

Because little was known about the development of Chinese Buddhism, Beal, in his *Catena of Buddhist Scriptures from the Chinese*, published in 1871, grouped together successive translations of works bearing on various phases of the Buddhist religion from the time of the primitive teachings of Sakyamuni to the mysticism of the nineteenth century.[98] By 1870 or 1875 scholars were only beginning to delve into the vast literature of Chinese Buddhism.   Missionaries were especially interested in the reasons why Buddhism, a foreign religion, gained such a strong foothold in China.   They thought Christianity might profit by observing the tactics and methods of the early Buddhist misisonaries.

Just as Christianity embraced the Occident, Buddhism swept the East. Why Buddhism had been able to do this was a theme for speculation.   Confucianists attributed the rapid growth of Buddhism to the love of the common people for the marvellous and the tendency of the multitude to follow any leader.   Edkins wrote that the "Buddhists from India came peaceably, teaching the Chinese to revere their pompous ritual, and their placid, benevolent, and thoughtful divinities.   They spread among them the doctrine of the separate existence of the soul, and its transmigration into the bodies of animals. They also pleased their imaginations with splendid pictorial scenes of far-away worlds, filled with light, inhabited by Buddhas, Bodhisattwas and angelic beings, and richly adorned with precious stones and metals.   In this way they enticed the Chineses into idolatry."[99]   Watters thought that this religion was able to make great headway in China because of the excellence of many of its doctrines and the enthusiasm and zeal of its early missionaries.[100]

Monasticism was a popular element in Buddhism.   The monastery was a refuge for the unhappy, those who had not succeeded in any vocation, sickly children, and any who wished to lead a cloistered life.   The renunciation of the world and the absorbing preoccupation of a religious life had a peculiar

[98] "Beal on Chinese Buddhism," *Sat. R.* (1871), 32, p. 248.
[99] Watters, "Buddhism in China" *op. cit.*, 2, 81.
[100] *Ibid.*

attraction for the mystical and the religious.[101] The social character of Buddhist worship appealed to many of its devotees. In the presence of images, the monks met for morning and evening prayer. The pleasing appearance of the altars and the lofty, gilt images supposed to represent powerful beings, which would protect the faithful, enhanced the religious atmosphere of the temples.[102] These and other elements which aided the spread of Buddhism deserved the careful study of Western students of religious history, wrote Edkins. China had done more for the development of Buddhist thought than any other country with the exception of India.[103]

Another question, constantly debated by Christian writers, was whether or not Buddhism had been an aid to the development of civilization in China. Hardwick said that he could not accept the point of view of some Christian writers who maintained that the spread of Buddhist doctrines was adverse to the higher interests of humanity. To say of this religion that its adherents were people "whose business is to do nothing, and to live as much as possible on nothing is a representation meagre, hasty, and one-sided." Hardwick also wrote:

The stress which it originally placed on ethics in their social and political aspect; its contempt for principles which long created an impassable gulf between the different orders of Hindu society; its fuller recognition of the rights of woman; its mild and inoffensive spirit, its equanimity under suffering, its forgiveness of injuries, are some of the peculiar features which adorn its moral code. Instead of ministering to all the grosser passions, like the theories of Islam, it carried its appeal directly to the intellectual and contemplative province of man's nature; instead of finding its chief stimulus in struggles after fame and in the offer of material prosperity, it preached the vanity of earthly goods, the hollowness of human approbation; instead of teaching man to hoard the produce of his industry, it not unfrequently suggested the devotion of superfluous treasure to the founding of a refuge for the blind, the destitute, the crippled, the diseased. Some kings are mentioned, who, starting from the worship of the "Three Precious Ones," had carried their

---

[101] Edkins, *op. cit.*, Preface, xx.
[102] *Ibid.*, xxi.   [103] *Ibid.*, Preface.

philanthropy and tenderness from every kind of animal life to most absurd extremes, and even were accustomed to dole out in alms not only the immense accumulations in the royal coffers, but the whole of their personal ornaments.[104]

Because of these practices of early Buddhism and its great service to humanity, Hardwick agreed that Western admirers of Buddhism were almost justified in calling this religion the Christianity of the East.[105] The teachings of Sakyamuni impressed many Western writers. Students of all creeds praised the simplicity and purity of his moral precepts and practiced rules. The stability with which they withstood the onslaughts of philosophy, infidelity, and Mohammedanism was conclusive proof of their inherent value, and the favor and support lent them by the governments of Asia were cited as evidences of their tendencies to make men peaceful citizens and loyal subjects.[106]

Other Western writers severely condemned Buddhist teachings especially their ideas on morality. In a Buddhist work on morals, *Merits and Demerits Examined,* an individual was directed to keep a debtor and creditor account with himself of each day's acts and at the end of the year to close the record. If the balance were in his favor, it served as the foundation of a stack of merits for the following year and, if against him, it was to be liquidated by future good deeds. Various lists and comparative tables were given of both good and bad actions in the several relations of life. To kill a person was reckoned at one hundred on the demerit side. To save a person's life was fixed at one hundred on the opposite side. A single act of charity rated as one on the merit side. To repair a road, make a bridge, or dig a well ranked at ten and to cure a disease at thirty on the same side. To censure a person unjustly counted as three, to level a tomb at fifty, and to dig up a corpse at one hundred on the debtor's side. This method of keeping a score

---

[104] Hardwick, *op. cit.,* II, 107 *et seq.;* "Beal on Chinese Buddhism," *op. cit.*

[105] Hardwick, *op. cit.,* II, 109; Abel Rémusat, *Mélanges posthumes d'histoire et de littérature orientales* (Paris, 1843), p. 237.

[106] "Beal on Chinese Buddhism," *op. cit.*

with Heaven was branded by Sir John Davis as a foolish and dangerous system of morality.[107] It should be observed, however, said this author, that these notions of morality were not peculiar to Buddhism but prevailed almost universally among the Chinese.[108]

Although students of Buddhist literature appreciated this religion, Western missionaries of the nineteenth century argued that Buddhism for centuries had been in a state of retrogresssion and decay.[109] The priests came from the lowest strata of society and were often almost illiterate.[110] Solitary, unsocial, and contemplative, they lived in idleness and strove for total abstraction or quietism. The idiotic smile and vacant countenances of the majority of these men made them appear little above the animal world in intelligence. Only a few by serious study rose above the general level of mediocrity.[111] Reciting their prayers in Pali, a dialect of Sanscrit, they performed their ceremonies punctiliously and mechanically without any comprehension of their meaning and object.[112]

The Buddhist convents differed little from the monasteries in the mode of worship and the way in which they were supported and conducted. As to the character and practices of the votaries, it was said that with a few exceptions their reputations were not above suspicion.[113]

Besides the monastic establishments, a large number of temples both large and small were scattered throughout China.

[107] Davis, *China*, II, 49 *et seq.*; "Tenets of the Buddhists," *C. Repos.* (1850), 19, p. 548.

[108] Davis, *op. cit.*, II, 50; Williams, *op. cit.*, II, 253.

[109] Hardwick, *op. cit.*, II, 107 *et seq.*

[110] F. E. Forbes, *Five Years in China* (London, 1848), p. 156; C. Gutzlaff, "Remarks on the Present State of Buddhism in China," *JRAS* (1856), 16, p. 73.

[111] Laurence Oliphant, *Narrative of the Earl of Elgin's Mission to China* (New York, 1860), p. 166 *et seq.*; George Smith, *A Narrative of an Exploratory Visit to Each of the Consular Cities of China* (New York, 1847), p. 162.

[112] W. T. Power, *Recollections of Three Years' Residence in China* (London, 1853), p. 283; Williams, *op. cit.*, II, 252; Davis, *op. cit.*, II, 48.

[113] J. L. Nevius, *China and the Chinese* (New York, 1869), p. 102; W. C. Milne, *Life in China* (New ed., London, 1859), p. 116.

Although some were extensive and well supported,[114] most of them were in a state of ruin. Buddhism was not in a flourishing state at the time.[115]

Occidentals, especially Protestant missionaries, often remarked that Buddhism was only a counterfeit of Christianity. Its external ceremonies were supposed to bear a striking resemblance to Roman Catholicism.[116] The monastic habit, holy water, counting rosaries to assist in prayer, the ordinances of celibacy and fasting, masses for the dead, and the canonization of saints were cited as features of both religions. Both burned candles and incense. Both Roman Catholic and Buddhist priests used a dead language for their liturgy.[117] Huc, a Catholic missionary, admitted that certain features of Lamanist worship showed a remarkable similarity to Catholicism. The cross, the mitre, the cope worn by the grand Lamas on their journeys and at ceremonies outside the temple, the service with double choirs, the Psalmody, the exorcisms, the censor suspended from five chains, the priest's benedictions given by extending the right hand over the heads of the faithful, the chaplet, ecclesiastical celibacy, spiritual retirement, and fasts are similar to certain practices of the Roman Catholic religion. Huc thought these characteristics of Buddhism were of Christian origin althought he admitted that he did not have sufficient evidence to prove his point.[118]

The forms of worship used in these two religions were supposed to be similar. In a Buddhist temple, wrote an eyewitness, seven priests, clothed in flowing robes, stood erect and motionless before the altar. While chanting, three priests kept time with the music, one beating an immense drum, another a large vessel, and a third a wooden ball. Afterwards they leaned upon low stools and bowed before the colossal image

---

[114] Robert Fortune, *Two Visits to the Tea Countries of China* (3rd ed., London, 1853), I, 147.   [115] Davis, *op. cit.*, II, 52.

[116] E. J. Eitel, "Buddhism versus Romanism," *C. Recorder* (1870), 3, p. 142 *et seq.*

[117] Williams, *op. cit.*, II, 257 *et seq.*

[118] E. R. Huc, *Souvenirs d'un voyage dans la Tartarie, le Thibet, et la Chine pendant les années 1844, 1845 et 1846* (2nd ed., Paris, 1853), II, 110.

of Buddha. The solemnity of the service in many respects resembled that in a Roman Catholic chapel.[119]

Because of its image worship, external observances, and its teachings in regard to a future existence, Buddhism seems to have taken hold of people's minds particularly those who needed something more colorful and more emotional than the practical morality of Confucianism or the abstract philosophy of Taoism.[120] The three religions came to be on almost the same footing in the nineteenth century. The Lama maintained a small throne in his principality in Tibet and exercised spiritual power over his religious followers. The chief of the Taoists, residing in a beautiful palace in the province of Kiangsi, had the rank of a great mandarin. Many pilgrims visited him to obtain cures for illnesses and the secret of life. The literati or Confucianists, ever invoking the teachings of their master, sometimes adopted in their private life superstitions borrowed from the other two religions. Their symbol was said to be the *Book of Rites* and their divinity was China one and indivisible.[121]

RELIGION—GENERAL CHARACTERISTICS

Westerners, missionaries in particular, made many comments upon general religious notions and practices of the Chinese. Many of their ideas, such as the explanations of the creation of the world and the origin of the first man seemed very odd to Occidentals. The Chinese story of creation began like the scriptural account with the time when the earth was without form and void. Chaos was succeeded by the operation of a dual power, rest and motion, the one female, *Yin*, the other male, *Yang*. Of Heaven and earth, of men and all creatures, animate and inanimate, *Yang* and *Yin* were the father and mother. All things were either male or female.[122] One of the most sensible of their authors, wrote Wells Williams, gives the following account of creation:

[119] Williams, *op. cit.*, II, 257 *et seq.*
[120] "China," *No. Brit. R.* (1847), 7, p. 405.
[121] Théodore Pavie, "Les trois religions de la Chine," *RDM* (1845), 9, p. 475 *et seq.*
[122] "The Chinese Adam," *Liv. Age* (1855), 45, p. 54.

Heaven was formless, an utter chaos; and the whole mass was nothing but confusion. Order was first produced in the pure ether, and out of it the universe came forth; the universe produced air, and air the milky way. When the pure male principle *yang* had been diluted, it formed the heavens; the heavy and thick parts coagulated and formed the earth; the refined particles united very soon, but the union of the thick and heavy went on slowly; therefore the heavens came into existence first, and the earth afterwards. From the subtle essence of heaven and earth the dual principles *yin* and *yang* were formed; from their joint operaton came the four seasons, and these putting forth their energies gave birth to all the products of the earth. The warm effluence of the *yang* being condensed, produced fire; and the finest parts of fire formed the sun. The cold exhalations of the *yin* being likewise condensed produced water; and the finest part of the watery substance formed the moon. By the seminal influence of the sun and moon, came the stars. Thus heaven was adorned with the sun, moon and stars; the earth also received rain, rivers, and dust.[123]

But such an explanation, Williams said, did not satisfy the common people who needed a more simple and concrete exposition. They deified and personified these powers and operations, but from the Western point of view, their mythological creations were coarse and grotesque. The first man, Panku, performed a herculean task; he put into order the chaos producing him and chiseled into form the earth to contain him. The Rationalists pictured Panku holding a chisel and mallet with which he split and fashioned vast masses of granite floating confusedly into space. Behind the openings which he made were the sun, moon, and stars. At his right were the dragon, phoenix, tortoise, and sometimes the unicorn, divine progenitors with himself of the animal creation. The Heavens rose; the earth spread out and thickened, and Panku grew in stature. After his labors were ended he died for the benefit of his handiwork. His head became mountains; his breath formed the wind and clouds, and his voice was thunder. His limbs were changed into the four poles and his veins into rivers, his

[123] Williams, *op. cit.*, II, 195 *et seq.*

sinews became the undulations of the earth's surface, and his flesh made the fields. His beard was turned into stars and his skin and hair into herbs and trees. His teeth, bones, and marrow were converted into the metals, rocks, and precious stones. His perspiration formed rain, and the insects which clung to his body were transformed into people.

This story afforded none of the pleasing images and personifications which Greek mythology and Egyptian religion contained. Chinese myths fatigued without entertaining and illustrated their authors' childish imaginations. Panku was followed by the three rulers called the celestial, terrestrial, and human sovereigns, impersonations of a trinity of powers whose reigns continued for approximately eighteen thousand years. During that time good government was established, and men learned the rudimentary elements of civilization.

An important feature of Chinese religion is the absence of any hierarchy of gods. There was no conclave on Mount Olympus nor any judgment of the mortal soul by Osiris. No human emotions were attributed to the powers above. All was ascribed to disembodied agencies whose works progressed in quiet order. No religion and little imagination were to be found in this cosmogony. Chinese mythology, Williams remarked, might be considered as reasonable as the Greek mythology if sense were looked for in such legends, but it was not explained in sublime poetry, represented in exquisite sculptures, or preserved in faultless and imposing temples.[124] Williams's criticisms obviously show that he rated the Chinese far below the Greeks and even below the Egyptians in imagination and loftiness of sentiment. Other writers have given little attention to the Chinese beliefs in regard to the origin and creation of the world. Huc dismissed the entire subject by asserting that the Chinese cared little for long philosophical speculations and little for questions concerning the origin, creation, and end of the world.[125] The Chinese who were indifferent toward religion were supposed to be absorbed in material matters and the

[124] Ibid.
[125] E. R. Huc, The Chinese Empire (London, 1859), p. 382.

enjoyment of life.[126]   Little religious intolerance, therefore, existed in China.[127]

Two negative features of the Chinese religious systems were noteworthy. The Chinese offered not only no human sacrifices but made no offerings to atone for sin. They did present gifts to win the favor of the gods. This purpose in making offerings was natural; the Chinese had no conception of the meaning of atonement. Sin was committed against man rather than the gods. They were magistrates who punished, and the culprits might escape punishment by flattery and gifts. The Chinese, therefore, bribed their gods. This is the usual interpretation which Westerners gave to the purpose and significance of Chinese offerings.[128]

Another negative feature of the Chinese religion was the absence of what Westerners termed the deification of vice. The Chinese although supposed to be a licentious people did not exalt immorality. They stressed chastity and seclusion as a means of attaining perfection.[129] These features, very commendable from the European point of view, strikingly distinguished the Chinese religion from those of many heathen nations, ancient and modern.[130] Another peculiarity of the Chinese religion is that no sect is a state religion in the Western sense. In Europe an established Church was considered an essential auxiliary of the Government, but in China the state tolerated although it did not support a priesthood, and no religious groups were endowed by the state.[131] In brief, the civil and religious institutions of China were almost wholly inde-

---

[126] *Ibid.*, 381; Williams, *op. cit.*, II, 367 *et seq.*; W. L. G. Smith, *Observations on China and the Chinese* (New York, 1863), p. 197 *et seq.*

[127] Huc, *op. cit.*, 405; G. W. Cooke, *China* (London, 1858), p. 122; "Der Tempel der Landwirtschaft in Pekin," *Land u. Meer* (1868), 20, p. 454; J. M. Mackie, *Life of Tai-ping-wang* (New York, 1857), p. 54; William Gillespie, *The Land of Sinim* (Edinburgh, 1854), p. 59.

[128] M. S. Culbertson, *Darkness in the Flowery Land* (New York, 1857), p. 127; Williams, *op. cit.*, II, 230 *et seq.*; Justus Doolittle, *Social Life of the Chinese* (New York, 1865), I, 293 *et seq.*, II, 394 *et seq.*

[129] Williams, *op. cit.*, II, 230 *et seq.*

[130] Doolittle, *op. cit.*, II, 395 *et seq.*

[131] James Holman, *Travels in China* (2nd ed., London, 1840), p. 276.

pendent of each other. The state, it was said, rarely appealed to the authority of religion.[132]

Although Williams commented upon the absence of a state-supported hierarchy as a remarkable feature, he remarked that a state religion which consisted largely of ceremonies had existed in China since a very ancient date. The objects of state worship were chiefly things although persons were included. There were three grades of sacrifices, the great, the medium, and the inferior. The objects to which the great sacrifices were offered were the heavens or sky, the earth, the great temple of ancestors in which the tablets of deceased monarchs were placed, and the gods of the land and of grain, and the special patrons of each dynasty. The medium sacrifices were offered to eight objects, the sun, moon, manes of the Emperors and Kings of former dynasties, Confucius, the ancient patrons of agriculture and silk weaving, the gods of heaven, earth, and the passing year. The inferior sacrifices were made to the ancient patron of the healing art, to the innumerable spirits of deceased philanthropists, to eminent statesmen, martyrs, virtue, clouds, rain, thunder, and many other things.[133]

The Emperor's assistants in his worship of the four superior objects belonged to the Imperial clan and the Board of Rites. Only one altar was consecrated to heaven and one to earth. Both were in Peking. Annual sacrifices at the time of the solstices were offered. During the equinoxes a prince of the Imperial clan was commissioned to perform the requisite ceremonies and to offer the necessary sacrifices. The statutes prescribed penalties, fines, or blows for informality or neglect. But heavier punishments such as strangulation or banishment were meted out to common folk who dared to state their wants to high heaven or to worship these objects of Imperial adoration because such acts implied Imperial ambition. The Chinese idea of heaven seemed to be pantheistic. In worshipping heaven, earth, and terrestrial god, the Chinese hoped to propitiate all superior powers. The state religion of China was, therefore, a

[132] "China and the Chinese," *Westm. R.* (1857), 67, p. 549.
[133] Williams, *op. cit.*, II, 233 *et seq.*

mere pageant and could not be called a religion. It was closely connected with the learned group, the Confucianists, who were deeply versed in the classical writings. This sect had no temples, no priests, and no creed. They could worship at Buddhist shrines and with the Rationalists without losing connection with their own learned class.[134] Justus Doolittle considered the state religion a fourth in addition to Confucianism, Taoism, and Buddhism. This author stressed the intimate connection of the so-called state religion with the administration of the government. This religion included the various superstitious and idolatrous acts which the mandarins performed as government officials by order of the Emperor.[135] Hegel also wrote that the Chinese religion was essentially a state religion. Because the religious functions belonged primarily to the Emperor, he was the priest for the whole nation.[136]

European notions of Chinese religion were often confusing. Most writers admitted that the lines of demarcation among the religions were not clear cut.[137] Western authors usually mentioned three principal sects of China, the systems of Confucius, Lao Tzŭ, and Buddha. But the religious ceremonies which appealed most strongly to the people were the rites offered at the family shrine to the two "living divinities" who presided in the hall of ancestors.[138] The first two religions, Confucianism and Taoism, were indigenous, but Buddhism known in China before the Christian era was not formally introduced until the first century A.D. From time to time each religion had its

---

[134] *Ibid.;* Culbertson, *op. cit.*, 33 *et seq.*

[135] Doolittle, *op. cit.*, I, 353 *et seq.*

[136] *Hegel's Philosophy of the State and of History*, G. S. Morris, ed. (Chicago, 1887), p. 144.

[137] Escayrac de Lauture, *Mémoires sur la Chine* (Paris, 1865), Religion, p. 17; "The Paper Wall of China," *All the Year* (1860), 3, p. 319; J. J. M. de Groot, *Religion in China* (New York, 1912), p. 1 *et seq.* Two minor religious groups mentioned by writers of the period are Mohammedans and Jews. The Mohammedans had long been tolerated by the Chinese. The Chinese literature on this religion, however, was not extensive. See Williams, *op. cit.*, II, 285; T. Watters, "Chinese Mahometan Literature," *CR* (1872-73), 1, p. 197. A Jewish colony had existed in Honan for centuries. See Williams, *op. cit.*, II, 287; W. C. Milne, *Life in China* (London, 1859), p. 336 *et seq.*   [138] Williams, *op. cit.*, II, 259.

period of ascendancy, but Confucianism was the dominant factor at court and was generally considered the state religion.[139] Westerners considered the teachings of Confucius, however, a system of philosophy rather than a religion.[140]

[139] W. H. Medhurst, *China; Its State and Prospects* (Boston, 1838), p. 152.
[140] *Supra*, p. 182.

CHAPTER XI

MUSIC AND THE ARTS

BEFORE 1875 no Westerner seems to have made an
exhaustive, interpretative study of Chinese music.[1] Travellers and others occasionally commented upon Oriental music,
but their remarks showed little understanding or appreciation of
its spirit and its meaning. Sir John Francis Davis wrote that "of
all burlesques upon harmony, the Chinese music is perhaps the
most atrocious; every man would seem to be playing a different
tune, or rather, making a different noise, and the predominance
of the tones of the Scottish bagpipe does not lessen the evil by
any means."[2] The Chinese, although they gave music a very
conspicuous place in their social and political system had not as
much variety and completeness in their music as the ancient
Greeks, according to Faber.[3] Huc admitted that Chinese music
had a certain softness and melancholy in its tones but became
intolerably monotonous after a time.[4] A story current in London in 1869 well illustrates European opinion of "Celestial"
musical appreciation. A Chinese attending a concert in that city
thought that the noise which the musicians made in tuning their
instruments was the finest part of the performance.[5]

It is hardly believable with the great interest at the present
time in Chinese painting, ancient bronzes, and porcelain vases
that Westerners almost totally ignored Chinese art throughout
the greater part of the nineteenth century. Critics had not come
in contact with the finest Chinese art then but only with the in-

[1] J. A. van Aalst's *Chinese Music* was published in 1884. Ernst Faber,
"The Chinese Theory of Music," *CR* (1872-73), 1, pp. 324-29, 384-88
(1873-74), 2, pp. 47-50.
[2] J. F. Davis, *Sketches of China* (London, 1841), I, 195; J. K. Duer,
"Chinese Sketches," *Knicker.* (1860), 50, p. 298 *et seq.*
[3] Faber, *op. cit.*, 325.
[4] E. R. Huc, *The Chinese Empire* (New ed., London, 1859), p. 455;
"Kulturgeschichte," *J. d. Lit.* (1848), 121, p. 147.
[5] "Chinese Notions of Music," *N. & Q.* (1869), 3, pp. 381, 447.

ferior pieces which traders had brought from the Orient. After the second Anglo-Chinese War during which the Summer Palace with its vast art treasures was looted, rare specimens were carried to England and France, and some were displayed at the international exhibitions at London in 1862 and at Paris in 1867. But the interest in Chinese art was not great enough to produce a significant work in that field before 1875. The criticisms on the subject which are summarized in the following pages are not by art critics, with the exception of Ruskin, but by writers who devoted a few paragraphs now and then to their impressions on Oriental art.

The chief defect of Chinese paintings from the Occidental point of view was the disregard of perspective and the principle of proportion.[6] Yet the Orientals were not altogether strangers to these subjects. As draughtsmen, they could portray some single portion of natural scenery with extraordinary fidelity.[7] The garden scenes of the fan painters at Swatow were remarkable for their beauty. Here was found a very fine class of Chinese art; it was pure and simple without a trace of any foreign element.[8] The Chinese did not understand light and shade and even objected to shadows in their pictures.[9] Because of their deficient knowledge of the principles of perspective and their aversion to the use of light and shadow, their landscapes and portraits, measured by European standards, were crude and elementary.[10]

The majority of Westerners who expressed themselves on the subject of Chinese art agreed that their vivid and striking colors were unusual.[11] Ruskin, who made occasional references

[6] John Ruskin, *Works* (Library ed., London, 1903-12), III, 144; Alexandre Bonacossi, *La Chine et les Chinois* (Paris, 1847), p. 280.

[7] G. T. Lay, *The Chinese As They Are* (Albany, 1843), p. 90; J. F. Davis, *China: A General Description* (New ed., London, 1857), II, 214.

[8] John Thomson, *The Straits of Malacca, Indo-China, and China* (New York, 1875), p. 281.

[9] W. B. Langdon, *Descriptive Catalogue of the Chinese Collection* (London, 1844), p. 118 *et seq.*

[10] Julia Corner, *The History of China and India, Pictorial and Descriptive* (3rd ed., London, 1847), p. 160.

[11] H. C. Sirr, *China and the Chinese* (London, 1849), I, 106.

to Oriental art in his general discussions of the subject of art, criticized the over-emphasis of color. He thought it detracted from Chinese art by causing it to border on the grotesque. He also attributed the weakness of Chinese artists in form to the influence of foolish terror and fanciful imaginations.[12] Other writers praised the Orientals for the unusual artistic skill which they displayed in their drawings of flowers, butterflies, insects, and fish.[13] One observer wrote that the Chinese had a strong appreciation of beauty in form and by studying the lines of trees and of various figures could combine them into very beautiful and graceful compositions.[14]

The Western writer most appreciative, probably, of Chinese painting was Sirr who highly commended a contemporary artist's work because of the exquisite coloring of his oil paintings. Many of his portraits of both Chinese and Europeans were excellent likenesses and, although deficient in light and shade, were executed in a masterly manner. Westerners' chief criticism of portraits by Chinese painters was the lack of life and expression.[15] Sirr commended the Chinese proficiency in oil painting, but Europeans were not generally aware of this particular talent. A good example of this type of art was a painting in oil which represented the interior of a Chinese dwelling. For clearness of design, truthfulness of composition, accuracy of perspective, and subdued tone coloring, it was not surpassed by a master of the ancient schools. The figures and costumes were perfectly portrayed while the objects of still life, flowers, and animals were depicted with great faithfulness and exactness.[16]

Foreigners now and then extravagantly praised Chinese art, but it was not appreciated by the West as a whole. Western critics set up the principles of European art as a standard and

[12] Ruskin, op. cit., X, 219, XIX, 383, XX, 227.
[13] John Henry Gray, Walks in the City of Canton (Victoria, 1875), p. 295.
[14] Arthur Fisher, Personal Narrative of Three Years' Service in China (London, 1863), p. 125.   [15] Sirr, op. cit., I, 107 et seq.
[16] Ibid.; Martha N. Williams, A Year in China (New York, 1864), p. 217; Arthur Cunynghame, An Aide-de-camp's Recollections of Service in China (London, 1844), II, 97; Fisher, op. cit., p. 124; Sinibaldo de Mas, La Chine et les puissances chrétiennes (Paris, 1861), I, 63.

pronounced Chinese art good only in so far as it conformed to the prescribed rules of the former. Most Occidentals seemed to think the art of Canton superior to that of any other part of the Empire because it was influenced by foreign painters.[17]

The West was no more impressed by Chinese sculpture than by painting. The stone figures were uncouth in form and proportion.[18] The Chinese, it seemed to Occidentals, could only express strength and power by size.[19] Although the Orientals were not great sculptors, they were excellent modellers and had access to a very fine clay from which they made admirable figures.[20] This art was highly developed at Tientsin. The colossal clay statues of that city were remarkable for their gigantic proportions and their expressions.[21] The Chinese also moulded tiny clay figures which were good images of men and women. Their humorous characteristics were often faithfully portrayed.[22] Genuine Western appreciation of Chinese painting and sculpture, however, belongs to a period later than 1875, and little real appreciation is apparent before the first decade of the twentieth century.

Throughout the nineteenth century, a few Westerners admired the Chinese method of ornamentation and marvelled at the power to balance colors, the fullest tones of the most delicate shades, with striking effects. The Chinese were most successful, perhaps, in the management of the lighter tones of pure colors of which pale blue, pink, and green predominated.[23] Ruskin, however, thought that the Chinese stressed color too much, and as late as 1856 Owen Jones, who was for a long

[17] Davis, op. cit., II, 213 et seq.; James Holman, Travels in China (2nd ed., London, 1840), p. 242; S. W. Williams, The Middle Kingdom (New York, 1848), II, 174; "Chinese Artists," Illus. London News (1859), 34, p. 428. [18] Davis, op. cit., II, 216.

[19] W. T. Power, Recollections of Three Years' Residence in China (London, 1853), p. 183. [20] Bonacossi, op. cit., p. 281.

[21] J. E. Bingham, Narrative of the Expedition to China (London, 1842), I, 337.

[22] Thomson, op. cit., p. 502; Maurice d'Irisson d'Hérisson, Études sur la Chine contemporaine (2nd ed., Paris, 1869), p. 157.

[23] Owen Jones, The Grammar of Ornament (London, 1856), Chap. XIV; Williams, op. cit., II, 117.

time unimpressed by this field of art, made the following comment:

> In their ornamentation, with which the world is so familiar through the numerous manufactured articles of every kind which have been imported into this country, they do not appear to have gone beyond that point which is reached by every people in an early stage of civilization; their art, such as it is, is fixed and is subject neither to progression or retrogression. In the conception of pure form they are even behind the New Zealander. . . .
>
> The general forms of many of the Chinese porcelain vases are remarkable for the beauty of their outline, but not more so than the rude water bottles of porous clay which the untutored Arabian potter fashions daily . . . and the pure form of the Chinese vases are often destroyed by the addition of grotesque or other unmeaning ornaments, built up upon the surface, not growing from it: from which we argue, that they can possess an appreciation of form, but in a minor degree.
>
> In their decoration both painted and woven, the Chinese exhibit only just so much art as would belong to a primitive people.[24]

After the second Anglo-Chinese War and the T'ai P'ing Rebellion, some magnificent specimens of ornamental art were sent to Europe. The unusual skill in the technical processes, the beauty and harmony of the colors, and the general perfection of the ornamentation of these objects were remarkable, Jones wrote in 1867.[25] Because of more intimate acquaintance with Chinese art, this critic had changed his views in a very short time and popularized to a certain extent the Chinese style of ornamentation in England and other countries of the West.

No comprehensive work on Chinese architecture was published in the West before 1875, but books on the general subject

---

[24] Jones, op. cit.; J. R. Peters, Miscellaneous Remarks upon the Government, History, Religions, Literature, Agriculture, Arts, Trades, Manners, and Customs of the Chinese . . . (Philadelphia, 1847), p. 125; Langdon, op. cit., p. 68 et seq.; Davis, op. cit., II, 205.

[25] Owen Jones, Examples of Chinese Ornament (London, 1867), Preface, p. 5; "China," Asiat. J. (1840), 32, Part II, 48; J. B. Waring, Masterpieces of Industrial Art and Sculpture at the International Exhibition, 1862 (London, 1863), I, p. 35.

of architecture, as well as descriptive works on China, summarized the more obvious features of its buildings.[26] Fergusson wrote that "China possesses scarcely anything worthy of the name of architecture." The reasons for no remains, he attributed to the want of taste rather than to the lack of power. Another reason for no real appreciation of architecture was probably the absence of a dominant priesthood which ordinarily gives impetus to a strongly developed sacred art which, in turn, lends inspiration to architecture.[27] Many temples did exist in China, but they were very similar to the domestic style of building. Huc believed the Chinese to be incapable of comprehending the majestic, solemn, and melancholy style of the Western religious edifices. The Orientals built their pagodas on gay sites which they planted with trees and flowering shrubs. Such a place had the atmosphere of a rural dwelling in the midst of a park or garden.[28]

Goethe's satirical epigram, "The Chinaman in Rome" (1796) is a succinct expression of the European attitude, which also prevailed in the nineteenth century, toward Chinese architecture:

A Chinaman I saw in Rome; all the buildings without an exception ancient and modern alike seemed to him heavy and gross. "Ah!" he exclaims with a sigh, "Poor souls! will they some day learn that elegant pillars of wood are the only support for a roof, that a compound of paper and laths and fretwork painted and gilded gives to the liberal sense of the cultured its only delight?" In him I seemed to behold how many a frivolous aesthete! who the light webs he spins out of his brain would compare with Nature's eternal woof, who labels the sound and the healthy morbid, and he, the diseased, he is the only one sound![29]

[26] James Fergusson, *The Illustrated Handbook of Architecture* (2nd ed., London, 1859), pp. 133-43; Eliza Chalk, *A Peep into Architecture* (London, 1845), pp. 165-67. Daniel Ramée in *Histoire générale de l'architecture* (Paris, 1860) does not discuss Chinese architecture. Examples were not displayed at the Exposition Universelle (Paris, 1867). Alfred Normand in *L'Architecture des nations étrangères. Exposition universelle de Paris en 1867* does not mention China.

[27] Fergusson, *op. cit.*, 133 *et seq.*   [28] Huc, *op. cit.*, 400.

[29] Adolf Reichwein, *China and Europe* (New York, 1925), p. 137.

Thomas Allom undoubtedly appreciated many features of Chinese architecture or could not have portrayed its details with such precision and understanding. Many of Allom's drawings in *The Chinese Empire Illustrated* (1843) were inspired by Alexander's sketches, published in 1796. Allom's "Playing at shuttle cock with the feet" follows in general Alexander's drawing on the same subject. Allom's figures, however, are more gracefully and more clearly depicted. The deftly drawn pagoda and junk in the background give a subtle atmosphere to the picture. Allom's "Great Wall" is similar to Alexander's in its main outlines, but the figures in the foreground blend into the scene more artistically than Alexander's. Other drawings of Allom are based upon sketches of landscapes made by other Europeans in China and probably upon his own observations in the East. The unusual limpid and delicate beauty of Allom's drawings made the books in which they appeared very popular not only in England but in other European countries.[30] The beauty of the Chinese landscapes also inspired a number of drawings by the French artist, Auguste Borget who lived for many years in China. Several of his Chinese landscapes sketched from nature were in the exhibition opened at the Louvre in 1841. Borget's *Sketches of China and the Chinese* (1842) contain some excellent drawings which Allom used as themes for some of his sketches.[31]

Because of the non-existence of a hereditary nobility and the equal division of a man's property at his death among his children, no durable domestic architecture developed in China. Even the wealthiest men did not build mansions, designed to last longer their their own lives.[32] Because of the security of property, no fortified strongholds like the castles of medieval

[30] *China, historisch, romantisch, malerisch* (Carlsruhe im Kunst-Verlag); Thomas Allom, *L'Empire chinois* . . . Description par Clement Pelle (Paris, 184?); Henri Cordier, *Bibliotheca Sinica* (Paris, 1904-08), col. 80 *et seq.*

[31] "Auguste Borget," *Mo. Chron.* (1841), 2, p. 285; "China, in a Series of Views . . . Drawn by T. Allom . . . ," *C. Repos.* (1849), 18, p. 420. See "Harbour of Hong Kong" and "Bamboo Aqueduct at Hong Kong," Thomas Allom, *China* . . . (London, 1843), I, 17, 33; see "Baie et Île de Hong-Kong," Auguste Borget, *Sketches of China and the Chinese* (London, 1842), illustrations IV, III.   [32] Fergusson, *op. cit.*, p. 134.

Europe dotted the country of China.[33] These are Fergusson's explanations for the absence of lasting domestic architecture in that country.

Almost the only buildings which could be classed as real representatives of Chinese architecture were the pagodas of which the celebrated "porcelain" tower of Nanking was the finest example. But the pagoda owed its fame chiefly to the coating of "porcelain." This glaze covered the brick walls as well as the under and upper sides of the projecting roofs which marked the division of each of its nine stories. This covering produced an unusual brilliancy and was the type of decoration on which the architect almost wholly relied to produce the desired effect.[34] Because the pagoda is original and because any tower of great height is usually pleasing, the "tapering, octagonal form, the boldly-marked divisions, the domical roof, and general consistence in design and ornament, of these towers, entitle them to rank tolerably high among the tower-like buildings of the world."[35] The feature of Chinese architecture which Westerners most admired was not its form, which lacked both durability and grandeur, but its brilliant colors and the beauty of its carvings and ornaments.[36]

The grounds surrounding the temples and other buildings were very much admired by Europeans and Americans.[37] Davis said, however, that the Chinese style of ornamental gardens had been very much overdrawn by Sir William Chambers who popularized the Chinese method of landscape gardening in England about a century earlier.[38] Davis quoted Barrows's description of the Emperor's extensive pleasure ground northwest of Peking. Barrows, who admired the Chinese taste in landscape design, gave the following description of these grounds:

The grand and agreeable parts of nature were separated, connected, or arranged in so judicious a manner as to compose one

[33] Ibid., 135.

[34] Ibid., 135-36.   [35] Ibid., 137.

[36] Ibid., 140; Corner, op. cit., p. 160; George Mogridge, The Celestial Empire (London, 1844), p. 251.

[37] W. C. Milne, Life in China (New ed., London, 1859), p. 68; Power, op. cit., p. 181; R. J. L. M'Ghee, How We Got to Peking (London, 1862), p. 211.   [38] Davis, op. cit., II, 215.

whole, in which there was no inconsistency or unmeaning jumble of objects, but such an order and proportion as generally prevail in scenes entirely natural. No round or oval, square or oblong lawns, with the grass shorn off close to the roots, were to be found anywhere in these grounds. The Chinese are particularly expert in magnifying the real dimensions of a piece of land, by a proper disposition of objects intended to embellish its surface. For this purpose tall and luxuriant trees of the deepest green were planted in the foreground, from whence the view was to be taken; whilst those in the distance gradually diminished in size and depth of colouring; and in general the ground was terminated by broken and irregular clumps of trees, whose foliage was varied, as well by the different species of trees in the group, as by the different times of the year 'in which they were in vigour; and oftentimes the vegetation was apparently old and stunted, making with difficulty its way through the clefts of rocks, either originally found, or designedly collected upon the spot.

The effect of intricacy and concealment seemed also to be well understood by the Chinese at Yuen-ming-yuen; a slight wall was made to convey the idea of a magnificent building, when seen at a certain distance through the branches of a thicket. Sheets of made water, instead of being surrounded by sloping banks, like the glacis of a fortification, were occasionally hemmed in by artificial rocks, seemingly indigenous to the soil. . . .[39]

The Chinese were not great artists in any field with the possible exception of ornamentation, from the Western point of view. But Europeans did admire their ingenuity and skill in various kinds of craftwork.[40] In all kinds of manufactures with the exception of cutlery, locks, and other iron objects which were crudely wrought, the native craftsmen were extremely deft and versatile. Despite the inferior quality of their iron work, their tools such as chisels, planes, and axes were sharp and, notwithstanding their clumsy appearance, many were of good quality.[41]

[39] Ibid.
[40] Sirr, op. cit., I, 394; Lay, op. cit., 93; G. T. Staunton, Miscellaneous Notices Relating to China (2nd ed., London, 1822-50), Introduction, p. 10.
[41] "Chinese Tools and Mechanics," Penny M. (1843), 12, p. 151; Justus Doolittle, Social Life of the Chinese (New York, 1865), I, 60 et seq.

Some of the manufactures in which the Chinese excelled were silks which included damasks, flowered satins, crêpes, and pongee.[42] Their embroidery was not only unequalled but was even superior to that of any other nation, wrote Sirr.[43] The matchless skill of Chinese craftsmen in the carving of such materials as ivory, mother-of-pearl, tortoise shell, jade, stone, and wood is demonstrated in articles of great beauty both for ornamental and utilitarian purposes.[44] Few examples of their skill are more remarkable than the ivory balls, containing ten or more, carved one within the other.[45] While Occidentals admired the delicate workmanship of all kinds of manufactures and crafts which they attributed to sheer mechanical skill, they argued that any kind of work which required profound thought and mathematical exactness was beyond Chinese ability.[46]

The industrial arts in which the Chinese showed themselves expert craftsmen, Europeans and Americans had admired since their first contacts with China. The early traders returned to their native countries with various examples, probably not the best, of porcelain, cloisonné, ivory, wood and jade carvings, embroideries, and fine qualities of manufactured silk. The great international exhibitions held at London in 1851 and 1862, at Paris in 1867, at Vienna in 1873, and at Philadelphia in 1876 displayed some very beautiful specimens of the fine arts, which included painting and sculpture, and also examples of the various branches of industrial art. These expositions, therefore,

[42] Davis, op. cit., II, 204; Langdon, op. cit., 120; Williams, op. cit., II, 123; Isidore Hedde, Description méthodique des produits (Saint Étienne, 1848), p. 101 et seq.

[43] Sirr, op. cit., I, 385; Robert Fortune, Two Visits to the Tea Countries of China (3rd ed., London, 1853), I, 66; Williams, op. cit., II, 123; Hedde, op. cit., 237 et seq.

[44] Corner, op. cit., 157; New York Tribune . . . Guide to the Exhibition (New York, 1876), p. 2.

[45] Williams, op. cit., II, 140 et seq.; W. H. Medhurst, China; Its State and Prospects (Boston, 1838), p. 99; Milne, op. cit., 22; Davis, op. cit., II, 199; Frank Leslie's Historical Register of the United States Centennial Exposition, 1876, Frank H. Norton, ed. (New York, 1877), p. 247; International Exhibition, 1862. Official Catalogue of the Fine Art Department (London).

[46] The People of China (Philadelphia, 1844), p. 159 et seq.

introduced Chinese art on a large scale to the West and popularized Chinese crafts such as cloisonné work.[47]

[47] Waring, *op. cit.*, vols. I, III; *Paris Universal Exhibition, 1867. Complete Official Catalogue* (2nd ed., London, 1867), pp. 217, 223, 239, 249,
261, 268, 285, 303, 411; *Frank Leslie's Historical Register, op. cit.*, 244;
International Exhibition, 1862. Reports by the Juries . . . , (London, 1863),
Class XXX, Sections A and B, p. 12.

CHAPTER XII

SCIENCE

CHINESE scientific knowledge was confined almost entirely to arithmetic and geometry. In antiquity medical art vied with science in importance. It was always an art, however, rather than a science in China.[1] Few Western scholars admitted that the Chinese had advanced very far in abstract science, but Wylie wrote that further investigations would establish more correct views on this point. He emphasized Chinese progress in the development of arithmetic. When the Roman Catholic missionaries, Ricci, Schall, and others arrived in China, the exact sciences were in a state of decline, and the missionaries introduced much European science into the East. The Western system of astronomy and methods of computation impressed the native mathematicians to such an extent that the Astronomical Board came largely under the control of the Jesuits. They greatly influenced the development of mathematics in China. Wylie also mentioned a few important native scholars of the nineteenth century. Some of these mathematicians applied themselves to certain branches of mathematical science which had been entirely independent of all Western progress along the same lines, since the introduction of European scientific principles by the Jesuits.[2] Occidentals knew very little about Chinese science, and the general opinion prevailed that the Chinese cared very little for abstract science. They seemed to recognize its value only in so far as it was useful for practical purposes.[3]

In the seventeenth century Chinese medicine had a certain vogue in Europe, and a few treatises on the subject were printed.

[1] R. K. Douglas, "The Progress of Science in China," *Ecl. M.* (1873), 81, p. 745.

[2] Alexander Wylie, "The Science of the Chinese," *C. & J. Repos.* (1864), 1, p. 411 *et seq.*

[3] Douglas, *op. cit.*, 747; A. W. Loomis, "Medical Art in the Chinese Quarter," *Overland* (1869), 2, p. 500.

Specimen Medicinae Sinicae was edited by Andreas Cleyer and published at Frankfurt in 1682.[4] A further proof of the interest in Chinese medicine was a memoir on acupuncture by Willem Ten Rhyne, a Dutch surgeon, who had just returned from Batavia. It was published in 1683 in his work, *De Athritide*.[5] Since that time, Westerners have been curious about Chinese medical practices. A number of articles on diseases and their methods of treatment were published by physicians in the medical journals of the West.[6] Because the public was always interested in the odd and bizarre customs, general accounts and periodical articles capitalized the comical side of Chinese medical practices. An example is the paper, "John Chinaman, M.D."[7] He was described as "a happy compound of pedant, quack, fortune-teller, and spirit-rapper, flavored with a dash of Confucian priest."[8]

Most Westerners had a rather low opinion of Chinese medical science which was said to be inferior in the nineteenth century to medical art at the time of Hippocrates.[9] Chinese medicine was also said to find its exact parallel in the practices of Europe two centuries earlier.[10] Chinese doctors were supposedly ignorant of all that was then known of chemistry, physiology, and anatomy. Many false notions about these subjects were handed down undisputed from generation to generation. Because of vague and incorrect notions of anatomy, surgery scarcely existed, and only the most simple operations were performed.[11]

[4] Paul Pelliot, "Michel Boym," *TP* (1935), 31, p. 137 *et seq.*; see also Daniel Hanbury, *Notes on Chinese Materia Medica* (London, 1862), p. 1 *et seq.*

[5] J. J. L. Duyvendak, "Les Études hollando-chinoises au 17ième au 18ième siècle," *Quatre esquisses détachées relatives aux études orientalistes à Leiden* (1930), p. 36 *et seq.*; Henri Cordier, *Bibliotheca Sinica* (Paris, 1904-08), col. 1473.   [6] *Ibid.*, 1462 *et seq.*

[7] J. W. Palmer, "John Chinaman M.D.," *Atlan.* (1868), 21, pp. 257-68.   [8] *Ibid.*, p. 258.

[9] William Lockhart, *The Medical Missionary in China* (2nd ed., London, 1861), p. 154; W. H. Medhurst, *China; Its State and Prospects* (Boston, 1838), p. 98.

[10] F. P. Smith, "Chinese Medicines," *N. & Q. on C. & J.* (1869), 3, p. 117.

[11] J. G. Kerr, "Chinese Medicine," *CR* (1872-73), 1, p. 176 *et seq.*; James Henderson, "The Medicine and Medical Practices of the Chinese,"

Europeans were surprised that, as late as the middle of the nineteenth century in a country where learning played such an important part, medicine was not studied scientifically, no recognized system of teaching the subject existed, no certificate was required of practitioners,[12] and such ignorant and mediocre doctors were tolerated.[13] Any one could set himself up as a doctor if he chose to do so.[14] The practitioner usually concentrated on the pulse. It afforded some clue to the malady, and the doctor could conceal his ignorance by pretending in this way to determine the exact nature of the disorder.[15] Through the whole range of the voluminous medical literature, ignorance and conceit were evident; their best theories were based upon empty speculations.[16]

Because Chinese doctors' practical knowledge was far in advance of their theory, they quite often successfully treated certain diseases. Huc mentioned the successful treatment of hydrophobia by medical men but did not describe the remedies used.[17] They were also rather skillful in setting broken bones.[18] Some of their treatises on dietetics and medical practices contain good advice from the Western point of view. Although their theory was imperfect, they found, by tracing the history of their cases, methods of treatment effective and the properties of certain medicines beneficial for particular diseases. They gradually came to use specific treatments for certain diseases.[19] Medical practice in China was therefore empirical.

A department of medicine which impressed many Westerners during the period from 1840 to 1876 was Chinese *materia*

JNCBRAS (1864), i, pp. 21-69; Loomis, *op. cit.*, p. 502; Lockhart, *op. cit.*, p. 112.   [12] *Ibid.*

[13] Kerr, *op. cit.*   [14] Douglas, *op. cit.*, 746.

[15] Kerr, *op. cit.*, 178.   [16] Henderson, *op. cit.*, 36 *et seq.*

[17] E. R. Huc, *The Chinese Empire* (New ed., London, 1859), p. 284 *et seq.*

[18] S. W. Williams, *The Middle Kingdom* (New York, 1848), II, 183.

[19] Lockhart, *op. cit.*, 113 *et seq.* A collection of Chinese medicines and medicinal vegetables, fruits, and animals were on display at the Exposition at Philadelphia, 1876. See *Frank Leslie's Historical Register of the United States Centennial Exposition, 1876*, Frank H. Norton, ed. (New York, 1877), p. 247; see also *International Exhibition, 1862. Official Catalogue of the Industrial Department* (London), p. 168.

medica. The *Pên Ts'ao,* the standard work on the subject, contains a list of almost twelve hundred substances derived from animal, vegetable, and mineral matters which were used in medicine. The description of their properties and their uses is taken from the works of more than eight hundred authors. Such a work as the *Pên Ts'ao* had scarcely a parallel in the world at the time that it was compiled.[20] This work, originally a *materia medica,* gives an almost complete record of the botany of ancient China because the Chinese used nearly every known plant as medicine.[21]

Interest in Chinese drugs and medicinal plants after 1840 was doubtlessly stimulated by the general development of the science of pharmacognosy which deals with crude drugs and other vegetable and animal raw materials used in medicine. Pharmacognosy owes its origin to the initial studies on the histology or microscopic anatomy of plants. Through researches on the structure of plants, scientists learned that drugs of different origins could be determined by their cellular differences. After scientists had discovered these facts, pharmacognosy developed rapidly in Europe. Many scholars made researches and published the results of their studies.[22]

Westerners were interested, long before the nineteenth century, in Chinese natural history especially botany.[23]   Boym wrote a short treatise on Chinese botany, *Flora Sinensis* (1656); Martini in his *Atlas Sinensis* and Kircher in *China Illustrata* gave some information on the plants, animals, and minerals of China. The material on these subjects, furnished by the Jesuits, was incorporated in Du Halde's *Description de la Chine.* Later students of Chinese botany and zoology used these works, although they were not very scientific from the nineteenth-century point of view.

Wells Williams, who had a considerable knowledge of natural science, was one of the first students to try to identify

[20] Kerr, *op. cit.,* 178.

[21] Emil Bretschneider, "The Study and Value of Chinese Botanical Works," *C. Recorder* (1870), 3, p. 161 *et seq.*

[22] K. Kimura, "Important Works in the Study of Chinese Medicine," *CJ* (1935), 23, p. 109 *et seq.*   [23] Bretschneider, *op. cit.,* 242 *et seq.*

Chinese names of plants, animals, and minerals with European names. The three chapters in Bridgman's *Chrestomathy in the Canton Dialect* (1841) treating of botany, zoology, and mineralogy were compiled by Williams. In 1850 Tartarinov, physician at the Russian Ecclesiastical Mission in Peking, published a list of drugs obtained from Chinese shops. Knowing some Chinese, he studied botanical works and gathered many medicinal plants which the scientists in Saint Petersburg examined. This is the origin of Tartarinov's *Catalogus Medicamentorum Sinensium* (1856).[24]

Hoffmann and Schultes in a small treatise, *Noms indigènes d'un choix de plantes du Japon et de la Chine* (1853), tried to identify Chinese plant names with scientific names used in the West. Another small but valuable work, for its time, was Daniel Hanbury's *Notes on Chinese Materia Medica* (1862). The author admits that the work is very incomplete because the zoology, botany, and mineralogy of China had not been adequately studied.[25]

In 1870 Emil Bretschneider, a physician at the Russian Legation in Peking, published in the *Chinese Recorder* a series of papers, "The Study and Value of Chinese Botanical Works"[26] in which he tried to show how the Chinese treated the subject of natural science especially botany and what advantages European scientists and Sinologists could derive from Chinese botanical works. More than ten years later the same author published in the *Journal of the North China Branch of the Royal Asiatic Society* his "*Botanicon Sinicum*, Notes on Chinese Botany from Native and Western Sources" and later, "Botanical Investigations in the *Materia Medica* of the Ancient Chinese."[27] These treatises, based on extensive research extending over a long period of time, contained the fullest information then available and were very valuable contributions to Western knowledge of Chinese botany. Bretschneider collected his specimens in China

[24] Cordier, *op. cit.*, col. 1475.   [25] Hanbury, *op. cit.*, 1 *et seq.*
[26] *C. Recorder* (1870), 3, pp. 157-63, 172-78, 218-27, 241-49, 264-72, 281-94.
[27] *JNCBRAS* (1881), 16, pp. 18-230, (1893), 25, pp. 1-468, (1896), 29, pp. 1-623.

and had access to important books in Chinese and European languages at the libraries of the Russian Legation and the Russian Ecclesiastical Mission. He also collaborated with both native and Western scholars. Because of these advantages, even though he was not a botanist, he believed himself better prepared to make a study of the subject than the scientists of Europe.[28]

Frederick Porter Smith's *Contributions toward the Materia Medica and Natural History of China* (1871) was one of the first books on this subject by a Western author. Smith, a medical missionary, lived for a long time in the central provinces of China. He studied such works as the *Pên Ts'ao* and also used the works published by Europeans on the subject of Chinese botany. His compilation of a list of drugs used for medicinal purposes in China was primarily for the use of Western physicians in that country and native medical students. The wealth of material on plants and minerals in this book was valuable to European scientists.[29]

Because of the advance of Westerners in all fields of science especially in applied science during the nineteenth century, Europeans viewed Chinese science with disdain. The Western writers, Davis, Huc, and Williams gave the Chinese only a moderate amount of praise for their achievements, which were largely practical, in the field of natural science. Loomis wrote that the Chinese with almost no knowledge of chemistry had stumbled on ways of reducing many of the ores, methods for extracting a few oils, and special techniques for mixing colors.[30] Davis compared the state of science in China with the condition of science in Europe previous to the use of the inductive method of philosophy.[31] Bretschneider wrote that because the Chinese

[28] Emil Bretschneider, "*Botanicon Sinicum*, Notes on Chinese Botany, from Native and Western Sources," *JNCBRAS* (1881), 16, p. 18 *et seq.*

[29] Jules Mohl, "Contributions toward the Materia Medica," *JA* (1873), 1, pp. 123-24.

[30] Loomis, *op. cit.*, 500; Williams, *op. cit.*, II, 154; Huc, *op. cit.*, p. 194; R. S. Maclay, *Life among the Chinese* (New York, 1861), p. 30; T. Watters, "Chinese Notions about Pigeons and Doves," *JNCBRAS* (1867), 4, p. 225.

[31] J. F. Davis, *China: A General Description* (New ed., London, 1857), II, 221; Smith, "Chinese Medicines," *N. & Q. on C. & J.* (1869), 3, p. 118.

style of writing was ambiguous and because they possessed little talent for careful observation, their works on natural science were inferior to the Greek and Roman treatises on this subject.[32]

Numerous books, dealing with botany and the closely related sciences, such as agriculture, contain much material on the uses of plants for food, clothes, and manufacturing purposes.[33] With the exception of Hervey-Saint-Denys' little book on Chinese agriculture, no general work on the subject was published during the years from 1840 to 1876. Enough comments have been found on agriculture in general and on certain phases of the subject in Robert Fortune's books, in the Reports of the United States Department of Agriculture, and in general descriptive accounts to show a definite Western interest in Chinese methods of agriculture and in plants which Occidentals hoped to introduce in their respective countries. Europeans had extravagantly praised Chinese agriculture since their earliest contacts with the Orient. The imaginations of the early missionaries and later travellers were stirred by the Emperor's participation in the annual ceremonies. Each spring he went to a field near Peking to plow a furrow into which he threw some rice seed; he then covered the seed with the freshly upturned earth. In this way the Emperor demonstrated the Government's interest in the cultivation of the land to supply food for the teeming population.[34]

Hervey-Saint-Denys said that the Chinese taste for agriculture and horticulture entered into all of their customs, and their respect for these occupations were read into every page of their history. The most ancient monuments of their literature as

[32] Bretschneider, "Study and Value of Chinese Botanical Works," C. Recorder (1870), 3, p. 161 et seq., 172.

[33] ———, "Botanicon Sinicum. . . ," JNCBRAS (1881), 16, p. 21; Le Comte d'Escayrac de Lauture, Mémoires sur la Chine (Paris, 1865), Coutumes, p. 64.

[34] Robert Fortune, Two Visits to the Tea Countries of China (3rd ed., London, 1853), I, 221 et seq.; S. W. Williams, "Notices on Chinese Agriculture," Report of the Commissioner of Patents, Agriculture (1860), p. 467. The annual report on agriculture until 1861 formed a part of the report of the Commissioner of Patents, and after 1849 the report on agriculture made a separate volume. After 1862 the Department of Agriculture, which was created in that year, issued an annual report.

well as the most recent decrees of their Emperors show the
sovereign constantly protecting agriculture, the science *par excellence* of China.[35] The Chinese developed agriculture to the
highest point of perfection with very crude implements. No
European laborer could use their plow which was merely a
sharpt point set in a rude piece of bent wood. Every acre,
nevertheless, was supposedly cultivated. Sometimes a hill was
entirely covered with rice plots one above the other in the form
of terraces. Even the top of the hill was often a rice field,
and if no river were near by reservoirs were dug to supply
water in cases of drought.[36] Williams considered the Chinese
gardeners rather than farmers. Although they were almost
entirely ignorant of the scientific principles of agriculture, they
raised good crops by careful plowing, irrigation, and fertilizer
which restored the elements taken out of the soil by growing
crops.[37] The progress and advance in agricultural methods,
according to both Davis and Fortune, were overrated by the
early Catholic missionaries whose opinions frequently found
their way into the works of later writers.

Serious study of Chinese agriculture was very much neglected in the West. Boym did publish a notice of Chinese
plants, but the missionaries, even with their vast knowledge,
lacked the special training necessary for an adequate treatment
of agriculture. Any observations they made in this field were
usually of more interest to the man of letters than to the scientific and practical student of the subject.[38]

That portion of Chinese literature devoted to agriculture was
first investigated by the French Orientalists. A treatise on the
silkworm translated by Julien (1837)[39] had such a favorable
effect on the industry in France that scholars thought other
branches of French agriculture might benefit from further trans-

---

[35] M. J. L. Hervey-Saint-Denys, *Recherches sur l'agriculture et l'horticulture des Chinois* (Paris, 1850), p. 9 *et seq.*; "Agriculture in China,"
C. Repos. (1834), 3, pp. 121-27.

[36] "Notices of China," *ibid.* (1840), 9, p. 400.

[37] Williams, *op. cit.*, 468.

[38] Hervey-Saint-Denys, *op. cit.*, 12 *et seq.*

[39] This work was translated into almost all of the languages of Europe.
Ibid., p. 28.

lation of Chinese material in this field.[40]   Hervey-Saint-Denys thereupon decided to translate portions of two horticultural and agricultural encyclopaedias[41] which would summarize the methods of scientific agriculture in China, but because of many difficulties connected with the translation of such works full of botanical and technical terms, the author published only a simple memoir, *Recherches sur l'agriculture,* in which he gives a short analysis of the encyclopaedias and some practical information on fruits, legumes, and trees.   He also discussed the possibility of the introduction of many Chinese plants into France and Algeria. The bamboo, he argued, would be a valuable product for Southern Europe and especially for Northern Africa.   The gigantic reed-like tree, because of its quick growth and many uses, might partially replace wood which was costly, rare, and also indispensable to African colonization.[42]   Other writers, likewise interested in the agricultural development of their respective countries, stressed the similarity of the climate of China and parts of the United States, Southern Europe, Northern Africa, and India which would make possible the introduction of many Chinese plants.

The East India Company in 1848 sent Robert Fortune, who ten years previously had visited China, as botanical collector for the Horticultural Society of London, to study the tea industry and to obtain tea plants, seeds and manufacturers' implements for the recently established plantations of Northern India.[43]   In the United States in the same year, a single attempt, indifferently managed and early abandoned, was made to grow the tea plant by Junius Smith near Greenville, South Carolina. Smith's experiment was by no means a conclusive test.   His

[40] Jules Mohl, "Rapport," *JA* (1851), 18, p. 182 *et seq.*

[41] A work of sixty books dating from 1607, and a later encyclopaedia of 178 volumes published by order of the Emperor, Ch'ien Lung, to propagate the best things that science had produced in agriculture and horticulture, formed a part of the Chinese collection of the Bibliothèque Royale.   See Hervey-Saint-Denys, *op. cit.,* 26 *et seq.*

[42] Hervey-Saint-Denys, *op. cit.,* 183 *et seq.*

[43] Fortune, op. cit., Preface (3rd ed.), I, iii; Poulain de Bossay, "Rapport sur le voyage . . . de M. Robert Fortune," *BSG* (1854), 7, p. 113.

soil was poor, and his plants without proper care and nourishment soon died.[44]

About ten years later the Bureau of Agriculture sent an agent to China to collect tea seeds and shrubs which were to be propagated on a portion of the public grounds in the city of Washington. Later they were removed to the sites where the experiments were to be made ultimately.[45] This project, as the preceding one in tea culture, seems to have had no permanent results. Again in 1874 many thousands of young tea plants were distributed throughout parts of the United States, but the main difficulty in making the tea crop a commercial success was the cost of labor. Many hoped to overcome that obstacle by the adoption of improved methods of curing.[46]

Wells Williams, the Protestant missionary, who in 1848 had been asked to obtain seeds of valuable plants and trees for the United States Government's experiments, recommended in 1850 the importation of camphor, cassia, tallow, and varnish trees which were of commercial value.[47] The Southern states were especially interested in the acclimatization of semitropical Chinese fruits which Williams thought might be important commercially.[48] None of these trees at the time were introduced into the United States on a large scale. But certain vegetables like the Chinese yam became favorites in the West.[49] A number of Chinese grains were also successfully grown in France and Algeria.[50]

Occidentals were much more interested in the products of Chinese agriculture and horticulture than in their methods which were decidedly inferior to those of the West. Almost all Europeans and Americans commended the thrift and industry of the Chinese farmer. Although a few French Sinologists, such as Hervey-Saint-Denys, who had delved into the Chinese agricultural literature dating from the seventeenth century, were im-

[44] *Report, Agriculture* (1848), p. 168; (1859), p. 7. See note 34.
[45] *Ibid.* (1858), v.
[46] *Ibid.* (1874), 7; (1855), xlii *et seq.*
[47] *Ibid.* (1850), 450 *et seq.*
[48] *Ibid.* (1850), 450-53.   [49] *Ibid.* (1855), 223.
[50] "L'Envoi des graines de la Chine," *BSG* (1852), 3, p. 88.

pressed by their methods,[51] Williams, Fortune, and other observers of Chinese agriculture admitted that until the eighteenth century it was probably superior to that of the West. Since that time no great advance had been made, and Chinese methods remained backward and stationary in the nineteenth century.[52]

[51] Hervey-Saint-Denys, *op. cit.*, 17, 27.
[52] Fortune, *op. cit.*, I, 222 *et seq.*; Davis, *op. cit.*, II, 325.

CONCLUSION

THE attitude of the West toward China during the years from 1840 to 1876 is largely determined by the spirit of the times. The Victorian Age was a period of self-satisfaction, prejudices, and limitations. Chinese civilization during this period was for the most part commendable in so far as it measured up to European standards of excellence. Chinese art was not studied in its own setting but was compared to that of the West. Foreigners considered Cantonese art, which showed traces of Western influence, superior to pure Chinese art. Occidental criticisms of Chinese civilization also reflect the point of view of the age. Europeans did not realize that the prodigious development of the West in science, for example, was very recent. Legge, commenting upon the limitations of Confucius's scholarship, pointed out that he knew nothing of natural science; in Confucius's day, the study of natural science scarcely existed in any country. Westerners' conceptions of China were much less favorable in the nineteenth century than Europeans' conceptions in the sixteenth, seventeenth, and first part of the eighteenth centuries. Influenced by Jesuit reports, Europeans during the earlier period were impressed by the highly civilized condition of the "Celestial Empire." Certain factors in the history of both Europe and China partially explain this shift from a favorable point of view to an unfavorable conception of Chinese civilization in the late eighteenth and nineteenth centuries.

When the missionaries and other travellers left for the Orient in the latter part of the sixteenth century, they left behind them a Europe disrupted by religious and political wars. During a large part of that century France was engaged in both civil and foreign war which left the country almost in a state of collapse. The state was virtually bankrupt. Trade had stopped. Towns were in ruins, and roads and bridges were out of repair. Discharged soldiers and lawless bands pillaged the country. In the same century Spain had to contend with various revolts among her subject peoples. Rebellions of the Moriscos and Aragon were suppressed after a few years, but the Dutch Revolt in 1568 continued for many years.[1]

The Thirty Years' War (1618-1648), the last of the so-called religious wars, seriously weakened the power of the Holy Roman Empire politically and economically. "About two-thirds of the total population had disappeared; the misery of those that survived was piteous in the extreme. Five-sixths of the villages in the empire had been destroyed . . . in the north quite one-third of the land had gone out of cultivation, and trade had drifted into the hands of the French or Dutch. Education had almost disappeared; and the moral decline of the people was seen in the coarsening of manners and the growth of superstition, as witnessed by the frequent burning of witches." In the latter part of the seventeenth and in the eighteenth century, dynastic and colonial rivalries led to a series of wars in which practically all of the important countries of Europe took part at one time or another.[2]

In contrast to these conditions in the West, the order and prosperity of the Chinese Empire made a deep impression upon Europeans. The Mings, who were in power until 1644, ruled a vast territory which included all of China Proper. Silver and copper were plentiful; both metals were used as mediums of exchange. Because of the peace and prosperity of the country, China reached a high standard of culture under this dynasty. Jade and ivory carving showed unusual skill in craftsmanship. The architecture of the period displayed in temples, pagodas, bridges, and city walls was imposing.[3] The Great Wall, much admired by foreigners, was rebuilt under the Ming Emperors.[4] In other fields China unquestionably showed

[1] Carlton J. H. Hayes, *A Political and Cultural History of Modern Europe* (New York, 1932, 1936), Vols. I, II, Part IV.

[2] *Ibid.*, I, 275.

[3] Kenneth Scott Latourette, *The Chinese, Their History and Culture* (New York, 1934), I, 316-24.

[4] *Oeuvres complètes de Voltaire* (Paris: Armand-Aubrée, éd., 1829) (*Essai sur les mœurs*, I), XII, 212; Latourette, *op. cit.*, I, 323.

progress. Chinese craftsmen produced unusual cloisonné. Rugs
and carpets were superior to those of earlier periods. In cer-
amics, the Orientals especially excelled; Chinese porcelain with
its unusual colors and designs was much admired in the West.
At this time the East came to be regarded as a treasure house
not only of spices, jewels, and medicaments but also a factory
of marvellously beautiful products which included porcelain,
silks, satins, carved ivory and jade, and metal work.

The Ming dynasty laid the foundations of the huge Empire
which the Manchus consolidated in the seventeenth century.
Under the latter rulers the Empire reached its greatest territorial extent and attained a level of prosperity probably never
equalled before. In the latter part of the seventeenth and
through most of the next century, China was the most populous
and possibly the wealthiest country in the world. Most European travellers, missionaries, and other writers, until about 1750,
commended Chinese law and its administration which compared
favorably with that of contemporary Europe. It is important
to remember that penal codes were not reformed, administration of justice was not obviously improved, and prison conditions remained unsatisfactory in the West until the nineteenth
century. The Jesuits and, later, Voltaire praised the Chinese
system of civil service which they believed was in part responsible for the good government of the Chinese Empire.

For almost a century and half two great Manchu rulers,
K'ang Hsi and Ch'ien Lung, ruled China. K'ang Hsi during
his reign (1662-1722) not only maintained his authority within
China but protected and expanded his frontiers. He promoted
the material welfare of his people, tried to establish a sound currency, and instituted public works. He encouraged literature by
financing the publication of new compilations, new editions of
the *Classics*, and rare books. He also had many Chinese works
translated into Manchu. After a short reign of comparative
unimportance, another able Emperor, Ch'ien Lung, ruled China
(1736-1795). During these years the Manchu dynasty reached
the zenith of its power and entered upon a state of decline

which became more pronounced in the course of the nineteenth century.[5]

China presented a striking contrast to Europe from the sixteenth until the latter part of the eighteenth century. It is not strange that the Jesuits extravagantly praised many features of Oriental civilization. Intellectual conditions in Europe at that time were, however, in some respects superior to those of China. European learning seemed less stereotyped than Oriental, and the Europeans were ahead of the Chinese in mathematical science and astronomy. Sixteenth century Europe was distinguished for its artists, its humanists, and its scientists who revolutionized astronomy and made important contributions to mathematics, physics, medicine, biology, and political theory. The Jesuits who went to China in the latter part of the sixteenth and in the following century introduced many principles of mathematics and astronomy which native scholars adopted. European science at the time was largely abstract and interested only a relatively small number of scientists and intellectuals. Only when applied science began to be used for practical purposes, did the West as a whole become conscious of its superiority in that field of knowledge.

At the very time when China was entering upon a period of stagnation and retrogression, Europeans and Americans were making great progress especially in material civilization. Before the eighteenth century Europe had made no great advance. During that century the material conditions of Europe were similar to those of the sixteenth century. The individual peasant cultivated his land much as his ancestors had and introduced no improvements. He knew little about the use of fertilizer to make the land more productive; his farming tools were simple and crude. Primitive methods of agriculture continued down to and after the French Revolution. At that time agricultural conditions in France were deplorable. The yield of crops per acre was low. Peasants were poor and had only the rudest tools. Because of the heavy taxes and obligations to the

[5] *Ibid.*, I, 299 *et seq.*

nobles, they had no incentive to improve their holdings. In Eastern Europe, the lot of the peasants was even worse, but their conditions had been improved to some extent by the middle of the nineteenth century.

Agricultural conditions in England were changed by the agricultural revolution of the eighteenth century. Then, capitalistic, large scale, scientific farming appeared. Rotation of crops, better tools, and use of fertilizer to restore the natural elements of the soil were introduced. After the close of the Napoleonic Wars in 1815, a temporary decline in agriculture ensued. After 1840 it showed a remarkable revival in England as a result of the application of machinery and science to methods of farming. This agricultural revival approximately parallels the main phase of the Industrial Revolution.

This movement, which likewise had its beginning in the latter part of the eighteenth century in England and a little later on the Continent and in America, progressed by leaps and bounds and revolutionized life in the West. Machinery was applied to agriculture, industry, and commerce so that economic production and the exchange of commodities were greatly increased. The standard of living for many Westerners was perceptibly raised.

A close relationship between the Industrial Revolution, the development of agriculture, and natural science particularly physics and chemistry is apparent. Natural science, which in earlier times was primarily theoretical, now became more practical. Industrialists became interested in science, and scientists applied their knowledge to agriculture and industry. Agricultural experiment stations were established in Western countries to conduct scientific experiments with soils and plants.[6] In the material aspects of civilization, the West in fifty or sixty years had far outstripped China. Westerners seemed to forget that Europe, until about the last quarter of the eighteenth century, had been just as backward or possibly more so than China was about 1850. In the nineteenth century many writers asserted that contemporary Chinese society was much as it was in Con-

---

[6] Hayes, *op. cit.*, II, Chap. XV.

fucius's day and also in the thirteenth century when Marco Polo visited "Cathay."

Traders, merchants, and capitalists, who had almost no interest in the intellectual life of China and were unappreciative of its culture, regarded it as an extremely backward country because it had poor transportation facilities, still used primitive tools in farming, possessed no large factories, and had not developed its mineral resources. Western capitalists sought concessions for the development of mines and the construction of railroads. By industrializing and modernizing China, they hoped to create a demand for Western manufactured products so that they would have available markets. Traders and merchants deplored the slowness of missionary methods of "civilizing" China, and emphasized the importance of Western inventions, such as steamboats to facilitate river transportation and thereby hasten economic development of China. A few officials, notably Sir John Francis Davis and Thomas Taylor Meadows, genuinely admired many elements of Chinese civilization, and their books contributed toward an understanding of the Chinese people and an appreciation of their achievements.

The more able missionaries, such as Legge, Wylie, Faber, Edkins, Eitel, Doolittle, Milne, and Wells Williams did study the customs, philosophy, religion, and literature of the Chinese. They commended many features of their culture. But the missionaries were also influenced by the materialistic civilization of the West. Their writings indicate that they attributed their own advanced civilization to the fact that they were Christian. By converting the Chinese, they were conferring upon them the blessings of Western civilization, in addition to teaching them the principles of Christianity.

In the nineteenth century a certain humanization of religion is perceptible. A Christian's duty and obligation to society were strongly emphasized.[7] A number of clergymen, both Protestant and Catholic, concerned themselves with the social betterment of humanity. Among Anglican clergymen were Denison

[7] J. R. Seeley, *Ecce Homo* (Boston, 1866), pp. 339-55; Arthur Cushman McGiffert, *The Rise of Modern Religious Ideas* (New York, 1921), Chap. XIII.

Maurice and Charles Kingsley who inaugurated the "Christian Socialist" movement. In the forties this group conducted a campaign against bad conditions in factories and sweatshops. They pleaded for the moral and educational betterment of the masses. In France the "Social Catholic" group, including Frédéric Ozanam, demanded drastic social legislation to improve the lot of the laboring groups.[8] In America at the time when slavery was a pre-eminent issue, many clergymen notably Henry Ward Beecher threw themselves into the anti-slavery conflict because as preachers of religion they felt it their duty to support all righteous causes which affected the welfare of any part of the human race. The missionaries in China under the influence of the humanitarian movement of the nineteenth century naturally concerned themselves with the social betterment of the Chinese. They established hospitals and schools and taught them the material benefits of Western civilization oftentimes before they presented the abstract doctrines of Christianity.

Missionaries and others at this time contrasted the justice of the English code of laws with the horrible treatment of Chinese criminals and the dreadful conditions of prisons in China. England had just revised the criminal code in 1821; the death penalty was replaced by milder punishment in many cases. Prison conditions were made more humane, and the use of the pillory and the whipping-post were legally abolished. Missionaries believed that, if the Chinese accepted Christianity, they would also introduce the reforms which Christian countries had adopted.

Not only in material civilization and social reform was China backward in the nineteenth century but also in theories of government. In the preceding century the Chinese Government, which was in its essentials patriarchal and benevolent, made a definite appeal to the proponents of enlightened despotism. Voltaire asserted that the organization of the Chinese Empire was the best that the world had ever seen.[9] The reigns

---

[8] Hayes, *op. cit.*, II, 86, 144.

[9] *Oeuvres complètes, op. cit.* (Dictionnaire philosophique, II), XXXI, 416; G. F. Hudson, *Europe and China* (London, 1931), Chap. X; *Hegel's*

of K'ang Hsi and Ch'ien Lung furnished strong support to Europeans who saw in enlightened despotism the ideal form of government. But the decline of China and the growing inefficiency of its administration contrasted very unfavorably with the carefully organized governments of Western Europe. By 1830 official service in the West was, in the phrase of the time, "open to talent," and most of the states of Europe developed trained bureaucracies which made for much more effective government and administration.[10]

With the development of more ably administered European governments was closely identified the principle of liberalism which gained important victories in the thirties in Great Britain and France. By 1847 liberalism had invaded Central Europe and caused a series of revolutions to break out in 1848. Although many of the revolutionary movements were failures, some forms of constitutional government survived in Prussia and other continental countries. While the conservative governments of Europe were combatting liberalism from about 1830 to 1850, they thought little about colonial empires or countries outside of Europe. Many of the intellectuals devoted their energies to the discussion of liberalism. Finding no inspiration for their ideas in China because its patriarchal form of government had tended to thwart individual initiative, they concentrated their attention upon European history.

When liberals were agitating for more individual liberties, Europe particularly England was in the process of industrialization. Wherever the Industrial Revolution made the greatest headway, liberalism was strongest. The manufacturers for selfish reasons accepted the principles of liberalism which, if applied to commerce and industry, would give them a free hand in individual enterprise without governmental restriction. In their own countries because of the over-supply of workers, they could treat labor as a commodity with little regard for the condition of the working classes. Their policy in dealing with

<hr>

Philosophy of the State and of History, G. S. Morris, ed. (Chicago, 1887), p. 139 *et seq.*
[10] Hayes, *op. cit.*, II, 63 *et seq.*

"backward" countries was just as ruthless. Although they talked about "civilizing" China and other countries, they had, with few exceptions, no altruistic motives. They were primarily interested in them as regions of wealth to be exploited for their own gain.

In harmony with the principles of economic liberalism, the monopoly of the British East India Company was abolished in 1834, and traders rushed to the East to participate in the China trade. The Home Government placed almost no restraint upon their activities, and the merchants had little respect for or knowledge of Chinese laws and customs. The misunderstandings which arose from their policies were one factor in the outbreak of the first Anglo-Chinese War. Traders, especially the British and the Americans, continued throughout this period to have an interest in the Oriental trade because it was profitable, but the West with the exception of special groups lost interest in China from about 1830 until 1860 or later.

With the rise of Romanticism during the late eighteenth century and its development in the following century, Europeans turned away from the East and looked to the Middle Ages of Europe for inspiration. Many painters, such as the Pre-Raphaelites, went to the Middle Ages for their themes. Europeans also became tremendously interested in the history and characteristics of their own nationalities and in the development of their respective cultures. Artists depicted episodes in the lives of their heroes and memorable incidents in their national history. This cultural nationalism, which emphasized medieval civilization, enhanced the development of political nationalism which tended to focus attention upon national problems and upon European affairs. Intellectuals engrossed in their own culture with the exception of a few scholars forgot about China during the period of Romanticism.[11]

The powers of the West did not show very much interest in China, until 1860 and even later, although they had gained some commercial privileges after the first Anglo-Chinese War. Germany, engrossed with problems of unification, social legis-

[11] *Ibid.*, Chapters XVI, XVII.

lation, and European diplomacy, did not acquire an overseas dominion until the eighties. France during the same period was concerned primarily with domestic affairs and continental politics. But in the decade of the fifties, Napoleon III did have visions of a second colonial empire, and in 1856 France joined Great Britain in an expedition against China which culminated in the further opening of China to Western trade.

During the first half of the nineteenth century, the political group which dominated British policy for a number of years believed that colonies were a liability and should be given their freedom. In connection with British policy in China, it is significant to note that R. M. Martin and other English officials emphatically stated that they did not want Chinese territory because of the tremendous expense and responsibility. They wanted unrestricted freedom of trade in the Chinese Empire.

In the sixties the British became not only more directly concerned about their outlying possessions but also more ambitious for new colonies. As a result of the Industrial Revolution which speeded up production of manufactured articles, most of the European countries became tremendously interested about 1870 and later in colonies as sources of raw materials, as places for the investment of capital, and for markets. Because of the development of nationalism, European countries wanted colonial empires for the enhancement of their prestige. China at the time because of its vast population, its relatively undeveloped resources, and its lack of transportation facilities attracted still more forcibly Western manufacturers and capitalists.

After 1842 Western countries signed a number of treaties with China which gave them commercial privileges within the Chinese Empire. During the T'ai P'ing Rebellion the position of foreign merchants was precarious, and their trade was in jeopardy because of the weakness of the Imperial authority. The traders appealed to their Home Governments for protection. Certain areas around Shanghai, Ningpo, and other cities were set aside for foreign residents. The commercial groups, probably to influence their Home Governments to demand privileges and concessions from the Chinese, emphasized the bar-

barisms of Chinese law, the corruption of official administration, and the general backwardness of Chinese civilization. Because of the primitive state of Chinese law, "civilized" Christian powers demanded the right of extraterritoriality. As China was not in a position to resist Western demands, concessions of territory and extraterritorial privileges were greatly increased in the last half of the nineteenth century.

The Russians at this time advanced rapidly into Central Asia. To protect the frontier trade which had sprung up between China and Russia in the vicinity of Kuldja and Tarbagatai, the latter in 1871 moved troops to Kuldja and occupied the territory of Ili. They assured the Chinese that the occupation was temporary and that the territory would be restored when the latter was able to maintain order. At that time it was thought that China would never be able to recover control of the distant region, but under the leadership of the celebrated general, Tso Tsung-t'ang, the reconquest of the vast region astonished the world. This victory made Western nations realize that the Empire had recuperative powers and that its collapse was not imminent. When Western European countries approached China from the sea and Russia advanced eastward toward a Pacific port, the Chinese policy of exclusion was doomed. China to maintain itself was forced to make some adjustments to new conditions.[12]

The Chinese at this time began to realize their inferiority in armaments. Their war junks opposed modern ships, and their soldiers, equipped with bows and matchlocks, tried to defend walled cities against the well-drilled, well-armed regiments of Western nations during the first and second Anglo-Chinese Wars. But not until Japan, which had modelled its military and naval organization upon that of Western powers, delivered a crushing blow to the Chinese in the latter part of the nineteenth century, did China make a great change in its military organization.

[12] Payson J. Treat, *The Far East* (New York, 1928), p. 146 *et seq.*; Edward Thomas Williams, *A Short History of China* (New York, 1928), p. 344 *et seq.*

The domestic policy of China was not greatly changed by the treaties of 1858 and 1860 with Western countries, but many changes took place in Japan partly as a result of the opening of the country after Perry's visit in 1853. The whole social and political structure of the Empire was profoundly modified, and Japan entered upon an astounding course of development. The ruling classes, which for centuries had held undisputed sway, gave up their special privileges so that their country might be strengthened and centralized to cope with the powers of the West.[13]

Many Westerners admired the Japanese because they reformed their Government and introduced Western inventions and methods of warfare. They contrasted the progressive Japanese with the unprogressive Chinese. Intellectuals became enthusiastic about Japanese arts especially color prints which were popularized by such writers as Baudelaire, the Goncourt brothers, Zola, and Burty, and by the painters, Monet, Degas, Manet, and Whistler.[14]

It has always been extremely difficult for both the East and the West to view a different civilization with an open mind, but following the date, 1876, there was a general intensification of interest among Western intellectuals in the civilization of Japan and China. It was evidenced not only by an appreciation of art, especially Japanese, and literature but also by an interest in Oriental philosophy and religion. At the same time China and Japan began to use Western inventions, to adopt Western business methods, and to send students to the universities of Europe and America. When both the Orient and the Occident began to appreciate the civilization of the other, their relationships entered upon a new era.

[13] R. K. Douglas, *Europe and the Far East* (Revised ed., New York, 1913), Chapters IX, X.

[14] William Leonard Schwartz, *The Imaginative Interpretation of the Far East in Modern French Literature* (Paris, 1927), Chap. II.

INDEX

AUTHOR INDEX

VITA

Mary Gertrude Mason was born in Kentucky in 1900. She received the degree of Bachelor of Philosophy from the University of Chicago in 1923 and the degree of Master of Arts from Columbia University in 1927.